Lengthened Shadows

LENGTHENED SHADOWS

AMERICA AND ITS INSTITUTIONS IN THE TWENTY-FIRST CENTURY

Edited with an Introduction by

ROGER KIMBALL
and
HILTON KRAMER

Encounter Books
San Francisco 2004

ENCOUNTER BOOKS

First paperback edition published in 2004 by Encounter Books, an activity of Encounter for Culture and Education, Inc., a nonprofit corporation.

Encounter Books website address: www.encounterbooks.com

Manufactured in the United States and printed on acid-free paper.

The paper used in this publication meets the minimum requirements of ANSI/NISO Z39.48-1992 (R 1997) (*Permanence of Paper*).

Library of Congress Cataloging-in-Publication Data:
Kimball, Roger, 1953– . Kramer, Hilton.
    Lengthened shadows : America and its institutions in the twenty-first century / edited with an introduction by Roger Kimball and Hilton Kramer.
      p. cm.
    Includes bibliographic references and index.
    ISBN 1-59403-054-5 (alk. paper)
      1. United States-Civilization-21st century. 2. United States-Civilization-1970– I. Title.
E169.12 .L437 2004
306'.0973'09051-dc22

                                    2004054338

10 9 8 7 6 5 4 3 2 1

To James Piereson

Contents

INTRODUCTION: LENGTHENED SHADOWS   *ix*

THE BURDENS OF EMPIRE
Keith Windschuttle   *3*

MODERNISM & ITS INSTITUTIONS
Hilton Kramer   *25*

THE ART OF WAR
Frederick W. Kagan   *43*

"ALL SAIL, NO ANCHOR":
ARCHITECTURE AFTER MODERNISM
Michael J. Lewis   *67*

TENDING THE GARDENS OF MUSIC
Jay Nordlinger   *93*

EXPENSIVE ILLITERATES: VICTIMHOOD & EDUCATION
Mark Steyn   *119*

RELIGION IN AMERICA: ANCIENT & MODERN
David B. Hart   *143*

Of Lapdogs & Loners: American Poetry Today
　　Eric Ormsby　　　　　　　　　　　　　*169*

Olympians on the March:
the Courts & the Culture Wars
　　Robert H. Bork　　　　　　　　　　　　*195*

Institutionalizing Our Demise:
America vs. Multiculturalism
　　Roger Kimball　　　　　　　　　　　　*225*

Contributors　　　　　　　　　　　　　　*251*

Acknowledgments　　　　　　　　　　　　*253*

Index　　　　　　　　　　　　　　　　　*255*

Introduction:
Lengthened Shadows

"A N INSTITUTION," Emerson proclaimed in "Self-Reliance," "is the lengthened shadow of one man." Like much that Emerson wrote, "Self-Reliance" is longer on attitude than argument. Its mode is hortatory. But Emerson's *mot* about institutions hints at some important characteristics of those curious joint ventures. For one thing, institutions tend to exist beyond themselves in a penumbra of interests: they *loom*. Then, too, institutions tend to owe their identity, in large part, to the animating energies of individuals. ("*One* man"? Well, sometimes.) They are impersonal entities enlivened by the personalities that created and maintain them. We thought of Emerson's fertile if sobering phrase when we began contemplating the series of essays on America and its institutions that we published in *The New Criterion* from September 2003 to June 2004 and that we offer in revised form in this volume.

Even before the terrorist attacks of 9/11, it had become clear that a new chapter was opening for American institutions: cultural and social as well as economic and military. The jagged velocity of twentieth-century life had unaccountably catapulted the United States to a rare, perhaps unprecedented, preeminence on the world stage. How that preeminence would be negotiated—to what extent it would even be acknowledged—was a question more often answered by neglect than by engagement. Whatever else can be said about the events of September 11—events whose reverberations continue to sound nearly three years later—they had the effect of which Dr. Johnson spoke when he observed that the prospect of hanging "concentrates the mind wonderfully." Exactly what was this richest, most powerful, most influential of countries? Its reach was far—how far? And how far beneficent?

Lengthened Shadows: America and Its Institutions in the Twenty-first Century offers a wide-ranging and provocative assessment of the engines of American cultural and political life in the post-9/11 world. Seen from one perspective, the ten essays composing this book are bulletins from the trenches. Moving from the institution of the military to the fate of modernism in the visual arts, from the law to music, from religion and poetry to diplomacy, architecture, education, and the battle over that contested concept, American identity, *Lengthened Shadows* presents expert testimony about numerous discrete aspects of the American experience at the dawn of the twenty-first century.

Taken together, however, the essays in this volume are more than a series of critical snapshots. They are more like themes in a musical composition, answering to and elaborating upon one another. In sum, they offer an embracing moral and intellectual diagnosis, by turns affirmative and admonitory.

The book opens with an essay by the Australian historian Keith Windschuttle on "The Burdens of Empire." Among much else, Mr. Windschuttle sets the stage for what follows by placing the future of American power in the context of its past and the past of other great military and economic powers. His conclusion is simultaneously hard-headed and far-seeing: he acknowledges both the burdens of empire—which means the responsibilities of power—and their limitations. In other words, he steers a middle course between the enemies of American power and cheerleaders for the idea of an American imperium. He acknowledges that, although "rogue states and terrorists could inflict serious damage if they got the opportunity, none of them threaten America's world hegemony now or in the future."

America's Islamic opponents pose as much threat to its strategic position as the Dervish brotherhood posed to the British in 1898. Kitchener at Omdurman and Napier at Magdala knew what to do. They confronted the enemy and destroyed him utterly. Similarly, the proper response today should be confined to the military. Only if another rival imperial force arose again, one that posed a threat on the scale of international communism during the Cold War, might the case for a more formal imperial role by America make sense. But without an imperative of this kind, America has no need to emulate the British Empire, or any other for that matter, and hence is unlikely to do so.

It is within the boundaries that Mr. Windschuttle limns— under the dispensation of a robust but self-limited power— that the future of American institutions can best flourish.

Formidable though the threat of terrorism remains, the more significant long-term danger to American institutions may come from within. This is not to underestimate the strength and resiliency of those institutions. In economic, military, and political terms, America has never been stronger (though Frederick W. Kagan issues some well-considered warnings about contemplated transformations in the U.S. military). Culturally, America is energetic and extraordinarily influential, though perhaps in many areas its activity is less a sign of strength than of anxious enervation. There are, to be sure, some indisputable bright spots. Jay Nordlinger celebrates one conspicuous success story in his tour of the world of classical music performance (though Mr. Nordlinger has noted that his assessment would have been far darker had he dilated on the state of classical music composition). Hilton Kramer, writing about modernism and the visual arts, and Eric Ormsby, writing about poetry, offer more equivocal if not entirely gloomy prognoses.

THE STORY SHIFTS to a decidedly minor key when the focus moves to education and the law. In "Expensive Illiterates,"

Mark Steyn shows how even primary education in this country has become more and more in thrall to the imperatives of political correctness. As an example, Mr. Steyn tells the story of the Madison School in Skokie, Illinois, where the children had been planning a Thanksgiving celebration replete with homemade Pilgrim and Indian costumes. After receiving one parental complaint, Pete Davis, the school's principal, forbade the event because it would promote (in the words of the Native American Educational Services College) "Hollywood-type stereotypes of American Indians"—a laughable objection because, as Mr. Steyn explains, "you'd have to be well into late middle-age to remember any 'Hollywood-type stereotypes' like poor old Tonto." So instead of a traditional Thanksgiving celebration the kids got a bit of sensitivity training from a Plains Indian, who came and lectured them about "his culture"—a culture, by the way, that has nothing to do with the Pilgrims or the New England Indians who formed the historical basis for Thanksgiving. As one parent complained, the whole Thanksgiving Day commemoration was "hijacked." "But," Mr. Steyn observes, "it's not really about Thanksgiving, is it?"

> On receiving the lone complaint about his school's decades-old holiday celebration, Principal Davis could have done what I did—mooched around in a reference book for ten minutes. Instead, the moment he heard the Sensitivity Police were on his case, he ran to the relevant ethnic-grievance bodies. . . . So now the first graders learn nothing about American history, nothing about that remarkable celebration when the Pilgrims gave thanks for their unlikely survival in this difficult climate with the Indian people who had helped them raise enough food to do so. . . .
>
> Every day small acts of historical vandalism are perpetrated at grade schools across the country by the likes of Principal Davis: something that is true is replaced by something that is "sensitive"—even if, as in this case, "sensitivity" involves being entirely insensitive to historical reality. In diving straight for

the refuge of the American Indian Center, Mr. Davis was merely the latest "educator" to embark on the flight from facts to feelings.

An analogous process is transforming the institutions of American law from a bulwark of democracy to an activist body bent on remaking society. As Robert H. Bork shows in "Olympians on the March: the Courts & the Culture Wars," the Court is increasingly "dominated by a gentrified form of Sixties radicalism."

> The Supreme Court is enacting a program of radical personal autonomy, indeed moral chaos, piece by piece, creating new and hitherto unsuspected constitutional rights. . . . Since each individual must be permitted to define meaning for himself, it must follow that there is no allowable truth, legal or moral. . . . Partly as a consequence of the Supreme Court's extra-constitutional adventures, we are losing our community of ideas about moral behavior. The result is a species of legal triumphalism: When law has disintegrated the bonds of society, its common moral assumptions, there will be nothing left but law to sustain us, and law alone cannot bear that weight.

That "community of ideas" of which Judge Bork speaks goes to the heart of our concerns in *Lengthened Shadows*. The future of the institutions that define American political and cultural life depend upon a foundation of shared values about what matters and, indeed, about who we are. This pertains as much to the life of art as to the life of law. In many respects, we stand at a crossroads: the future of our cultural institutions, the fabric of our social and political life are fiercely embattled even as we write. What answers prevail will deeply shape the future of American society.

Patrick, Lord Devlin put the case well in his neglected classic, *The Enforcement of Morals* (1964):

[S]ociety means a community of ideas; without shared ideas

on politics, morals, and ethics no society can exist. Each one of us has ideas about what is good and what is evil; they cannot be kept private from the society in which we live. If men and women try to create a society in which there is no fundamental agreement about good and evil they will fail; if having based it upon a common set of core values, they surrender those values, it will disintegrate. For society is not something that can be kept together physically; it is held by the invisible but fragile bonds of common beliefs and values.

Events of the past few decades have dramatized both the fragility of which Lord Devlin speaks and the importance of those common beliefs and values for which he argues. In the long run, material strength is fruitless without an illuminating spiritual power to guide it. *Lengthened Shadows* is an effort—a series of efforts—to show that truth at work in the pulse of American and social life.

August 2004

Lengthened Shadows

The Burdens of Empire

Keith Windschuttle

O N SEPTEMBER 2, 1898 at Omdurman on the banks of the Nile just outside of Khartoum, an Anglo-Egyptian army under the command of General Herbert Horatio Kitchener faced a Sudanese army led by the Khalifa, the local leader of the fundamentalist Wahabbist sect of Islam. The British were clearly outnumbered. Their twenty thousand soldiers faced fifty-two thousand troops of the Dervish Islamic fraternity. The British were the better armed, with fifty-five Maxim guns supported by gunboats in the river, but the Dervishes had two Maxim guns of their own plus an extensive arsenal of field artillery. Kitchener's troops, in uniforms of red jackets and white helmets, formed battle squares, their backs to the Nile. A mile away behind some low hills, the Dervishes, in ascetic white robes, their heads shaven, formed a line five miles long. At dawn a hilltop observer, the twenty-three-year-old Winston Churchill, who had joined the British expedition as a correspondent for the *Morning Post*, saw the Dervishes charge over the hills, chanting in unison: "There is one God and Muhammad is the Messenger of God."

The Sudanese army was no match for the well-drilled, well-armed British troops. Churchill watched wave after wave of Dervishes "struggling on through a hell of whistling metal, exploding shells and spurting dust—suffering, despairing, dying." British guns quickly reduced the desert tribesmen to what Churchill called "dirty bits of newspaper" strewn across the plain. Within five hours it was all over. Ten thousand Dervishes were killed outright. Ninety-five per cent of their army suffered casualties. On the British side, there were four hundred casualties and of these only forty-eight were dead.

Kitchener's expedition to Omdurman had been in retaliation for the death of General Charles George Gordon in Khartoum in 1885. Gordon and a small Anglo-Egyptian force had been victims of the Mahdi, a charismatic Islamic leader who had revived the militant Wahabbist sect in the Sudan in the early 1880s. During the thirteen years the British government deliberated over its response, the Mahdi died and it fell to his successor, the Khalifa, to confront the infidels. The victorious Kitchener showed no respect for Islamic sensitivities. After the battle, he destroyed the Mahdi's tomb and carried off his head in a kerosene can as a trophy. There were no more Muslim uprisings. The Sudan soon became a British colony, one more link in a chain of African territory that by 1920 stretched from the Cape to Cairo.

The Battle of Omdurman was not unique. It was largely a repetition of a number of similar events that punctuated British expansion throughout the nineteenth century. Another had taken place in 1866–1867 in Abyssinia where the Emperor Theodore seized British and European officials and diplomats and held them hostage in his mountain fortress at Magdala. Sir Robert Napier led a 13,000-strong British-Indian force that overran the fortress and rescued the hostages, leaving 2000 Abyssinian casualties, the Emperor dead, and Magdala in flames, all for the cost of twenty British soldiers wounded and none killed.

These incidents from the history of the British Empire bear a number of obvious similarities to the outcomes of the American incursions into Afghanistan and Iraq in our own time. The United States demonstrated in both places that it could inflict rapid military defeat on its enemies with minimal losses to itself. The easy victories of both past and present tell the same cautionary tale: weak, backward countries with delusions of grandeur who take on the world's leading military power usually suffer the consequences; the loser subsequently becomes a dependent of the victor, whose realm of political liability expands accordingly.

In his speech to the American Congress on July 17, 2003, the British Prime Minister Tony Blair tried to argue that the situation the world faced today was unprecedented. There was no immediate danger of conflict between the world's most powerful nations, he said. Instead, the threat to security came from disorderly states and political movements among the less powerful. "There never has been a time," Blair said, "when, . . . except in the most general sense, a study of history provides so little instruction for our present day." He went on: "When we removed the Taliban and Saddam Hussein, this was not imperialism. For these oppressed people, it was their liberation."

While Blair's final comment was certainly true, a more historical perspective might have given the Prime Minister a better insight into the imperial ramifications of these events. The logic of Britain's world role in the nineteenth century has enough correspondence to the position of the United States today to repay the effort to examine their respective historical positions.

INDEED, in the wake of its defeat of Iraq in April 2003, it is noticeable how many commentators have ignored Blair and applied the imperial tag to the United States. A label once confined to the vocabulary of the radical left is now deployed all the way across the political spectrum, from liberal to conservative. Even more conspicuous is the fact that imperialism's long-standing bad reputation is now being quickly reappraised.

Contributors to this debate have ranged from Peter Beinart in *The New Republic*, Paul Kennedy in *The Financial Times*, Michael Ignatieff in *The New York Times*, Max Boot in *The Wall Street Journal*, John O'Sullivan in *National Review*, Stephen Peter Rosen in *The National Interest*, and Paul

Johnson in *The New Criterion*. Some of these commentators even speak as if the issue were already a forgone conclusion. Michael Ignatieff asks: "What word but 'empire' describes the awesome thing that America is becoming?" All that remains, Ignatieff says, is for Americans to face the reality of what they have created. "It is an empire without consciousness of itself as such, constantly shocked that its good intentions arouse resentment abroad. But that does not make it any less of an empire." The Yale historian Paul Kennedy acknowledges that Washington denies it has imperial ambitions. But, he adds, "if the US increasingly looks like an empire, walks like an empire and quacks like an empire, perhaps it is becoming one just the same."

This is the most dramatic conceptual turnaround in recent times. A subject which, as little as two years ago, was almost universally regarded as a dirty word, has now become one whose merits and prospects can not only be rationally examined but also positively advocated.

A proper discussion needs to be clear about what an empire actually entails. All the empires of history have been great powers, either in their geographic region or across the world itself. The concept refers, however, to more than just a powerful nation or one with the ability to bend others to its will. Similarly, economic influence is not enough. Some historians speak of Britain's nineteenth-century "informal empire" of trade but many of those subject to it retained their own political control. American and European actions to force an open-door policy on Japan and China in the nineteenth century have often been denounced as acts of imperial power, but they left those countries politically intact and largely free to determine their own futures.

Overall, a real empire is one that rules over many lands and many peoples, with or without their consent. It can do this either directly or indirectly, through various combinations of imperial viceroys, local satraps, and indigenous collaborators, as long as these people hold their office at the will of the central power.

Most people today identify imperialism with the nineteenth-century western European variety, with colonies dispersed around the globe. But there have been powerful land empires whose reign was confined to dependencies adjacent to their own home territory, such as those of the Russians, the Ottomans, and the Habsburg dynasty of Austria. In the nineteenth century, the United States itself underwent a similar kind of imperial expansion. As the thirteen original colonies expanded westwards, they acquired and came to rule territories once held by Britain, Mexico, Spain, France, Russia, and the Indians. Once this process had been consolidated, however, it made more sense to speak of the United States as a nation, not an empire. In the twentieth century it gave up all the substantial overseas territories, including the Philippines, Cuba, and Japan, it had acquired in foreign wars.

NONETHELESS, the United States still bears many of the qualities that characterized the British Empire in its heyday. It has the same liberal political culture and the same desire to spread the benefits of that culture around the world. Moreover, some of the forces that appear to be pulling America into an imperial role today are similar to those that acted upon Britain in the early nineteenth century. In the decades after it lost its American colonies, Britain was a reluctant imperialist. It wanted to trade around the world but was not enthusiastic about shouldering the military and financial burdens of full-blown imperial rule. Adam Smith and the classical liberal school of economics argued that imperialism distorted market forces and was against the long-term financial interests of the home country itself. The British hoped to establish the benefits of their civilization by example rather than by force. The wish proved illusory because some of its trading partners began to resist and some of its imperial rivals encouraged them. Almost before it realized it, Britain had acquired colonies across south Asia and the Pacific and a chain of coaling stations around the globe.

Similarly, the dominant cultural and political values of the

United States have long been anti-imperialist. President Bush told military veterans at the White House last November that America had no territorial ambitions. "We don't seek an empire. Our nation is committed to freedom for ourselves and for others." Nevertheless, circumstances seem to be conspiring against these ideals. The need to guarantee American security and international interests appears to be applying pressures that are hard to resist. Already, Iraq, Afghanistan, and the Balkans look like becoming long-term dependencies, just like many of those that Britain found it necessary to acquire 150 years ago. Indeed, the historian Niall Ferguson points out that it is no coincidence that a map of the principal American military bases around the world today looks remarkably like a map of Royal Navy coaling stations a hundred years ago.

Perhaps the most remarkable aspect of the new debate over imperialism is the turnaround in attitude. The period since the Second World War has been dominated by the idea that self-determination is a core human value, indeed the bedrock of human rights. The United States was a major influence in cementing this ideal. As well as endorsing it through various presidential speeches and United Nations declarations, America discouraged the old European empires from returning to the Asian territories they had lost to the Japanese. As recently as September 2001, the United Nations conference on racism, racial discrimination, and xenophobia declared Western imperialism the basis of most of the problems of the poor of the world:

> Colonialism has led to racism, racial discrimination, xeno-phobia and related intolerance. . . . Africans and people of African descent, and people of Asian descent and indigenous peoples were victims of colonialism and continue to be victims of its consequences.

By the time this declaration was made, however, the argument was beginning to wear thin. The failure of so many former colonies to thrive economically in the half century since they gained self-government suggested that their problems had deeper roots.

Moreover, in the past decade, some good historians have made a number of important reevaluations of imperialism and have contributed to a greater maturity of discussion about the subject. The contribution of imperialism to *advancing* the human condition can now be acknowledged. It is not hard to argue that, throughout the course of human history, the absorption of many small communities by larger polities has been the major single force for the evolution and progress of human culture. Imperialism can be seen as the ultimate form of this process. The Romans, for example, gave the forest tribesmen they conquered in Gaul, Illyria, and Germania the gifts of literacy, books, and all that the Latin language opened up. Roman notions of law, property, and government were established where few existed before, as were the habits of living in towns and using coin for exchange. Along with this came Mediterranean tastes in food, drink, and clothing as well as new concepts and forms in architecture and artistic expression. Much the same can be said for the early emperors who united the people of China. In short, history shows imperialism, rather than being a force of oppression, has often been the engineer of civilization.

Moreover, far from being a major cause of racism and racial discrimination, imperialism has usually pushed in the opposite direction. Emperors who have governed diverse peoples have often found it in their own interests to ensure the protection and status of their different tribes and races, including those of racial minorities. In the mature Roman Empire, a non-Roman ethnic origin was no barrier even to ascending to the purple robe of Caesar. The Austro-Hungarian Empire of the Habsburgs created a multiethnic society that guaranteed the civic, cultural, and property rights even of alien minority groups such as Galician Jews. Throughout history, it has been smaller, self-governed communities and nations, organized around kinship or ethnicity, which have most frequently regarded other tribes and peoples as sub-human, and therefore unfit to live.

The most far-reaching historical reappraisal of the imperial process has been applied in recent years to the British Empire. Between 1998 and 2000, Oxford University Press published its five-volume *Oxford History of the British Empire*, edited by William Roger Louis, which went a long way towards depoliticizing the debate and allowing the evidence of Britain's imperial record to be rationally evaluated. This year, Niall Ferguson's book and television series *Empire* has taken that process further. Ferguson presents a convincing case that the British Empire not merely was nothing to be ashamed of, but was a positive force that "made the modern world." Its history was characterized by the global spread of trade and wealth, technological and cultural modernization, and the growth of liberalism and democracy.

FERGUSON DOES acknowledge, sometimes in gruesome detail, British atrocities against those who attempted to defy their rule: the mass hangings of Indian mutineers in 1857, the shooting of unarmed protestors at Amritsar in 1919, and several others. But he argues that the real debate over the Empire should be less over the morality of individual events and more about the major changes it brought and the differences it made to the lives of most people it affected.

Ferguson is an economic historian. But in addition to recording the flows of commodities, capital, and labor from the imperial center to the colonies, he also emphasizes the importance of the flows of knowledge, culture, and institutions. For the transition to modernity to occur, legal and administrative institutions such as the rule of law, credible monetary regimes, transparent fiscal systems, and competent bureaucracies were essential. Institutions of this kind were the cultural products of Western Europe, especially Britain itself. The only way for the world to gain their benefits, he argues, was for Europe's most powerful military and economic nation to impose them on the countries it made part of its empire. Imperialism encouraged investors to put their money in developing economies, places that would otherwise have been sites of great risk. The extension of empire into the less developed world had the effect of reducing this risk by imposing, directly or indirectly, some form of British rule. In practice, money invested in a *de jure* colony such as India, or a colony in all but name such as Egypt, was a great deal more secure than money invested in a *de facto* colony such as Argentina.

In fact, if those international political activists who now protest at the policies of Western financial institutions like the World Bank and the International Monetary Fund were serious in their concern for the poor of the world, they would be seeking an imperial revival in many of the former colonies. When the British Empire was at its peak it was a much greater positive force for international investment, especially in poor countries, than any of today's institutions. In 1913 some 63 percent of foreign direct investment went to developing countries, whereas in 1996 the proportion was only 28 percent. In 1913, 25 percent of the world stock of capital was invested in poor countries; by 1997 it was no more than 5 percent. A very great deal of this investment went into the infrastructure needed for the transition to modernity: railways, power stations, urban water supplies, dams, and irrigation schemes. In India under the Mughal rulers, only 5 percent of agricultural land was irrigated. The British increased this by a factor of eight. By the time they left in 1947, irrigation was provided to a quarter of all agricultural land.

The British Empire was also a force for the spread of liberal democracy. While this did not work in all its colonies, especially in those parts of Africa and the Middle East acquired late in the imperial era and decolonized a few decades afterwards, the legacy still remains formidable. As the political scientist Myron Weiner pointed out in an oft-cited study in 1983, every country in the Third World that emerged from colonial rule after World War II with a population of at least one million and with a continuous democratic experience was a former British colony. France, in comparison, fostered little independent political development in its colonies and left few lasting political legacies apart from tyranny, civil war, and the *coup d'état*.

In contrast, the British gave their subject peoples the intellectual tools for their own emancipation. William Roger Louis observes that the very idea of colonial independence derived from British concepts. "Indians, as well as French Canadians and Afrikaners, quoted John Locke, Lord Durham, and John Stuart Mill." British law and parliamentary government were goals to which many anti-colonial political movements aspired. British rule encouraged the formation of collaborating elites who were themselves groomed to succeed to power, most notably in India. The major point of difference between rulers and ruled turned not on the fact of decolonization but on its timing.

It is clear, then, that a positive case can not only be made for the British Empire but also for the United States to perform a similar role in the world. As a successor sharing the same political and cultural heritage, an American empire would resemble the British more than any other. Advocates of an American Empire now have a persuasive historical model both to defend and advance their cause.

Indeed, Niall Ferguson writes as if this question were already largely resolved in the affirmative. He claims America has already taken on a *de facto* imperial role very much like the one Britain once played. But because the American political tradition has been largely anti-colonialist, Ferguson says that Americans have yet to recognize what they have become. They inhabit "an empire that dare not speak its name." America has assumed Britain's mantle, he argues, "without yet facing the fact than an empire comes with it . . . empire is as much a reality today as it was throughout the three hundred years when Britain ruled, and made, the modern world."

IF THE United States really is to be Britain's successor, we should expect some similarity in the intellectual debate over imperial policy. In fact, such a debate is already up and running, and its participants have quickly divided into camps similar to those that argued the pros and cons of Britain's imperial ventures.

Although radical-left critics have monopolized the field for the past fifty years, the most important debate over the founding of empire has always been between liberals and conservatives. In the British Empire, "liberals" meant the heirs of Adam Smith and the advocates of free trade. While they wanted British ideas and institutions to be exported as widely as possible, they insisted that an imperialism involving the outright rule of other countries was against the financial, military, and cultural interests of the home country. In particular, Smith warned them about the costs of "the whole annual expense of the peace establishment of the colonies."

This movement, sometimes known as "Radicalism" or the Manchester School, was originally a tendency within the Liberal Party. Its main support came from the manufacturing classes who had arisen during the industrial revolution, many of whom were located in the midlands and north of England. Their leading politicians, John Bright and Richard Cobden, were the staunchest defenders of laissez-faire capitalism, the small state, and individual self-reliance. Cobden was sure his philosophy had history on its side. He told an audience at Manchester in 1846: "I believe that the desire and the motive for large and mighty empires; for gigantic armies and great navies . . . will die away."

The British Tories were the main party of imperial expansion in the nineteenth century, but this was not because they had a coherent program. In the first half of the century, they shared the liberals' concerns about the costs of empire. They took decisions to expand British territory reluctantly and primarily on grounds of security, to preserve the sea lanes for maritime trade, and to protect the territory Britain already possessed against the ambitions of rival powers. The expansion of British territory throughout the Indian subcontinent at the time was largely the outcome of either direct warfare with the French or indirect conflict with France's Indian allies for the right to do business there.

In the last three decades of the nineteenth century all this changed. The Tories proclaimed a Roman model of empire, openly symbolized by the proclamation of Queen Victoria as Empress of India in 1876. They answered social discontent at home by procuring cheap food and raw materials from the colonies, by using the Empire as a captive market for British manufactured goods, and by exploiting popular culture through the appeal of manly exploits in exotic locations, an international civilizing mission, and the theatrical attraction of a queen and her government bestriding the world like a colossus.

NONETHELESS, the most profound political transformation took place within the Liberal Party. While mid-century Liberals like Lord Palmerston were prepared to use British arms in the Opium Wars to force China to accept British trade, it was the movement known as Liberal Imperialism that emerged in the 1880s that developed a full-blown ideology to justify imperial expansion. One-time liberal radicals like Joseph Chamberlain abandoned their earlier views to become the most zealous advocates of a British version of the Roman Empire.

To accomplish this, the Liberal Imperialists had to reinvent liberalism itself. They took their cue from the German idealist philosophy of G. W. F. Hegel that rose to influence at Oxford University. The leading Oxford Hegelian was T. H. Green of Balliol College, an institution that became renowned for its success in producing imperial proconsuls, high commissioners, and other colonial administrators. Between 1874 and 1914, no fewer than 27 percent of Balliol graduates went on to administrative positions in the Empire. Few had aristocratic backgrounds. Most had been born into the rising professional and bureaucratic classes.

This generation of liberals came to regard the state not as a nightwatchman or a necessary evil, but as the very source of freedom. Abandoning laissez faire, they proclaimed a new role for government. Liberty was no longer to be defined as freedom *from* the state but as something to be realized *through* the state.

At home, these ideas allowed the liberals in the 1900s to lay the foundations for welfare-state socialism. Abroad, they generated a new enthusiasm for imperial expansion and allowed liberals to support the occupation of Egypt in 1882, the scramble for Africa in the 1880s and 1890s, the Cape to Cairo scheme, and, after the First World War, the British annexation of much of the Arab lands of the Middle East. So, while the Tories could be described as opportunistic imperialists, willing to use the empire for domestic electoral purposes and to preserve British interests and security abroad, the real ideologues, the men driven by an intellectual theory and a determination to use it to change the world, were those Liberal Imperialists who rose to power in the late nineteenth and early twentieth centuries.

IN TERMS OF both ideology and policy, the biggest loser in all of this was classical liberalism. Its case against imperialism fell on deaf ears, its support of free trade was rejected in an age of protectionism, and for a long time it seemed to have been consigned to the dustbin of history. The reputation of classical liberalism did not revive until the 1980s when, reinvigorated by the arguments of the economists Milton Friedman and Friedrich von Hayek, it was given a political renaissance in the governments of Margaret Thatcher and Ronald Reagan.

The debate that has recently sprung up in the United States has been conducted within the same political boundaries, but with history reversing the position from which the major players have started. Today, the advocates of big government at home and state intervention abroad are the modern liberals or social democrats. The Clinton administration's intervention into the conflicts in Bosnia and Kosovo, where it had no immediate or foreseeable military interests, was an early case of action driven by the liberal ideology of international humanitarianism rather than strategic ends.

The same politics are now being invoked to draw America into Africa. According to the editor of *The New Republic*, Peter Beinart, "Africa's post-cold-war disaster zones suffer not from too much US imperialism but too little." Only when a former colonial power has stepped in to local conflicts, Beinart argues, have large numbers of African lives been saved. Beinart wants the United States to follow suit in Liberia and he is critical about those conservatives who oppose Liberian intervention, which they deem "foreign policy as social work." He calls this a "cold and narrow realism," which he contrasts with the generosity of the liberal spirit.

> Only the much-maligned liberal media, for instance ABC's Nightline, which in September 2001 broadcast a stunning five-part series from Congo, and liberal groups such as Human Rights Watch, have labored to keep Africa's crises in the spotlight. And it is primarily liberal internationalist voices, such as *The Washington Post* editorial page, which have pushed for intervention in Liberia and an intensified US role in Congo. If Africa's suffering represents a challenge to the conscience of the world, it is clear who on the US ideological spectrum is willing to face it and who would rather turn away.

As John Fonte's illuminating analyses have shown, until recently the leading ideology of these liberals was internationalism. Lawyers and human rights activists had hoped to integrate the United States into a global legal and economic order overseen by the United Nations, the International Criminal Court, the Kyoto protocol, and other international legal and environmental institutions. The unwillingness of the United States to surrender sovereignty to such institutions and to such an agenda, especially in the wake of the war against Iraq and the failure of the United Nations to take a positive role in that conflict, has cost this program much of its appeal.

INTO THIS VOID has come the idea of a global order conducted by an imperial United States itself. This is a concept that will have much the same appeal to the same kind of people, once they have pulled the appropriate mental levers to accommodate themselves to the switch of allegiance required. This is a liberalism not far removed from the variety that gave the graduates of Balliol the determination to spread British civilization to the world a century ago.

The moral rationale for such a movement has already been written. Its most prominent spokesman and perhaps greatest enthusiast is the British Prime Minister Tony Blair who, in both the UK and the US, has been advocating an optimistic program for reinventing the world. In the wake of September 11 he defined the appropriate American response not in terms of revenge but justice:

> Justice not only to punish the guilty. But justice to bring those same values of democracy and freedom to people round the world. . . . The starving, the wretched, the dispossessed, the ignorant, those living in want and squalor from the deserts of Northern Africa to the slums of Gaza, to the mountain ranges of Afghanistan; they too are our cause.

Blair has tied this appeal to the context of American security. Echoing lines from Paul Berman's recent book *Terror and Liberalism*, Blair told Congress in July: "The spread of freedom is the best security for the free. It is our last line of defense and our first line of attack." Blair's appeal struck a chord with a number of liberal commentators, including Richard Just who endorsed this "truly remarkable speech" in *American Prospect*. Just thought it a pity that Blair could not run for office in America. "But because a Blair presidency isn't possible, perhaps we can settle for the next best thing: a Democratic candidate who takes up the mantle of Blair's approach to world affairs and uses it to propel himself to the White House."

Even though some commentators like Peter Beinart have criticized conservatives for their less than enthusiastic endorsement of the same sentiments, there are a number of influential conservatives who differ only slightly in degree and definitely not in kind. The most prominent are Lawrence

Kaplan and William Kristol in their recent book, *The War over Iraq: Saddam's Tyranny and America's Mission*.

The authors try to distance themselves from Bill Clinton's "wishful liberalism," which led the United States to turn a blind eye to Saddam's murderous regime. But their support for the war goes much further than ousting a tyrant or enhancing the military position of the United States in the Middle East. America, Kaplan and Kristol argue, will liberate Iraq by force, create democracy in a land that has known only dictatorship, and apply Wilsonian principles to foreign policy. "The mission begins in Baghdad," they write, "but it does not end there." The Iraq war represents the dawn of a new historical era. It is "about more even than the future of the Middle East and the war on terror. It is about what sort of role the United States intends to play in the twenty-first century." The American occupation of Iraq, they acknowledge, is likely to take many years and will not be really complete until the whole Middle East is liberated from tyranny. America, they are convinced, should be the great democratic hope for mankind. "Not only is the United States a beacon of liberal democracy; every one of this country's leaders . . . has recognized the special role that America's principles play in its conduct abroad."

WHAT IS NOW known as American neoconservatism was born in the 1980s as a program to reform the economy, to revive the classical liberalism of free trade, small government, and the rule of market forces. It has been remarkably successful. Those countries that have adopted the neoconservative agenda have enjoyed the most sustained period of economic growth in a century. They broke down the inertia and dependency of the welfare state and helped win the Cold War. Modern liberals and social democrats have not dared to challenge them. Both Clinton and Blair adhered to the same successful formula. In economic policy today, Adam Smith rules.

In the wake of September 11, however, some neoconservatives want to cast off a crucial part of this legacy by ignoring

Smith's anti-imperialism. In doing so, they put their own success at risk. As the history of the British Empire demonstrated, once its liberals became imperialists, the first thing they abandoned was their liberalism. American neoconservatism is unlikely to avoid the same fate.

In other words, imperialism has always posed serious hazards for the imperial power itself. For a thousand years after the fall of Rome, the causes of its collapse occupied an important place in the Western mind. The main lesson was that there was always a point beyond which empires could not grow. On reaching this point, the imperial process would generate a malignancy that would eat away at the capital itself. Administration would become unmanageable, military forces would be spread too thin, and the metropolis would lose its original character and virtue.

Some felt Britain had reached this point around 1900, at the apparent zenith of its power and reach. Up to then, imperialism could be readily sold to the populace through its glamour, adventure, and its real economic benefits to the middle and lower classes. The Boer War, however, turned much of this sour. The war not only escalated the military costs of the empire but had a demoralizing effect at home, a combined impact that spawned a revived anti-imperial movement. This emerged, however, not amongst traditional liberals but on the far left of the political spectrum. When combined with a concern for a further escalation of the same costs during the First World War, anti-imperialism became a principal agenda of those political groups that thought their society so flawed it deserved to be transformed by socialist revolution.

A similar scenario, but with a much compressed timetable, would probably face an American empire at home. American history is grounded in anti-imperial sentiment. The foundation myth of the United States is an anti-colonial struggle. At various times in US history, appeals against imperialism have struck an electoral chord. Popular sentiment forced the hurried decolonization of Cuba after America acquired it in the 1898 war with Spain. After the Second World War, Americans saw themselves as opponents of the old European empires and actively resisted their return to their Asian territories.

Moreover, since the American radical left of the 1960s has not only survived but thrived thanks to its subsequent long march through the institutions of education, the media, and the arts, the point at which anti-imperialist sentiment could be turned against both American liberals and conservatives to rebuild a radical leftist constituency would be much lower than it was for Britain. A real American empire, rather than the imaginary version conjured by radical critics during the Cold War, would be a gift to the far left that would rebuild its constituency back to the levels it enjoyed during the campaign against the Vietnam War.

There is also America's track record as an imperial power to consider. In 1898, the war against Spain left the United States responsible for two substantial colonies, Cuba and the Philippines. In Cuba, the United States instituted a process that gave the country its first elected president, built schools and hospitals, and provided some modern infrastructure in the form of roads, bridges, and harbor facilities. In less than two and a half years, it handed administration back to the Cubans. Nevertheless, Cuban politics were volatile and a local rebellion led to a second American occupation in 1906. Within three years, government was again handed back to the locals who established a regime, which, for the next fifty years, was noted for its graft, corruption, and fiscal irresponsibility.

Officially, the United States governed the Philippines for the thirty-five years to 1935. It effectively ran the country, however, for only the first decade and then largely handed over power to local officials and institutions. While these were liberal and democratic on the surface, most historians agree they were the creatures of the traditional land-owning oligarchy, who used them for their own ends. In short, a decade was not long enough to transform the traditional political culture of the country.

It is true that America produced a much better result with Japan after 1945. But the Japanese were already a culturally and politically unified people who had largely modernized themselves in dramatic fashion during the nineteenth century. America added liberal democracy to a country that already had most of the other trappings of modernization. In stark contrast, the latest American venture into nation building is the extraordinarily difficult case of Iraq, an artificial country riven by tribal conflict and hatred which for the past five hundred years has known only imperial or tyrannical rule. To start an empire with a dependent of this kind is to set it up to fail.

None of this, of course, denies the benefits the British showed could be brought to the subjects of an empire, as both the *Oxford History* and Niall Ferguson have demonstrated. Adam Smith always argued, however, that free trade and the example of "sweet commerce" would have been a better way to do it. The most critical requirement for an underdeveloped country seeking to modernize is to cultivate a commercial and trading middle class. British imperialism did help this process but it always had better foundations where the impetus came from within. As Owen Harries has warned, liberal democracy is not an easily exported commodity. It is essentially a do-it-yourself enterprise.

ANOTHER CRUCIAL issue is the time needed to get results. The time that the historical record suggests would be required is far greater than any of its current proponents either realize or are willing to admit. Britain did bring liberalism, democracy, and modernization to India and left that country much better than it found it under Mughal rule. But Britain was a significant force in India for more than 170 years. Fifty years in Africa and the Middle East were not long enough. Plainly, no democratic polity today can think in terms of time scales so great. Moreover, the fact that so many of the former European colonies have suffered major economic and political relapses since gaining independence is evidence that, for much of the world, the stability and development they enjoyed under Britain would have required an imperial presence in perpetuity.

The strongest case made by both liberal and conservative advocates of empire is on grounds of security. The example of September 11 and the prospect of weapons of mass destruction becoming available to non-state terrorist movements, they argue, puts the survival of western urban civilization at risk and justifies pre-emptive military action against any country thought to harbor or to assist such groups. This is a powerful argument, and the war against Iraq was well justified on these grounds.

Nevertheless, whether American imperialism and the social transformation of terrorist homelands are appropriate responses to these threats is another question entirely. In particular, the idea that liberal democracy or even economic prosperity will provide an antidote to terrorism appears to be wishful thinking that runs counter to experience. In the 1960s, the liberal democracies of Germany, Italy, and the United States all spawned terrorist groups of their own, whose members were mostly well-educated and middle-class young people. Their cause was generated not by social deprivation but by political ideology. The September 11 al Qaeda suicide bombers had similar backgrounds. In Indonesia, the authoritarian, American-backed regime of General Suharto experienced no attacks by Islamic terrorists. It is newly democratic Indonesia that has suffered the bombings at Bali and Jakarta's Marriott Hotel.

Other assumptions in the debate over terrorism also need to be questioned. None of the proponents of empire have offered a good argument why contemporary terrorism needs any more response than a military one. Moreover, it is not clear why the toppling of one regime obliges the victor to take responsibility for rebuilding the political and economic infrastructure of the loser. A security threat requires a military response. To advise America to respond to Islamic fanaticism by embarking on a program of imperial expansion, while at the same time attempting to transform the countries of the

Middle East and Africa into liberal democracies, is to urge an oversized, misdirected, and extremely blunt instrument to deal with such an opponent.

At the end of the Second World War, America and its allies did feel it was necessary to restore the civil society of its enemies, Germany and Japan. But their most pressing reason was to curb the expansion of the Soviet Union. Today, that threat no longer exists. This, in fact, is the most critical difference in the respective positions of America and Britain as world leaders. It is the absence today of any current or foreseeable rival to American power which provides the strongest reason why it has no need of an empire.

The force that transformed Britain from an overseas trader with a handful of minor colonies into the major international player of its day was imperial rivalry. Starting with the Seven Years War of the 1750s, Britain and France embarked on the imperial equivalent of an arms race. Initially, the British presence in India had amounted to a small number of trading ports: Bombay, Madras, and Calcutta. Subsequently, conflict with France and its Mughal allies escalated to the point where victory in the resulting wars meant Britain acquired the territory of both the French and the Mughals. By the mid-nineteenth century, this process left most of the subcontinent in British hands. Eventually, to prevent its rival from gaining a strategic naval advantage, Britain felt compelled to establish a chain of naval stations around the globe, as well as colonies extending far into the Pacific Ocean.

Similarly, the scramble for Africa had more to do with guaranteeing the sea route to India and curbing the emerging imperial ambitions of the Germans and Italians than with securing Rhodesian gold and diamond mines. After Kitchener's victory at the Battle of Omdurman, Britain made the Sudan its colony not in order to improve the lives of the Sudanese but to keep the French out of the eastern Sahara and to protect Britain's far greater financial interests in neighboring Egypt.

The United States today is not in a comparable position.

There is no other serious contender on any horizon. Indeed, America's current place in the world is historically unique. There has never been a world power so far ahead of its competitors in economic and military terms. In 1913 Britain's share of world output was eight percent; the equivalent figure for the United States in 1998 was twenty-two percent. Present American military budgets are fourteen times that of China and twenty-two times that of Russia. Britain never enjoyed such a lead over her imperial rivals.

While it is true that rogue states and terrorists could inflict serious damage if they got the opportunity, none of them threaten America's world hegemony now or in the future. America's Islamic opponents pose as much threat to its strategic position as the Dervish brotherhood posed to the British in 1898. Kitchener at Omdurman and Napier at Magdala knew what to do. They confronted the enemy and destroyed him utterly. Similarly, the proper response today should be confined to the military. Only if another rival imperial force arose again, one that posed a threat on the scale of international communism during the Cold War, might the case for a more formal imperial role by America make sense. But without an imperative of this kind, America has no need to emulate the British Empire, or any other for that matter, and hence is unlikely to do so.

Modernism & Its Institutions

Hilton Kramer

I couldn't portray a woman in all her natural loveliness. I haven't the skill. No one has. I must, therefore, create a new sort of beauty, the beauty that appears to me in terms of volume, of line, of mass, of weight, and through that beauty interpret my subjective impression. Nature is a mere pretext for a decorative composition, plus sentiment. It suggests emotion, and I translate that emotion into art. I want to expose the Absolute, and not merely the factitious woman.
—Georges Braque, circa 1908

Subject, with her, is often incidental.
—Wallace Stevens, on the poetry of Marianne Moore, 1935

Content is a glimpse of something, an encounter like a flash. It's very tiny—very tiny, content.
—Willem de Kooning, 1963

Although we have lately been advised that "the days when one could sit down with an easy mind to write an account of something called modernism are over,"[1] there nonetheless remains very little in our experience of the arts even in this first decade of the twenty-first century that can be separated from the traditions that were established by what

---

1 *Art in Its Time: Theories and Practice of Modern Aesthetics* by Paul Mattick (Routledge, 2003), page 9.

used to be called the modern movement but that nowadays tend to be known collectively as modernism. As I shall be using the term here—that is, modernism as a movement in literature as well as the visual arts—it was never monolithic in style, ideas, or impact. In its heyday, which by my reckoning dates from the 1880s to the 1950s, it encompassed a broad range of styles, from realism and symbolism to pure abstraction, and a variety of anti-styles we associate with the legacy of Marcel Duchamp and Dadaism.

In many respects, modernism is identified as much by the traditions it rejects as by the innovations it embraces. In his *Histoire de la littérature française de 1789 à nos jours* (1936), the French historian Albert Thibaudet highlighted the radical nature of the modernist enterprise when he spoke of the commitment to the idea of "indefinite revolution," of

> a right and duty of youth to overturn the preceding generation, to run after an absolute. If the poets were divided into "normal," or "regular," and free-verse, literature was divided into normal literature, and literature of the "avant-garde." The chronic avant-gardism of poetry, the "What's new?" of the "informed" public, the official part given to the young, the proliferation of schools and manifestos with which these young hastened to occupy that extreme point, to attain for an hour that crest of the wave in a tossing sea—all this was not only a new development in 1885 but a new climate in French literature. The Symbolist revolution, the last thus far, might perhaps have been definitively the last, because it incorporated the theme of chronic revolution into the normal condition of literature.

Thibaudet's announced subject was Symbolist literature; but his diagnosis of the way a commitment to "chronic revolution" had become "the normal condition of literature" pertains equally to the whole project of modernism. The ultimate aesthetic and spiritual fruitfulness of this chronic revolution differed sharply among genres. In the pictorial arts, revolution first of all entailed rejection of the moribund conventions of nineteenth-century academic instruction, which had elevated a narrowly conceived mode of depicting the observable world to the status of an aesthetic and cultural absolute.

What modernism rejected in architecture was ornament, decorative embellishments, and explicit references to historical precedent. The Viennese architect Adolf Loos put the case against ornament with histrionic astringency in his 1908 essay "Ornament and Crime." "The evolution of culture," Loss wrote, "is synonymous with the removal of ornament from utilitarian objects." According to Loos, "freedom from ornament is a sign of spiritual strength." In the modern world, "art has taken the place of ornament," and a hankering after ornament is, for Loos, a sign of spiritual backwardness or criminality. "Anyone who goes to the *Ninth Symphony* and sits down and designs a wallpaper pattern is either a confidence trickster or a degenerate."

Loos may have written with tongue at least partly in cheek, but he nonetheless summed up a cardinal element in the brief of classic architectural modernism. We are now perhaps in a position to question how fruitful the rejection of ornament really was as an aesthetic desideratum: what seemed terribly brash and exciting in 1908 looks rather different when it succeeded in transforming whole cities into monotonous rows of rectangular glass and steel plinths.

As far as painting and sculpture are concerned, modernism introduced a radical revision in the very concept of representation, the implications of which are admirably summarized in George Heard Hamilton's introduction to his classic history, *Painting and Sculpture in Europe 1880–1940* (1967):

In the half-century between 1886, the date of the last Impressionist exhibition, and the beginning of the Second World War, a change took place in the theory and practice of art which was as radical and momentous as any that had occurred in human history. It was based on the belief that works of art need not imitate or represent natural objects and events.

Therefore artistic activity is not essentially concerned with representation but instead with the invention of objects variously expressive of human experience, objects whose structures as independent artistic entities cannot be evaluated in terms of their likeness, nor devalued because of their lack of likeness, to natural things.

But revolution and rejection do not tell the whole story of modernism. As I argued long ago in my essay "The Age of the Avant-Garde" (1972), the impulse to wage war on the past had a constructive as well as a rebellious side. What was most conspicuously embraced by modernism in the literary arts were so-called free verse (*vers libre*) in poetry, which entailed an abandonment of traditional rhyme and meter, and the "stream of consciousness" technique in fiction, which was introduced to literature in English by James Joyce but was made more accessible to public comprehension by the popularization of Freudian psychoanalytical therapy. These innovations entailed a rejection of nineteenth-century narrative conventions in favor of more hermetic literary structures based on myth, symbolism, and other devices more commonly found in poetry, especially modern poetry, than in prose fiction.

Moreover, owing to the resolute and often vindictive resistance that such innovations met with in the arena of public taste, it was probably inevitable that ways would be sought to circumvent that resistance. It was, in any case, in direct response to such prohibitions that the modernist impulse was driven to create institutions of its own in order to safeguard the survival and prosperity of its aesthetic initiatives. It was probably inevitable, too, that in the early history of these institutions, an attempt would be made to minimize the sometimes controversial content of modernism—not only its sexual explicitness but its political provocations as well. After all, in a period when even as blameless a book of short stories as Joyce's *Dubliners* met with refusal by its first printers on the grounds that certain passages were deemed to employ improper language, and a masterpiece like *Ulysses* was legally banned in the United States, there was ample reason to be cautious about publicizing the content of certain modernist works.

On the large and thorny question of modernism's content and its relation to modernist form, however, it must also be said that certain modernists have themselves been complicit in minimizing its content even under conditions where prudence was no longer required, as the epigraphs quoted above from Georges Braque, Wallace Stevens, and Willem de Kooning suggest. For anyone who was present on the New York art scene in 1953, for example, when de Kooning exhibited the first of his sensational *Women* paintings at the Sidney Janis Gallery, the much-quoted claim made ten years earlier, obviously in reference to abstract painting, that the content in the creation of a work of art is "very tiny," would have sounded absurd. The ferocity with which de Kooning attacked his subject in the *Women* series left no one in doubt about the importance of its content—both for the artist and viewer—and the unraveling of de Kooning's talent in the aftermath of the *Women* paintings, when he returned to a mode of abstraction that was sadly depleted of both form and content, only underscored the point.

Similarly, Wallace Stevens's observation that in the poetry of Marianne Moore, "Subject . . . is often incidental," may indeed apply to some of the poet's minor later work, but elsewhere Moore's poetry positively bristles with difficult subjects. In the early masterpiece from the 1920s called *Marriage*—a work that, in my view, occupies a place in Moore's literary oeuvre akin to that of *The Waste Land* in Eliot's—the intensity and indignation prompted by the subject of matrimony is anything but "incidental." Its treatment is ferocious, as the poem's opening lines attest:

This institution,
perhaps one should say enterprise
out of respect for which
one says one need

not change one's mind
about a thing one has believed in,
requiring public promises
of one's intention
to fulfill a private obligation:
I wonder what Adam and Eve
think of it by this time,
this fire-gilt steel
alive with goldenness;
how bright it shows—
"of circular traditions and impostures,
committing many spoils,"
requiring all one's criminal ingenuity
to avoid!

In a new edition of *The Poems of Marianne Moore*, edited by Grace Schulman (Viking, 2003), *Marriage* runs to eight and a half pages, and remains to its very last lines one of the most caustic poems in the language—one of the scariest, too.

Georges Braque was a far gentler soul than either Willem de Kooning or Marianne Moore, and it was characteristic of his moral delicacy to wrap his statement about the artist's subject in a mantle of modesty, only to disclose in the end that, like so many other modernists, his too had been a pursuit of the Absolute. Braque's version of the Absolute no doubt differed from that of the true firebrands of modernism —among them, Piet Mondrian, Mies van der Rohe, Ad Reinhardt, and Donald Judd—yet where would any of them have been without the prior existence of Cubism, the creation of which was owed to Braque's collaboration with Picasso? It might even be said that Braque created the foundation upon which these firebrands were able to take their stand.

The great irony, as I pointed out in "The Age of The Avant-Garde," is that this effort to place tradition under the pressure of a constant revaluation had an unexpected effect. It resulted in the virtual dissolution of any really viable concept of tradition. And this sense of dissolution—of the muteness or sterility of tradition—is at the heart of the situation in which we find ourselves today. Without the bulwark of a fixed tradition, modernism found itself deprived of its historic antagonist. Much to its own embarrassment, it found that it had itself become a tradition—albeit one without obvious progeny. With its victory over the authority of the past complete, its own raison d'être had disappeared, and it had, in fact, ceased to exist except as an imaginary enterprise engaged in combat against imaginary adversaries.

In fact, in its most fruitful manifestations, the modernist attitude toward tradition was as much a distillation or transformation as a rejection of tradition. Indeed, a revaluation of the past is precisely what the modernist masters were forcing upon the official guardians of taste. One thinks in this context of T. S. Eliot, himself a modernist pioneer, who outlined in "Tradition and the Individual Talent" (1919) a vision of originality in which "not only the best, but the most individual parts of [a poet's] work may be those in which the dead poets, his ancestors, assert their immortality most vigorously." "No poet, no artist of any art," Eliot wrote in one of the most famous passages of that famous essay,

> has his complete meaning alone. His significance, his appreciation is the appreciation of his relation to the dead poets and artists. You cannot value him alone; you must set him, for contrast and comparison, among the dead. I mean this as a principle of esthetic, not merely historical, criticism . . . [for] what happens when a new work of art is created is something that happens simultaneously to all the works of art which preceded it. The existing monuments form an ideal order among themselves, which is modified by the introduction of the new (the really new) work of art among them.

Eliot's effort was not to subvert tradition but, on the contrary, to salvage it from the sclerotic imperatives of an exhausted antiquarianism or impotent gentility. To what extent Eliot succeeded may be open to question—his conception of an

"ideal order" of "existing monuments" may in the end have
been too purely aesthetic to bear the existential burden of
vitality with which he invested it. Nevertheless, Eliot's example illustrated the apparently unavoidable paradox that the
advent of modernism brought with it the seeds of its own
perpetual renovation: the anti-institutional impulse of
modernism would ultimately be brought to bear on the
seemingly unassailable institution that was modernism itself.
The question that confronts us today is to what extent the
institutions of modernism can survive the consuming effects
of their own self-immolation—survive, I mean, as vital
sources of cultural renewal, not simply as vacant bureaucratic
placeholders.

WHAT ARE the institutions that either created or were com-
mandeered to accommodate modernism's battle of the Absolutes? Some of them have become so well established as fix-
tures of our cultural landscape that we can hardly imagine a
time when they didn't exist—among them, the art galleries,
with their one-man shows of new art; the art museums that
vie with each other for the privilege of being the first to
embrace what is certain to be controversial; the "little
magazines," literary quarterlies and small presses without
which modernist literature would never have prospered; the
more problematic writers' "workshops," which seem now to
have degenerated into an academic racket (one recalls
Kingsley Amis's remark that much of what was wrong with
the twentieth century could be summed up in the word
"workshop"); and the Armory Show-type of large international exhibitions that grew out of the various "independent"
and "secessionist" modernist movements of a century or more
ago.
  Virtually all of these institutions were created by artists
working in collaboration with amateur, non-institutional collectors, just as the little magazines, small presses, and literary
quarterlies were created by poets and critics who understood
that mainstream publishers were not in a position to respond

to the challenges of modernist literature without the kind of spadework that only non-institutional amateurs could provide. As Lionel Trilling wrote in his essay "The Function of the Little Magazine":

> To the general lowering of the status of literature and of the interest in it, the innumerable "little magazines" have been a natural and heroic response. Since the beginning of the [twentieth] century, meeting difficulties of which only their editors can truly conceive, they have tried to keep the roads open. From the elegant and brilliant *Dial* to the latest little scrub from the provinces, they have done their work, they have kept our culture from being cautious and settled, or merely sociological, or merely pious. They are snickered at and snubbed, sometimes deservedly, and no one would venture to say in a precise way just what effect they have—except that they keep the new talents warm until the commercial publisher with his customary air of noble resolution is ready to take his chance, except that they make the official representatives of literature a little uneasy, except that they keep a countercurrent moving which perhaps no one will be fully aware of until it ceases to move.

Now, nearly sixty years after Trilling wrote "The Function of the Little Magazine" to mark the tenth anniversary of *Partisan Review*, the kind of "little magazine" he described in that essay is virtually extinct—as, of course, is *Partisan Review*. Some literary quarterlies have survived, but have diminished in number and—with the shining exception of *The Hudson Review* and (if I may say it) *The New Criterion*—in quality, too, as the blight of deconstructionist, post-structuralist, and other varieties of anti-literary "theory" has triumphed over literary intelligence. When we look back today on the much-maligned New Criticism, which was largely the creation of modernist poets—among them, T. S. Eliot and Ezra Pound—it looks like a Golden Age compared to the kind of academic obscurantism and political shadow-boxing that have supplanted it.

As for the fate of literature itself in the hands of the mainstream book publishers, we find that virtually all of the major houses in this country are now wholly owned subsidiaries of foreign conglomerates whose standard of achievement has less to do with literary quality or innovation than with access to media promotion, movie and television tie-ins, prize-winning, and other coefficients of high profitability. Mercifully, we can still count on a number of smaller presses and some of the better university presses to save the situation, but the downside of this benefit usually entails significantly reduced royalties for the worthy writers who do get published.

Exactly how it came to pass that a nation as prosperous as ours could not summon the resources to resist the takeover of its book-publishing industry by an ailing Europe remains to be explained, but that takeover is now a *fait accompli*, and we shall be obliged to suffer its consequences for a long time to come.

IN SOME RESPECTS, the institutions that serve the visual arts—especially the museums and the galleries—might seem to present a much rosier prospect, for even in periods of low economic growth they have continued to prosper. Indeed, headlong and often heedless expansion of both collections and exhibition space and the funds required to support them has been the rule in the art museums for some years now. Modernist art of various persuasions has been the driving force as well as the principal beneficiary of this very expensive expansiveness as museums have hastened to respond to new artistic developments while at the same time attempting to catch up on the earlier innovations they missed out on. This museological scenario is now so familiar to us that we sometimes forget that the compulsion on the part of museums to keep abreast of radical innovations in contemporary art—and even, when possible, to anticipate and assist in creating a demand for them—was itself a momentous innovation in the way museums come to identify their interests and responsibilities.

For this compulsion obligated the museums to become, in effect, not only collectors but also promoters of the art in which they were seen to have a vested interest—a vested interest, that is, in both the objects acquired for their collections and in the careers and celebrity of the artists who created them.

Hence the elements of hucksterism and entrepreneurial cynicism that have coarsened the character and spirit of so much museum activity today. Consider the advent of the museum called Tate Modern in London. Born in a blitz of publicity the like of which had formerly been reserved for pop stars and consumer gadgets, Tate Britain was the huge spin-off from the venerable Tate Gallery (now rebaptized Tate Britain). Housed in a gigantic renovated power plant on Bankside across the Thames from the original Tate Gallery, Tate Modern is ostensibly devoted to modern art. In fact, as the Tate's chief commissar Sir Nicholas Serota put it when announcing the bifurcation of the original Tate Gallery, Tate Modern is really devoted to "new narratives" of art—"new narratives," alas, in which the energy and seriousness of modernism is trivialized and distorted in order to accommodate its repackaging as a postmodernist exercise in chic cultural shallowness.

When we enter a monstrosity like Tate Modern in London, we are straightaway put on notice by the noise, the crowds, the theatrical lighting, and the general atmosphere of vulgarity and tumult that art has been used as bait to attract a segment of the public—free-spending youth—for which aesthetic achievement is, if not a matter of indifference, certainly not a compelling priority. And to assure a steady supply of the only kind of new art that is guaranteed to be a turn-on for this public, there are the proliferating productions of Charles Saatchi's gang of YBA's—Young British Artists—and the Tate's own atrocious Turner Prize winners, who can be counted upon to maintain the requisite standard of titillation.

Unlike the old Tate Gallery, our own Solomon R. Guggenheim Museum has not had to change its name but only its character to adjust to the new entrepreneurial standard. I wonder how many of the people who went to ogle Matthew Barney's freak show at the Guggenheim have any idea that this museum, with its once incomparable collection of paintings by Vasily Kandinsky, was founded in 1930 as an institution devoted to the achievements of abstract painting? (Its original name was the Museum of Non-Objective Painting.) Yet, just as its influence in that respect was contributing something important to the emergence of Abstract Expressionist painting in New York—the young Jackson Pollock, among other artists, worked there as a guard in its early days—the Guggenheim initiated the first of its ongoing efforts to reinvent itself. This project of reinvention has left the museum stripped of anything that can be called an identity and has required, among other depredations, the sale of a great many of its Kandinsky holdings and works by other modernist masters. Today it is an institution better known for its exhibitions of Norman Rockwell and Harley-Davidson motorcycles and its branch museums abroad than for anything that advances an understanding of modernist art.

Two of the other New York institutions that were founded to serve the interests of modernist art—the Museum of Modern Art and the Whitney Museum of American Art—are also at a crossroads that will determine their future course but for very different reasons.

MOMA is now in the throes of yet another of its periodic expansion plans, one of the biggest in its history. When the expansion is completed in 2005, it is expected to provide the museum with far more space for showing its permanent collection as well as for its temporary exhibitions program. Meanwhile, the museum and its public are making do with an abridged, unappealing facility in Long Island City, MOMAQNS, for a reduced exhibition schedule, and a theater on East Twenty-third Street in Manhattan for its popular film program.

At this point, we can only speculate about what this expansion will bring in the way MOMA's permanent collection—and thus modernism itself—is to be presented to the public for the remainder of the twenty-first century. If there is good reason to be hopeful about this outcome, it is mainly because John Elderfield—no doubt one of the most qualified senior curators in the field today—has been called upon to head the curatorial committee that will oversee the installation of MOMA's permanent collection in its new building. If there is also good reason to be anxious about the outcome, it is owing to the debacle of the museum's *MOMA2000* exhibitions, which radically recast the history of MOMA's permanent collection to conform to a "new narrative" emphasizing social content at the expense of aesthetic innovation. This was a shift in perspective that, among other losses, had the effect of consigning the history of abstract art—one of the central developments of modernist art—to the sidelines. Given the theme-park character that governed the organization of *MOMA2000*, there was no way that the aesthetics of abstraction could be given its due. It thus remains to be seen whether Mr. Elderfield will have sufficient authority to rectify such disastrous errors of judgment in the newly expanded MOMA.

About the future of the Whitney Museum, too, we can only speculate. Its recent history, marked by a succession of incompetent directors and a board of trustees that seemed at times to have lost its mind, has been so dismal that almost any change is likely to be a change for the better. The good news is that the Whitney's plan for a harebrained expansion of its own has been cancelled for financial reasons. The appointment of Adam D. Weinberg, a former curator at the Whitney, as the museum's new director also gives us reason to expect significant improvement. It will not be easy, however, for the Whitney to win back the respect it has lost among artists as well as the critics and the public. A good place to start would be either the overhaul or the outright abandonment of the Whitney's Biennial exhibitions, which in recent years have gone from being merely ludicrous to wholly contemptible.

As for the international exhibitions like Documenta in Germany and the monster Biennials in Venice and São Paulo, they have now become cultural dinosaurs with no useful functions to perform and therefore no reason to exist. There was a period, of course, when exhibitions like the 1910 Post-Impressionism exhibition in London, the 1913 Armory Show in New York, and the 1938 International Exposition of Surrealism in Paris, really did bring the public news of important avant-garde developments in modernist art. But the age of the avant-garde is long gone. Its celebrated scandals and audacities have passed into the possession of the academic curriculum, to be catalogued, codified, and otherwise processed for doctoral dissertations and classroom instruction. The pathetic attempts at artistic insolence, mostly having to do with sexual imagery and political ideology, that turn up in the Whitney's Biennial exhibitions and the art departments of colleges and universities are better understood as efforts to attract publicity and what in the business world is called market share than as anything that can be regarded as avant-garde. In a culture like ours, in which, alas, everything is now permitted and nothing resisted, the conditions necessary for the emergence of a genuine avant-garde no longer exist. It doesn't change anything, either, to adopt the term "trangressive" as a substitute for "avant-garde," for where boundaries no longer exist it is impossible to violate them. "Transgressive" is a term that belongs to the history of publicity rather than the history of art. Today there is no avant-garde, and the big international shows are mainly devoted to marketing and politics. Modern systems of communication have, in any case, rendered the big international shows irrelevant.

FAR MORE IMPORTANT to sustaining the aesthetic vitality of modernist art, however, has been the institution that we do not usually even think of as an institution: I mean the commercial art gallery. The art gallery as we know it today is, after all, a modern creation, barely a century old, and it performs a service for art unlike that of any other institution. It keeps the public in constant touch not only with current developments on the art scene but also with revivals of the work of earlier artists that the museums and the critics may have overlooked or underrated, and it does so at no financial cost to the viewer. More often than not, it is the gallery dealer, not the museum curator, who discovers significant new talent, for nowadays most curators make their "discoveries" in the dealers' galleries.

This is a cultural service more often enjoyed than acknowledged, but for many of us the art galleries have been a fundamental part of our aesthetic education. In this connection, it is worth recalling Clement Greenberg's tribute to the late Betty Parsons, whose gallery introduced Jackson Pollock, Hans Hofmann, Mark Rothko, Barnett Newman, and Richard Pousette-Dart, among other artists, to gallerygoers of my generation. In 1955, on the tenth anniversary of the Betty Parsons Gallery, Greenberg wrote:

> Mrs. Parsons has never lacked for courage. It is not a virtue signally associated with art dealers (or, for that matter, with art critics or museum directors either), but then she is not, at least for me, primarily a dealer. I have seldom been able to bring her gallery into focus as part of the commercial apparatus of art (I am not sneering at that apparatus); rather, I think of it as belonging more to the studio and production side of art. In a sense like that in which a painter is referred to as a painter's painter or a poet as a poet's poet, Mrs. Parsons is an artist's—and critic's—gallery: a place where art goes on and is not just shown and sold.

Just as modernist art in America was, initially, an extension and appropriation of European modernism, so was a gallery like Betty Parsons's in a tradition that grew out of the precedents set by Vollard and Kahnweiler in Paris and Alfred Stieglitz's "291" gallery, which introduced Cézanne and Matisse as well as Marsden Hartley and John Marin to the New York public even before the Armory Show and long before the museums awakened to the achievements of modernism. The same could be said of the Weyhe Gallery's efforts on behalf of Gaston Lachaise and Alfred Maurer and the exhibitions devoted to

Stuart Davis at Edith Halpert's Downtown Gallery. At every stage in the history of modernism in America, it was the galleries that set the pace in recognizing artistic achievement. This is not to suggest that all of our art dealers are sainted figures, but merely to point out that in New York, anyway, we are blessed with an extraordinary number of galleries that are places "where art goes on," and they should be given their due in any account of modernism and its institutions.

Finally, it is inevitable—or at least expected—in any discussion of modernism that the question of postmodernism will rear its ugly head. Or should I say, its wrong-headedness? For the entire concept of postmodernism is based on a fundamental misconception—a belief that the modernist era in art and culture is over and has been supplanted by something radically different. What we find this usually means when we get down to specific cases is a mode of art or thought in which some element of modernist sensibility has been corrupted by kitsch, politics, social theory, gender theory, or some other academic, pop-oriented, anti-aesthetic intervention. Modernism has aged to be sure, as modernity itself has aged, and in the process modernism has undeniably lost its capacity to shock or otherwise disturb us. But except for the short-lived antics of Dada and Surrealism, shock was never the essence of modernism. It was, rather, an inspired and highly successful attempt to bring art and culture into an affective and philosophical alignment with the mindset of modernity as we know it in our daily lives. Modernism endures, and does so, in part, anyway, by virtue of the institutions it has created to serve the needs of a public that is today more enlightened intellectually and aesthetically than at any other time in our history. Postmodernism, in contrast, has created no institutions of its own, largely because postmodernism is nothing but a mindset of deconstructive attitudes in search of a mission.

As I have noted elsewhere, we are far more aware than earlier generations of the many divisions, contradictions, and countervailing tendencies within modernism. We are more aware, too, that what goes under the name "postmodern" is really only modernism gone rancid—modernism with a sneer, a giggle, modernism without any animating faith in the nobility and pertinence of its cultural mandate. At any rate, it is a crowning irony that much that modernism in its original formulations took as essential to its identity should now appear just as dispensable as representation, narrative, ornament, and other traditional aesthetic accoutrements once did to the early modernists. It turns out that no style or genre has a monopoly on the modernist spirit. Its core is not synonymous with abstract art or plotless novels or Miesian glass boxes. On the contrary, the core of modernism lies in an attitude of honesty to the imperatives of lived experience, which means also an attitude of critical openness to the aesthetic and moral traditions that have defined our culture. The problem with postmodernism is not that it embraces architectural ornamentation or representational painting or self-referential plot lines. The problem is postmodernism's sentimental rejection of the realities of modern life for the sake of an ideologically informed fantasy world. In this sense, modernism is not only still vital: it remains the only really vital tradition for the arts. It is, in many ways, a broken or fragmented tradition, a tradition bequeathed to us not in a perfectly legible script that guarantees our continuity with the past, but in the hieroglyphic syllables of a past that must be continuously redeciphered in order to shed intermittent light on our half-plotted itinerary. We see, then, that what modernism requires is not a commitment to "chronic revolution" but rather permanent restlessness. It yields insights, but not finality. The traditions it recovers are partial, fragmentary, but also forthright and nourishing: "these fragments I have shored against my ruin."

LOOKING BACK on the history of modernism in the twentieth century, what is especially striking is the violence that was directed against its achievements by the most horrific totalitarian regimes in recorded history: the Nazis in Hitler's Germany and the Communists in Stalin's Russia. And if we ask the question of what it was about modernist art that prompted such a massively destructive response, I believe the answer is clear: modernist art was seen to provide a spiritual and emotional haven from the coercive and conformist pressures of the societies in which it flourished. Modernism represented a freedom of mind that totalitarian regimes could not abide. It is in this sense, perhaps, that the infamous *Degenerate Art* exhibition that Hitler devoted to modernist art in Munich in 1937 may now be seen to have marked the beginning of the "postmodernist" impulse. And just as modernism survived the determined efforts of Hitler and Stalin to impugn and destroy its artistic achievements, so, I believe, will modernism and its institutions continue to prosper in the face of the nihilist imperatives of the postmodernist scam.

The Art of War

Frederick W. Kagan

THE AMERICAN MILITARY today may be in the best position of any military in history. Its victories over Iraq and
Afghanistan have transformed not merely the way the U.S.
thinks about and conducts war, but the way the entire world
sees violent conflict. American technological prowess and the
skill of the professional American armed forces have opened a
gap in capabilities between the U.S. and its closest competitors
that many see as unbridgeable. Those triumphs, as well as the
American people's perception of the threats that the U.S. faces,
have also served dramatically to reduce the mutual mistrust and
hostility that had separated the military from the public since
the Vietnam War. Trusted by its people, emulated by its friends,
feared by its foes, unequalled in capability and skill, the American military is in many respects at the height of its power.
Properly handled, the U.S. armed forces might be able to maintain and even extend their preeminence into the distant future.

The challenges facing the military today, however, are no
less daunting than the opportunities are promising. Most
leaders and observers agree that the U.S. military will have to
"transform" itself in order to maintain its lead as well as to be
able to meet the challenges of the present and the future for
which it was not designed. At the same time, the U.S. is engaged in a war on terrorism, in peacekeeping operations in
Afghanistan, Bosnia, and Kosovo, and in a massive peace-

keeping, counter-insurgency, counter-terrorism, and reconstruction effort in Iraq. Tensions over nuclear proliferation remain high on the Korean peninsula and in Iran. Tensions also remain high over the cooperation of states like Syria in the war on terrorism and operations in Iraq.

These ongoing operations and threats have combined to stretch the U.S. armed forces beyond the breaking point. The Army has been compelled to deploy tens of thousands of soldiers for a full year at a time rather than the normal six months, to forego important training for those soldiers, and sometimes to send soldiers returning from one such deployment immediately into another. The National Guard and Reserves have been mobilized to an extent unprecedented since the 1970s first for "homeland defense" in the wake of the September 11 attacks and now in support of operations in Iraq, the Balkans, and elsewhere. The strain on soldiers and their families is growing, morale is declining, and it is hard to believe that these trends will not begin to take a serious toll on recruitment and retention in the near future, potentially exacerbating the problem.

The issues of transformation and military overstretch are inextricably linked. The Secretary of Defense has adopted a vision of transformation that relies on high-technology weapons systems rather than on soldiers. He has continued to pursue this program even as the armed forces have been stretched thinner and thinner. He has even resisted efforts by Congress to expand the military—a virtually unimaginable stance for a sitting Secretary of Defense—in order to preserve his program of military transformation. As a result, the U.S. is now attempting to transform its military in ways that hinder the conduct of current operations, even as those operations literally rip it apart. Worst of all, the current program of transformation turns its back on the approach that had brought America success so far, and flies in the face of the historical lessons about how to transform a military. If these problems remain unacknowledged and unaddressed, the U.S. may lose its predominance and endanger its security.

AMERICA ACHIEVED military dominance in 1991 with the collapse of the Soviet Union. Since no other state or group of states had been attempting to compete directly with the two superpowers, U.S. preeminence arrived unexpectedly and by default. The roots of the dominant position America holds today lie, therefore, in efforts American leaders made in the period from the late 1960s through the early 1980s to transform the military in order the better to face the USSR.

This first transformation had both a technological component and human element. In the twenty years from 1965 to 1985 America fielded a host of new weapons systems, created a global satellite constellation and advanced communications systems, and pioneered the development of entire new technologies such as stealth and precision-guided munitions (PGMs). In the midst of that technological transformation, a sociological transformation was also taking place within the armed forces. In the mid-1970s the U.S. abandoned the draft and recruited an all-volunteer professional military. Current military theory focuses almost exclusively on the technological aspect of transformation, but the human element was at least as important in bringing the American armed forces to their current level of excellence.

Almost all of the main weapons systems American forces used in Iraq and Afghanistan were developed and fielded in the 1960s and 1970s. The Air Force used new concepts of aircraft design and took advantage of computerization to produce the first generation of "super-fighters," including the F-15 and F-16, while the Navy developed its equivalent in the F-14. These aircraft, together with the F/A-18 fielded somewhat later, dominated the skies over Iraq and have led many of America's likeliest competitors to focus on air defense systems rather than on building their own aircraft with which to challenge the super-fighters. Fear of the Soviet air defense systems, through which American bombers would have to penetrate to strike their targets, led to an intense program in stealth technology in the 1970s and 1980s. That program bore fruit in the form of the F-117 fighter and the

B-2 bomber, used to great effect over Kosovo, Afghanistan, and Iraq.

The family of super-fighters and other advanced aircraft designed in the 1960s and 1970s was intended to provide versatility and redundancy. It reflected a determination to be the best at everything. The F-16 was designed to be the world's best dogfighter, able to achieve extremely high kill ratios either with its Sidewinder missiles or with its guns. The F-15 is an air-superiority fighter that was always meant to rely on its superior missiles and missile control technology to defeat enemy aircraft before they got within anything like dogfighting range. The F-14 attempts to duplicate the better characteristics of both planes in a naval version—the F/A-18 is an improvement on it, especially in the area of ground attack. Each plane overlaps the others in capabilities, but each is also designed to excel in a particular niche.

At the same time, the Air Force also fielded the A-10 ground attack aircraft. This ungainly, heavily armored plane with a 30mm anti-tank gun in its snout was designed to be the best tank-killer in the air. Its armor protects it from anti-aircraft machine guns and allows it to fly low to the ground and slowly enough to identify and engage its targets directly. It was enormously effective in Iraq, filling a specific niche that directly supported the Army's missions as well as the larger goal of destroying Iraq's armored forces. In short, it was not simply the development of PGMs that has made the U.S. Air Force the best in the world, but the quality of its aircraft across the board and in every specialty.

THE CURRENT American Army is also the result of changes made in the 1970s designed to allow it to excel in many areas. In the wake of the Vietnam War, Army Chief of Staff Creighton Abrams determined to revolutionize the Army's equipment by fielding a new generation of weapons systems including the M1 "Abrams" Tank, the Bradley Infantry Fighting Vehicle, the Apache and Blackhawk helicopters, the Multiple-Launch Rocket System (MLRS), the Stinger surface-to-air missile, and the Patriot air defense system. These were the main weapons systems Army forces have used to such success in all of the post-Cold War conflicts.

The goal of this technological transformation was to provide balanced capabilities to the Army. The M1 tank is a case in point. It was armored better than any other vehicle in the world at the time, and remains incredibly hard to kill. Its 120mm main gun firing depleted uranium anti-tank rounds gave it unprecedented destructive power—there are virtually no vehicles in existence today that an M1 cannot destroy. The M1 can move at up to fifty miles per hour, an extremely high speed considering the tank's seventy-ton weight. The M1, therefore, offered superb offensive and defensive power and excellent tactical mobility.

It has proven remarkably versatile. In open maneuver warfare in the Iraqi desert the M1 fulfilled its initial design goals. The Iraqis were unable to kill it even with direct hits from their T-72 tanks, and M1s killed almost every Iraqi vehicle they fired on with one shot. In 1991 as in 2003, American armored forces were able to move much faster than the Iraqis had expected.

The M1's defensive characteristics have also made it invaluable for a range of missions its designers had not foreseen. In peacekeeping operations in dangerous areas such as Bosnia and Iraq, the M1's virtual invulnerability has been important in deterring attacks and keeping critical areas secure. The Bradley Infantry Fighting Vehicle has also proved invaluable in this regard. It is no accident that almost all of the casualties American forces in Iraq have taken (apart from friendly-fire incidents) were to soldiers who were either dismounted or riding in trucks or Humvees.

The willingness to accept redundancy and inefficiency in defense programs that characterized the Army and Air Force transformations around the 1970s reflected a larger willingness to balance the development of capabilities, sometimes different, sometimes similar, across the services. At the same time the Army was developing the Patriot anti-aircraft missile, the

Air Force was fielding the planes that convinced all of America's subsequent foes not even to try to fly. As the Army was planning a tank that was both nearly indestructible and indescribably lethal to enemy armored vehicles, the Air Force was fielding an aircraft specifically to kill enemy tanks. The examples of redundant development are legion.

The most recent wars have made the virtues of this redundancy manifest. On numerous occasions, including as recently as the 2003 Gulf War, weather conditions restricted the Air Force's ability to fly sorties against enemy armored concentrations. The ability of the tanks and Bradleys of the 3rd Infantry Division to survive encounters with those enemy armored forces saved American lives. The Patriot has proven largely unnecessary in its role as a system to shoot down enemy aircraft. Its transformation into a ballistic missile defense system, however, gave the coalition much greater confidence in its ability to handle Saddam Hussein's missiles during the last war. Redundancy in war can yield flexibility and security. It ensures that when one system fails for whatever unforeseen reason, another can take its place. It provides the ability to meet unexpected challenges. In military affairs, redundancy is a virtue.

REDUNDANCY, of course, is expensive. During the Vietnam War and the Reagan buildup, the overriding threat of Soviet military power helped overcome America's traditional reluctance to spend money on its defense. Even Jimmy Carter, at the height of an economic recession that would cost him his presidency, felt obliged by the Soviet invasion of Afghanistan to begin the massive rearmament program that Ronald Reagan inherited and enlarged still further. The excellence of the American military in the 1990s owes a great deal to those days of open coffers.

The coffers inevitably closed with the fall of the Soviet Union. As Boris Yeltsin was attempting to forge a democratic Russian Federation on the ruins of the U.S.S.R., American defense officials and civilian experts were already talking of the "strategic pause" and the "peace dividend" that were supposed to follow that epochal event. Defense budgets dwindled and efficiency became the watchword in the Pentagon and on Capitol Hill.

The focus on efficiency and economics led to an effort to adopt "business practices" into the work of the military. This effort has a long history. Robert McNamara, himself a retired Ford executive, attempted to bring business models into the Pentagon in the 1960s. He applied new metrics to the Vietnam conflict, centering on body counts. He introduced a "game-theory" approach to war in the form of "graduated pressure" in which military forces were explicitly used to send messages to the enemy, whose responses could then be predicted. In general he preferred the advice of his "whiz kids," who understood the new way of thinking, to that of the professional military officers who clung to the "outdated" modes of conducting war. The results of this approach are well known.

Since then, the armed forces have adopted successively almost every major business fad, like "total quality management," "velocity management," and "just-in-time logistics," among others. Efforts to reduce the defense budget in the 1990s in order to expand the "peace dividend" led Secretary of Defense William Cohen to announce a "revolution in business affairs" in the Pentagon, to parallel and support the "revolution in military affairs" that he sought to bring about by transforming the military. The goal was to make the Pentagon more efficient and to use the funds recouped by that efficiency to support transformation.

At the same time that Cohen and his successors were attempting to bring business models once again to the economic side of the Pentagon, others were attempting to replicate McNamara's attempts to bring business models into the conduct of war. Throughout the 1990s a series of articles and books argued that the "information revolution" then sweeping the economy had an equivalent in the realm of war. Just as businesses had had to change their entire approaches to their work as a result of information technology, so too did armies. The "new economy," according to the wisdom of its advocates in the late 1990s, had its own new rules. Military thinkers like retired admirals William Owens and Arthur Cebrowski, among others, argued that war in the information age also had its own new rules. They argued further that the lessons of the new economy could be translated more or less directly to the business of waging war.

In *Network-Centric Warfare* (1999), a book central to the current U.S. program to transform its military, three defense analysts argued that the "information revolution" had fundamentally altered both business and war. In the past, they claimed, success relied upon the ability to move material objects around. Businesses that could produce items more rapidly and ship them faster and cheaper succeeded; those that could not failed. Similarly, armies succeeded by moving their forces to the decisive point and time and there concentrating them to defeat a similarly concentrated enemy.

The information revolution changed all that. Success in business now lay, they argued, in moving information around. Businesses that could acquire, disseminate, and analyze information would succeed; those that could not would fail. They described the reasons for Wal-Mart's success, pointing to its tightly integrated system for gathering information at the point-of-sale and disseminating that information not only to its own executives and other stores, but also to its suppliers.

Armies, they argued, now faced the same challenges. It was no longer necessary to concentrate forces—in fact, given the speed of events and the dangers of weapons of mass destruction, it had become dangerous. Instead, the successful army was the one that acquired the most exact possible knowledge of the enemy, that analyzed that knowledge to determine which "nodes" to attack, and that directed weapons systems launched from widely dispersed platforms to strike those nodes. It would not be necessary to move many forces around, only to ensure that they were within the thousand-kilometer range of their proposed targets.

These proposals received a powerful support when Donald Rumsfeld became Secretary of Defense in January 2001. Like McNamara, Rumsfeld came from the business community, and was determined to bring his business expertise to bear on the Pentagon bureaucracy. He believed enthusiastically in the Network-Centric Warfare model then being propounded, and he went even further. Determined to transform the military in accord with NCW ideas, Rumsfeld was also determined to do it at the lowest possible cost. He adopted a business approach to that problem as well.

A business can improve its bottom line by focusing its resources on the few things it does very well and abandoning markets in which it is performing poorly. Efficiency is all in business, a fact reflected in the many mergers that have taken place during the recent economic downturn. By eliminating redundancy and focusing on the areas in which they can excel, companies can dramatically improve their competitive position in some markets, even at the cost, sometimes, of abandoning others. Rumsfeld has adopted this approach in the area of military transformation.

AMERICA'S BIGGEST lead, the "market" in which the U.S. has the best competitive advantage, now lies in the realm of long-range reconnaissance and strike capabilities. No other state or group of states can begin to match America's ability to identify a huge number of targets and to attack them from platforms thousands of miles away.

The advantage in this area is greater than that in others. The U.S. has the best ground forces in the world, but China has larger ground forces, Germany has excellent tanks, Russia has large amounts of artillery, and so forth. America has the greatest ability to move and supply large forces to distant theaters, but Britain, France, and Russia can project force halfway around the world as well. None of those states, however, can come close to matching America's ability to identify, track, and destroy targets from great distances away.

Even if Rumsfeld had not been an enthusiastic supporter of

Network-Centric Warfare, it was only natural that his application of business principles to war would lead him to focus on America's capabilities with precision-guided munitions. This is currently the area of America's greatest competitive advantage. By directing funding into it, the U.S. can obtain an even greater competitive advantage—perhaps even the "lockout" that NCW advocates seek. In business, "lockout" occurs when one company attains such a predominant position that it can not be challenged.

The watchwords for the Rumsfeld Pentagon have, therefore, been focus and efficiency. The Pentagon has repeatedly stated that all new weapons systems will be evaluated primarily on the degree to which they further the armed forces' ability to conduct Network-Centric Warfare. Systems that bring other capabilities to the force have received less attention, less funding, and have sometimes been cancelled.

All of the services have participated in this race to a single goal. For example, the Navy now sells every new ship design on the basis of its ability to support Network-Centric Warfare. The Air Force has focused most of its development in the past decade on upgrading its PGMs and the ability of its aircraft to carry and control them. It now attempts to justify the F-22 and the Joint Strike Fighter on the grounds that they will support NCW the better, although the evidence for that claim is sketchy at best.

The result of these service changes will be to homogenize the armed forces. No longer will each service bring unique capabilities to the table, but all will now provide the same capability—the capability to identify and attack targets with PGMs at great distances. This homogenization will inevitably create redundancies that Rumsfeld's business model cannot tolerate in its search for efficiency. The Secretary of Defense recognized that fact early on. He cancelled the Crusader artillery system in part on the grounds that it did not provide capabilities different from those already provided by the air forces. He planned, prior to the Iraq war, to eliminate at least two and possibly as many as four of the Army's ten active duty combat divisions, since they, too, were becoming redundant as organizations that could identify and destroy enemy targets. Although the Joint Strike Fighter and the F-22 seem to be extremely redundant and do not really provide dramatically different capabilities, ironically, both systems have survived initial searches for efficiency on the grounds that they directly support the NCW concept.

THE RUMSFELD VISION of military transformation, therefore, is completely unbalanced. It will provide the U.S. with armed forces that do one thing only, even if they do it superbly well. They will be able to identify, track, and destroy enemy targets from thousands of miles away and at little or no risk to themselves. The suite of capabilities that the transformation of the 1970s and 1980s provided will be narrowed into a confined band of excellence. The business model that brought success to many companies in the 1990s will be adopted as the basis for this transformation, and all of America's future success will rest upon this one capability and the applicability of this single model. It is one of the most seductive and dangerous visions of modern times.

The Rumsfeld vision of military transformation suffers from a wide variety of flaws, some of which I have already considered in another forum.[1] One of the most significant flaws is the misunderstanding of the concept of the "revolution in military affairs" (RMA) that underlies this vision.

Although current documents mention a "revolution in military affairs" or the "information revolution" much more rarely these days, the concept remains central to present-day efforts to transform the military. All of the theoretical justifications for the current approach to transformation, written mostly at the turn of the millennium or just before, rely on this concept as their essential justification. The fact that it is slipping from current parlance reflects the reality that agencies responsible for transformation are focusing increasingly on

---

1 See "War and Aftermath" in *Policy Review*, August–September 2003.

the nuts-and-bolts of their task, and have stopped thinking seriously about the philosophical underpinnings and assumptions on which it is based.

The concept of RMA is a relatively new one in the history of military theory. Soviet military leaders coined it in the 1960s to describe the effects of mating thermonuclear weapons (hydrogen bombs) with intercontinental ballistic missiles. They argued that the unprecedented destructive power of thermonuclear weapons and the ability of ICBMs to penetrate even the densest air defense network created conditions for war so fundamentally different from those that had existed beforehand as to have brought about a revolution in the nature of war itself. Virtually overnight many of the basic guidelines that had led previous commanders to success had become irrelevant and new principles had to be sought.

The concept made its way slowly to the West, and really only came into vogue in the late 1980s to describe an entirely different revolution—the "information revolution" that we have considered above. In the interim, however, military historians have taken up the concept with enthusiasm, many to support it, a few to attack it. "Revolutions in Military Affairs" now form an important part of syllabi at defense educational institutions such as West Point and the National Defense University. Historians and military theorists have labeled everything from the advent of armored warfare to Napoleonic logistics and the development of the longbow as RMAs. Others have sought out the absurdities of some of these arguments to assail the entire concept as meaningless. Whatever the merits of those assaults, however, they will fall on deaf ears in the Pentagon, where the RMA has become the critical concept underpinning American defense policy today.

In truth, the concept of a revolution in military affairs is an important one for understanding the evolution of military development. In the course of military history there have been a series of dramatic breaks in the way war is fought at the most basic level. Warfare changed dramatically from 1700 to 1760, from 1813 to 1863, from 1870 to 1915, from 1942 to 1991.

Although many of the traditional guidelines to success continued to apply from one period to the next, many others also changed. In each change there were elements of long-term evolution, which has led some to argue that the term "*revolution in military affairs*" is inappropriate. Yet the nature of war changes most rapidly when major wars are actually being fought, so that for all the theorizing and development that preceded them, the outbreak of the American Civil War in 1861, the Franco-Prussian War in 1870, World War I in 1914, and World War II in 1939, for instance, led to sudden and dramatic changes nevertheless.

The problem with the current vision of military transformation, therefore, is not that it relies on the concept of a revolution in military affairs, but that it does not properly understand that concept. Since the 1980s, advocates of an "American RMA" based on information technology have tended to define the term as an "asymmetrical advantage" that one state acquires over its opponents. They have sought to develop transformation programs to extend that asymmetrical advantage indefinitely into the future, so that the other states of the world would never catch up, and American pre-eminence (or "lockout") would be secured, to all intents and purposes, forever.

HISTORY DOES NOT support such an interpretation of this concept, however. In each of the periods in recent history in which one might see a fundamental change in the nature of war, it is true that normally one state begins with a dramatic lead. Revolutionary France's ability in the 1790s to mobilize vast conscript armies and to sustain that mobilization for years gave her an important advantage over continental states unable to match such levels of mobilization. Prussia's early and enthusiastic development of a dense railroad net and of the general staff structure needed to plan for and control a railroad mobilization led directly to her crushing victories over Austria in 1866 and over France in 1871. The Nazis' creation of a technologically advanced and highly trained armored force, along with a significantly better armored warfare doctrine, led directly to the destruction of the Franco-British army in 1940.

In each case, however, we must also consider the sequel. Napoleonic France, Imperial Germany, and Nazi Germany all ultimately lost subsequent wars and were destroyed. The reasons for those failures are enlightening about the limitations of the current definition of revolution in military affairs.

Faced with the challenge of Revolutionary France, the other states of Europe were initially reluctant to make the social and political changes necessary to raise and maintain the large armies required to meet that challenge. Over years of sustained and unsuccessful warfare, however, France's enemies gradually changed their minds. Austria, Prussia, and Russia all eventually mobilized large forces. In Russia's case the army went from around 250,000 at the end of the eighteenth century to about 850,000 in 1815, a level at which it remained until an even more dramatic increase during the Crimean War. The mobilization and support of such large armies caused problems for all of the states of Europe, and led, in part, to the revolutionary disturbances that wracked the continent following Napoleon's final fall. The leaders of those states, however, ultimately accepted such costs in order to be able successfully to adapt to the new requirements of war. They were thereby able to defeat Napoleon.

The Germans went through a similar process twice. Their advantages in railway mobilization in 1866 and 1870 had been greatly reduced by 1914. France and Russia had spent fortunes upgrading their own railway systems and had developed general staff structures able to match the Germans' planning abilities. As a result, the German mobilization in 1914 was matched by equally skillful French and Russian mobilizations, the German war plan broke down, and Germany was ultimately crushed under the weight of superior allied forces. Germany's enemies had successfully adopted the methods that had led Germany to success in the mid-nineteenth century and then turned those methods against the Germans during World War I.

Hitler faced a kindred problem. The techniques that generated his initial successes against the French and the British, who had both developed inappropriate armored doctrines and tanks largely unsuitable for the sort of rapid mobile warfare the Germans fought, did not lead subsequently to victory against the Soviets. Problems of planning and confused objectives, among other things, vitiated initial German successes in 1941, and allowed the Soviets time to recover. When they did, they began to implement an armored warfare doctrine superior to the one the Germans had been using and to build tanks excellently designed to support that doctrine. Beginning with their victory at Stalingrad in late 1942, the Soviets conducted a virtually unbroken march to the west that resulted in the capture of Berlin in May 1945.

Even the "nuclear revolution" itself, the change in warfare that had led to the coining of the acronym RMA, saw a similar rapid balance. The U.S. and the Soviet Union fielded thermonuclear-tipped ICBMs at virtually the same time, and throughout the Cold War each advance by one side in this area was matched almost immediately by the other.

It goes without saying that each of these examples had much more complexity than can be explored in this article. Napoleon's adversaries made many changes to their armies other than simply increasing their size, including incorporating and improving on other aspects of Napoleonic warfare that had brought Bonaparte his early successes. Germany's Schlieffen Plan failed in 1914 not simply because the French mobilized well, but also because Schlieffen's successor had altered it in important ways. Hitler's invasion of the Soviet Union failed partly because of Hitler's inappropriate interference in the operation and because of his insistence on trying to achieve all of his ultimate objectives simultaneously, among other things.

The issues identified in this article, however, were central parts of the explanations for the outcome of all of these conflicts. If the allies in 1813, the French and Russians in 1914, and the Soviets in 1942 had not successfully adopted the critical features of the new military thinking that had brought their enemies victory, it is most unlikely that the other factors contributing to their success would have saved them from defeat. The key point is that the failings of Napoleon and the Germans would have been irrelevant if they had retained the asymmetrical advantages with which they had started. Their inability to react perfectly when they had lost those advantages was what led them to defeat.

History so far, therefore, has been very clear that "asymmetrical advantages" gained by one state do not normally last very long. Technology and technique inevitably spreads. Other states acquire either similar or counteracting capabilities. The final victors of each new "revolutionary" epoch have not usually been the states that initiated the revolution, but those that responded best once the technologies and techniques had become common property.

It also shows that the initial successes those "revolutionary" states achieved have tended to breed arrogance and overconfidence, hindering their ability to respond as other states began to match their capabilities. Napoleonic France, Imperial Germany, and Nazi Germany all ossified in their techniques after the initial victories, and lost to enemies who, forced by defeat, built on their own advances more successfully.

The search for an indefinite American "asymmetrical advantage," therefore, requires not merely a revolution in military affairs: it also requires a fundamental revolution in human affairs of a sort never seen before. It requires that America continue to change her armed forces so rapidly and successfully that no other state can ever catch up—indeed, that no other state in the world even try.

THIS UNREALISTIC requirement is central to the current vision of military transformation. Since, according to this vision, American armed forces will only be able to do one thing—strike targets precisely from great distances away—they will succeed only on two conditions. First, they will always have to fight wars in which striking targets precisely from great distances will lead directly to victory, and second, they will always have to fight enemies incapable of either matching that skill or of preventing the U.S. from using it. The precise weapons will *always* have to get through, their effects will *always* have to be decisive, and no enemy will *ever* be able to fire them effectively at American forces.

History suggests that these conditions will not be met for very long. But transformation enthusiasts today argue that the U.S. is in a unique position and that the rules really have changed. It is worth considering in some detail, therefore, whether or not it is likely that the U.S. will be able to retain its asymmetric advantages for decades to come.

The first question in this debate concerns the proliferation of the technology the U.S. relies upon now to maintain this advantage. The situation in this regard is both promising and alarming. On the one hand, American technological superiority rests primarily on computerization. Precision guided munitions are precisely guided because of the computer chips in their guidance systems and the communications systems that allow them to home in on either GPS coordinates or laser designators. The ability of American forces to identify, track, and strike targets also relies on such computer chips, and on the satellites that support the communications systems. The proliferation of microprocessors and satellites, therefore, could start an adversary on the road to challenging American technological preeminence.

It hardly needs stating that computerization is a revolution racing throughout the world, not just in America, or even that most microprocessors these days are made outside of the U.S. The American satellite constellation is the most sophisticated and dense of any, but many states have the ability to launch satellites themselves or to hire private companies to launch them. The real American advantage in this regard results from two things: money and time.

Building the current satellite constellation was exorbitantly expensive. The U.S. probably would not have undertaken it initially but for the fear of the Soviet Union. The development of PGMs and building large numbers of them was also extremely expensive. Very few states in the world today have the economic resources necessary even to begin such massive programs, let alone see them rapidly through to conclusion.

The very age of the American systems, moreover, is also an asset. The U.S. has had time not merely to computerize all of its major weapons systems and the weapons they fire, but to develop dense computer networks that connect them. That networking is an important part of America's technological advantage today, and it is not something that any would-be adversary could easily or rapidly replicate. Despite the ready proliferation of the technologies themselves, therefore, it would seem, after all, that the U.S. should expect to maintain its current technological lead for quite a considerable time.

SEVERAL FACTORS militate against this happy conclusion. For one thing, few if any of America's enemies will have the vast resource-stretching responsibilities that America has. They will be concerned only with their own region of the world and will focus their efforts on developing communications and target tracking systems only over a small portion of the globe. They will not need a dense global satellite constellation or the ability to project power over thousands of miles. The costs to them of developing systems comparable to America's, but only in a restricted geographic area, will accordingly be much smaller than the price the U.S. has had to pay to achieve that capability everywhere.

Then, too, other states can reap the benefits of modern communications systems without bearing the expensive burden of basic scientific research and development. Microprocessors, satellites, encrypted laser communications systems, cell phone systems, and the whole host of technologies that form the basis of American military superiority are now the property of the world. It will not cost America's enemies anything like what it cost the U.S. to develop its capabilities, either in money or in time. Since technology inevitably becomes less expensive as it proliferates and as time goes on, moreover, the situation for America's would-be adversaries will only improve in this regard.

Moreover, just as many European states drastically improved their railway networks in the nineteenth century, so now many states are improving their satellite constellations and naturally networking government and economic computer systems in order to support economic growth today. They are thereby also laying the groundwork for a rapid development of the military advantages that flow from those communications and networking capabilities. Many of the technologies that have led in the past to American success are now latent in every aspect of modern economic life, and this fact will reduce both the cost and the time required for a potential adversary to "revolutionize" its armed forces to match those of the U.S.

It should also be noted that technology is only part of the story of America's success. The way the U.S. military has integrated the technology into its professional, highly-trained armed forces has been at least as important as the quality of the technology itself. In this area, too, the U.S. has had an advantage since the mid-1970s, since most of America's likely enemies retained conscript militaries unable to match America's troops in skill, educational level, or experience. Even this advantage, however, is evaporating.

The first Gulf War started a global trend toward transforming large conscript armies into smaller professional forces. The second one has accelerated that trend. The Russians have struggled toward this goal, with only limited success, for a decade. The French abandoned their conscript military whose traditions harked back to the Revolution of 1789. Even the Chinese have recently announced that they would reduce their military and concentrate on developing a smaller, more professional and highly qualified force. The U.S. made the transition and garnered the advantages of that transition in about fifteen years. It remains to be seen how long it will take the rest of the world to do so.

When America's enemies have developed the technology and trained the people who will use it, they will also have to develop the doctrines and techniques to make it effective. In this regard, they have the most significant advantage of all. Much of America's tested doctrine has been published, much can be deduced from the CNN coverage of America's most recent wars. Once again, America's enemies can start from the position of proven success that the U.S. armed forces achieved, and build from there.

THEIR REAL ADVANTAGE in this area, however, results from the fact that they will be developing armed forces specifically designed to fight an enemy with the same capabilities. America's military has not done so. American military doctrine continues to foresee fighting enemies lacking any significant capacity to deploy precision guided munitions, without dense satellite constellations and communications systems, and without the ability to strike targets precisely at great distances. It is one of the more troubling lessons of the history of new military technology that the states that pioneer the new technologies and techniques generally fail to adapt successfully to the situation in which all major states have the same technologies and techniques. It remains to be seen whether America will do any better than her predecessors in this regard.

The problems identified above are nearly all inherent in any program of military transformation. They are not unique to Rumsfeld's vision. History suggests that whatever program America adopts to transform its armed forces, her enemies will tend to catch up and level the playing field. The problem with the current program is that it relies on maintaining an overwhelming advantage in a single area of military performance indefinitely. The failure to contemplate having to fight creditable opponents and the imbalance of the effort to transform the military both create serious risks and vulnerabilities for American armed forces in the future.

The solution is to refocus America's efforts at transforming its military on a program designed to produce balanced capabilities and to defeat a comparably armed and capable enemy. In the first instance, that will mean rebalancing the efforts to remake the ground and the air services. Right now, the initiative is primarily reliant on air- or sea-launched weapons. Advocates of this approach point out that it is cheaper and safer—cheaper because maintaining large ground forces divisions is costly, and safer because it obviates the need to put America's young men and women in harm's way. This is one of the main reasons that Rumsfeld and others have repeatedly advocated cutting the size of the Army and transferring the funds saved thereby into the purchase of advanced munitions, communications, and targeting systems for the Air Force and Navy.

It is easy to show the consequences of this approach in Iraq. Armies do more than destroy targets. They hold ground passively. They provide critical police functions. They can still conduct counter-guerrilla operations much more effectively than air-launched munitions. For a country engaged in nation-building, counter-insurgency, and counter-terrorism, there is no escape from the need to have a large and capable army, and America is suffering badly now from having an army that is too small.

It is not simply that current operations require significant ground forces, however, or even that the conditions that drive that requirement are likely to persist for some considerable time. The real reason to maintain a robust army that does more than simply add sophisticated launchers to the targeting mix is that it greatly complicates the enemy's ability to respond to America's movements and capabilities.

If the enemy knows that all he will face is a barrage of precision-guided munitions, he will find counter-measures— digging too deeply for the weapons to penetrate, jamming or blinding U.S. reconnaissance assets, etc. If the enemy must face advancing American ground forces as well as PGM strikes, however, his possible reactions are much more limited. He will have to concentrate his forces to a much greater extent in order to ensure that they can face an American ground attack. It will not be sufficient for him to blind American satellites or disrupt computer networks if the ground forces rolling forward can see his soldiers through their viewing prisms and kill them with their own weapons. Deeply dug bunkers may still protect vital command and control centers and weapons, but the importance of that fact will be greatly diminished when American soldiers have control of the enemy country above ground.

Recent history highlights the importance of this fact repeatedly. In 1991 Saddam Hussein withstood thirty-nine days of devastating aerial attacks and remained undaunted. After three days of a coordinated air-ground campaign, he made peace. In 1998 he withstood another barrage of cruise missile attacks following his expulsion of weapons inspectors, and did not change his policy in the least. In 2003 he had prepared himself and his country for yet another drawn-out bombing campaign, and was stunned not by the "shock and awe" of the air campaign, but by the incredibly rapid ground offensive spearheaded by the 3rd Infantry Division, the 101st Air Assault Division, and the 1st Marine Division.

Throughout the history of airpower, evidence abounds that unbalanced attacks are much less successful than balanced attacks. German strategic bombing of Great Britain in World War I and World War II failed to bring that country to the peace table. Allied strategic bombing in World War II was equally ineffective until it was combined with a massive ground campaign in Germany, or the threat of a massive invasion of the Japanese home islands. Strategic bombing directed at North Vietnam, un- accompanied by any meaningful threat of a ground invasion, failed completely to achieve its purpose.

The advocates of such bombing attacks are always ready to explain that if they had been given a little more time, a few more bombs, fewer political restrictions, and so forth, they would have brought the enemy to his knees without the need for ground forces. That assertion has never been proven. Even in Afghanistan, Bosnia, and Kosovo, ground forces or the threat of their use played the decisive role in bringing the enemy to surrender. In Afghanistan and Bosnia, the U.S. relied on local forces to supply the ground troops, which helped convince the hostile regimes to give in, but also left the U.S. politically beholden to its allies and unable to achieve its political aims as a result. During the Kosovo operation Slobodan Milosevic withstood the American air attack right up until it became clear that a ground attack might follow—and then he surrendered.

In this world, anything is possible. The U.S. might win a future war relying solely on airpower, for the first time in history, with no American or local ground forces involved and no meaningful threat of their deployment. That possibility cannot be excluded. The Rumsfeld vision of military transformation, however, does not pursue that as a possibility: it relies on it as a certainty. By focusing all of America's defense resources on the single medium of airpower, Rumsfeld is betting America's future security on the conviction that the U.S. armed forces will be able to do *every time* what no military to date has *ever* been able to do. In doing so, he is greatly simplifying the task of those preparing to fight the U.S. by presenting them with only one threat to defeat.

A sound program of military transformation would proceed in exactly the opposite way. It would recognize the value of America's technological advantage in the area of precision guided munitions. It would continue to enlarge and enhance them, much as Rumsfeld currently proposes. But it would not do so at the expense of the unique capabilities that ground forces bring to bear. It would focus, instead, on developing the capabilities of ground forces that are distinct from the capabilities provided by airpower. Ground forces can seize and hold terrain, separate hostile groups, and comb through urban areas with infinitely greater precision and distinction between combatant and non-combatant than can airpower. They can present the enemy with unacceptable situations simply by occupying a given piece of land, forcing the enemy to take actions that reveal his intentions and expose him to destruction. And it goes without saying that only ground forces can execute the peacemaking, peacekeeping, and reconstruction activities that have been essential to success in most of the wars America has fought in the past hundred years.

Above all, the U.S. must avoid the search for "efficiency" in military affairs. Redundancy is inherently a virtue in war. America's leaders should intentionally design systems with overlapping capabilities, spread across the services, and should intentionally support weapons that do not directly contribute to the overarching vision of war that they are pursuing. America should continue to try to build armed forces that are the best in every category and have the latent capabilities to meet challenges that cannot now even be imagined.

"All Sail, No Anchor": Architecture After Modernism

Michael J. Lewis

W HEN ARCHITECTURE gets a hall of fame, it needs to find a niche for a certain amiable rogue I will refer to as Palladio of the Wastepaper Basket. He made his mark during the 1960s at Yale's school of architecture. There it is the monthly task of students to design a hypothetical building, for which they make a model out of cardboard and foam core in a notoriously time-consuming operation. The process culminates in the *crit*, the stressful and often prickly review session in which visiting critics inspect the models and question the students, unfailingly finding the weak points of both. It is often the case that a verbally nimble student makes a better impression than an inarticulate designer, even one with a better design.

Our Palladio of the Wastepaper Basket found it more congenial to talk than cut cardboard. He prowled the halls of the architecture school at night, ransacking the trash for old models that had been discarded by their makers when the concept failed to stick. These he dusted off and submitted as his own work, often for a different class and a different assignment. A model of a circular drive-in restaurant might do duty as a church, for example, or—shifting the scale—a one-room beach house. Students watched their jetsam float back into the classroom but no one took it amiss. It seemed to fit the anarchic spirit of the times. But it also fits the spirit of *our* time, perhaps in a deeper way, when the words that fly around architecture seem fundamentally independent of it, and have precious little to do with its vital essence.

Fifty years ago there was no such split: architecture and the words written about it stood in harmonious concord. This is seldom true in art, where theory and practice normally race wildly after one another. But modern architecture reconciled the opposites of book and building to an astonishing degree and achieved a surpassing programmatic unity. Modernism's founding figures, especially Le Corbusier and Walter Gropius, were themselves theorists, and both wrote and designed. And the principles carefully spelled out in Le Corbusier's *Vers une architecture* (1923)—the open plan, the elimination of ornament, the rational use of modern materials—lent themselves to programmatic abstraction in a way that those of neoclassicism or the Baroque could not. This was more than mere intellectual consistency. It was the broad and comprehensive unity of the Modern Movement itself, of which architecture was but one lobe, and in which painting and sculpture, music and poetry aspired to the same radical emancipation from traditional structures of form and authority.

We take for granted the conquest of America by this high modernism, as something that was in the course of things inevitable, but in many ways it was quite alien to the American experience. A man of the 1920s would have scoffed at the notion that America needed a radical modernism, for America already was modern. Jazz, cinema, the radio (a national craze since 1925), and the affordable automobile were all quintessentially modern phenomena. So was the fanciful Art Deco skyscraper: the Chrysler Building with its winged chrome sentinels or the Empire State Building, whose soaring spire was to be a mooring mast for zeppelins, yet another modern phenomenon.

BUT THIS American modernism was organic rather than programmatic, and was accomplished without benefit of theory and manifesto; it was modernism without program. Its achievements were made possible by modern engineering and science, manufactured by the modern assembly line, and disseminated through mass-marketing (likewise modern), without central coordination. Its most striking aspect was its unpremeditated, even inadvertent character. Some of its accomplishments were not even the product of conscious thought, let alone theory. For example, the new skyscrapers: Prior to 1916, skyscrapers were permitted to rise without limit, to blacken the streets below and to cast their neighbors to the north into permanent shadow. In that year New York City passed a remarkable zoning ordinance that sought to protect property rights by restricting the height and bulk of skyscrapers. At each increment of height, a building was required to step back a prescribed number of feet (depending on the width of the street below); on only one quarter of its footprint could it rise without constraint. The result was the characteristic chiseled silhouette of the modern skyscraper (which fortuitously resembled ancient Mayan pyramids, then being studied, and brought about a charmingly incongruous fad for Mayan ornament). Here was an absolutely new architectural form, as distinctively American as the colonial saltbox, whose principal formal element—its forceful and expressive contour—was not an artistic invention at all, but a hard-earned armistice line between the demands of real estate and of legislation. Such was America's non-programmatic modernism.

The modernism that was simultaneously arising in Europe followed an entirely different trajectory, where it was both more urgent, in the wake of the First World War, and more centralized. To a continent mutilated by four years of cruel trench warfare, during which time it built little, the urgency was understandable. And the centralization was the normal state of affairs in Europe, where architectural patronage and industrial policy had always been a matter of state patronage, and was regularized in the state architectural bureaucracies that had arisen in Europe during the seventeenth and eighteenth centuries. The socialist or paternalist model of patronage on which modernism depended was the natural successor to this. Le Corbusier's audacious and daft proposal to demolish medieval Paris and replace it with serried ranks of rational towers differed from the urban interventions of Napoleon or Baron Haussmann only in degree.

In America, where architecture was historically a matter of private taste and commercial patronage, this model had but little applicability. Americans were hardly ignorant of European innovations but partook of them as consumers rather than believers, much as American painters had once discovered French Impressionism, stripped it of its social and theoretical content, and brought it home as a lighthearted and diverting fashion. When George Howe adapted the flat roof and abstract cubical massing of European modernism, it was for a fashionable suburban house. Most American architects were already moving in the general direction of their modernist counterparts, toward simplified volumes and flowing space. They needed no ukase from Le Corbusier prohibiting the cornice; the cornice had already fallen in disrepute by the early 1920s, as had the woman's bustle, and neither required a theoretical manifesto.

So long as capitalism thundered along, and the Twenties still roared, Americans had only passing interest in Europe's programmatic modernism. All this changed in October 1929. The Great Depression ravaged no American institution, the stock market excepted, as much as it did architecture. The violent, almost instantaneous contraction in building activity was stupefying. A single example from T. E. Tallmadge's 1936 *Story of Architecture in America* shows its magnitude. In 1927 the city of Chicago approved 12,025 building permits, for a total value of nearly $353,000,000. In 1932 the figure was only 467 permits, valued at $4,000,000—barely one percent of its pre-Depression activity. The figures for New York are similar. The Empire State Building, begun in 1929 and finished in 1931, was the end of the line. In short order, almost the entirety of the American architectural profession was unemployed. As private and commercial patronage stagnated, the American architectural world took on European lines. The state became by default the principal architectural patron; the buildings being built were schools, hospitals, community centers, and—above all—social housing projects, not skyscrapers or suburban manors. The whole world of Twenties eclecticism, of faience-tiled movie palaces, neo-Mediterranean villas, and *moderne* stores, had vanished, along with the capitalist patronage that had sustained them. Under these changed circumstances, European modernism looked different indeed.

The new state of affairs was captured in *The International Style*, the catalogue to the celebrated 1932 exhibition at the Museum of Modern Art, curated by Philip Johnson and Henry Russell Hitchcock. In it the buildings that were heralded a few years earlier as the very embodiment of American might and sophistication were subjected to malicious mockery. Instead of bold acrobatics in the sky, these were the vulgar acts of crass commercial clients. In the book's preface, Alfred H. Barr, the founding director of MOMA, did not try to mask his contempt: "We are asked to take seriously the architectural taste of real estate speculators, renting agents, and mortgage brokers." Of course it was easy to scoff at capitalism in 1932 when it lay prostrate. Only after their owners were penniless did the jaunty forms of Art Deco skyscrapers begin to look ludicrous. The Empire State Building was discredited not by the fanciful zeppelin mooring mast on its summit but by the apple vendors huddling around its base.

IT IS ONE of history's fateful coincidences that at the very moment of the collapse of America's architectural patronage, a stream of refugees began to make their way from Hitler's Germany to the United States. These included the key figures of the Bauhaus, Walter Gropius and Ludwig Mies van der Rohe, who found plum positions in America's schools of architecture and design, the former at Harvard and the latter at the Illinois Institute of Technology (IIT). To a remarkable extent, American conditions now recapitulated those of Europe in the 1920s: a dire economic crisis, enlightened government patronage, and an activist cadre of influential modernists in-spired by a sense of mission. Of course the prostrate condition of commerce would not last, but, when it recovered, Ameri-ca's architectural culture was permanently changed.

In terms of absolute numbers, the European émigrés were negligible, but they exercised a wildly disproportionate in-fluence. And if the great body of American architects was in-different or hostile, they were now jobless and therefore ir-relevant. In short order, other schools of architecture followed the lead of Harvard, and wherever they landed, modernist deans conducted swift and efficient purges of dissenters. A few anecdotes suffice: at Washington University, St. Louis, the modernist dean Buford Pickens opened his Saturday news-paper to see a rendering of a neo-Georgian office tower by one of his instructors—rank heresy; the man was fired on the spot. At the University of Pennsylvania, the chief instructor in design was Harry Sternfeld, the 1914 winner of the prestigious Beaux-Arts Institute's Paris Prize and the designer of Philadel-phia's most imaginative Art Deco and *moderne* buildings. Un-able to fire so prominent a figure, the new modernist dean relegated him to teaching "professional practice," an act on the order of requiring Cézanne to teach the care and cleaning of paint brushes. Every school has similar stories. And each school eliminated or drastically truncated its courses in the history of architecture, which had once been the mainstay of architectural literacy and their chief source of raw material for design.

These purges call to mind the political dimension of high modernism. Architecture was but one of many modernisms, each drawing strength from the others, but all were deeply conscious of the greatest modernism of all, the Russian Revo-lution, which always lay in the background. Modernism came to America at a time when world revolution still seemed dis-tinctly possible, if not imminent.[1] And it came surrounded by

---

[1] This is not to say that the early modernists were necessarily Com-munists, although many were, at the Bauhaus and elsewhere. After all,

that mightiest of accompaniments, the bold and silencing aura of inevitability. If the Russian Revolution could topple those principal pillars of western culture—religion, capitalism, class structure, the family itself—how much easier was it to sweep away music's tonality, poetry's meter, or architecture's gabled roof? Of all the arguments that modernism could bring in favor of its spacious claims, historical inevitability was the one that brooked no reply.

But even as modernism established itself in America, the cultural vanguard of the West was gradually losing faith in the Soviet Union—a prolonged process that stretched from the purge trials of 1937 to the invasion of Hungary in 1956—and the Modern Movement as a whole shed its presumption of historical inevitability. A bundle of separate and discrete modernisms, literary, musical, and so forth, remained, still omnipotent in the institutional compounds in which they were ensconced but without the bracing sense of being part of a collective movement that was reshaping the whole of civilization.

Ironically, this happened just as American modernism was enjoying its most conspicuous public successes, in the 1950s. America's commercial patronage had long since rebounded and made its peace with modernism; in fact, America's greatest monuments of modernism are those raised by corporations: the Seagram Building, Lever House, the TWA Terminal, the headquarters of Pittsburgh Plate Glass. Here was the high water mark of modernism, when modern architecture was endorsed equally by American business, government, and the academy. Thus Gropius could design both the Pan Am Building in New York and the American embassy in Athens, even as he presided over Harvard University's Gradu-

---

Mies van der Rohe blithely submitted projects for Nazi buildings before eventually fleeing Germany following the close of the Bauhaus in 1933. But this is nothing more than garden-variety artistic opportunism, the same sort that permitted the painter David to serve in turn the *ancien régime*, the French Revolution, and Napoleon.

ate School of Design. By then there was no longer any appreciable dissent. For a brief and startling moment, the architectural avant garde and establishment had merged and become identical.

PASSING IN turn through depression, world war, and prosperity, modernism's hegemony and overweening moral authority lasted but a generation. If one had to pick a death date, the point at which the collapse of modernism was irrevocable, one could do worse than 1968—a year when so many things seemed to go wrong at once. Since then no movement has enjoyed anything remotely comparable to its prestige and authority. In fact, the last point of common agreement on which the dissenters to modernism concurred before they fragmented into a welter of contending tendencies and movements was the fact of modernism's failure. Here was the last consensus, the last fixed navigational point on the horizon (the same role played in the pictorial arts by Clement Greenberg's formalism, which fell from favor at this same moment: in a trackless ocean, one navigates from the well-documented shipwreck).

THE CRITIQUE of modernism had both a theoretical and an empirical wing. The theoretical assault took modern architecture to task for its reductivism, its mad attempt to encompass the tempest of human experience within the hard matrix of rational form. Empirical critics had it easier; they only had to *look*, and soon assembled a vast roster of exhibits: malevolent social housing projects, totalitarian megastructures, and cities disfigured by blundering urban renewal campaigns. Jane Jacobs, that perceptive observer of urban life, produced the most damning manifesto of all, *The Death and Life of Great American Cities* (1961), a book with a startling international resonance, particularly in Germany. Other thoughtful observers of public life and culture, notably William H. Whyte, followed in her path.

The most deadly challenge of all, however, came from

within the ranks of modernism itself, and bore the imprimatur of the Museum of Modern Art, the keeper of the modernist flame. This was Robert Venturi's *Complexity and Contradiction in Architecture* (1966), a book that did much to extinguish that flame. As with Gorbachev's *perestroika*, there are some paths of reform that, once launched, soon acquire their own willful momentum. *Complexity and Contradiction*, an incendiary manifesto effectively disguised as an interminable art history lecture, used examples as diverse as Michelangelo and Levittown to show that the formal clarity of modernism—its chilly, ruthless idealism—represented a fatal diminution of architecture's expressive power: its infinite capacity to challenge the intellect, to bewilder, inform, and delight.

Venturi drew his examples across the whole of architectural history and geography, reproduced in tiny postage-stamp images. Having been banished from schools of architecture, history was now permitted in once more, although under a sort of probation—not as style (a formal and coherent system of design) nor as archaeology (forms derived from certain historical and cultural conditions), but simply as a great schoolhouse of graphic ideas, whose origin and authorship was ultimately irrelevant.

And so, one by one, the separate pillars of modernism were kicked away during the course of the 1960s. But to demolish an edifice is one thing and to raise one quite another, and here the critical facility proved mightier than the creative. While the past few decades have given rise to a sparkling pageant of styles and movements, none of them have enjoyed anything remotely like the moral authority of mid-century modernism.

Of course, not all modernists practiced the rarefied, haiku-lite minimalism of Mies van der Rohe, and one faction, the New Brutalists, sought to restore architecture's lost physicality. This they achieved with concrete, a material as modern as steel but with the visceral properties of weight, texture, and bulk. Beginning in England in the mid-1950s, and soon reaching the United States, the New Brutalists produced muscularly textured buildings clad in rippling corrugated concrete whose surfaces were coarse enough to draw blood. It took only a few conspicuous examples—Yale's Art and Architecture Building by Paul Rudolph and Boston City Hall by Kallmann, McKinnell, and Knowles—for the public to recoil violently from Brutalism and its claim that the expression of architecture's palpably physical nature was a gesture of humanism.

OTHERS HANDLED concrete more adroitly and serenely. The Philadelphia architect (and mentor to Venturi) Louis I. Kahn formulated a stately, substantial modernism, constructed of masonry, and evoking the weight and permanence of the great buildings of the past. At their best, his works have the tragic dignity of archaeological ruins. Kahn was a late bloomer; after having been schooled in the early 1920s according to the old Beaux-Arts system with its insistence on strong axes and geometric order, he cast this off to embrace the flowing space and dematerialized planes of modernism. Still, he never quite fit in as a mainstream modernist. Only in the 1960s did he find his voice, when he reconciled modernism with the classical principles he had encountered as a student and during subsequent travel to Europe. In such masterworks as the Kimbell Art Museum and the Salk Institute at La Jolla, he triumphantly rehabilitated those respective victims of Mies and Le Corbusier: the wall and the room.

The quiet introspective character of Kahn's work lent itself to civic commissions, but not to houses or commercial buildings. Moreover its essential seriousness made it suspect in the eyes of a generation wearied of Modernism's self-consciously heroic stance, and ultimately Kahn's legacy has been more inspirational than practical. Another paragon of concrete was Eero Saarinen, of Cranbrook, whose great TWA Terminal was itself a diagram of flight, concrete frozen into great liquid arcs, depicting a type of architectural energy that had not been exploited since the Baroque: torque. But this veered close to expressionism, which as a highly personal language was ill-suited to the formation of a collective language. Saarinen's forms are still reprised whenever a building needs to look like a snail or conch, such as hockey rinks, but his influence essentially ended with his premature death in 1961. (Nonetheless the writhing forms of Frank Gehry, a student when Saarinen was in his glory, betray a lingering influence.)

But these were late modernisms, not anti-modernisms. They still accepted the ethical imperative of modernism, that a radically new age required radically new forms. Ultimately it is skepticism or derision of this claim that distinguishes the non-modernist, or postmodernist, from the modernist. Even when otherwise using modernist materials, detailing, and planning—these lessons of modernism were not easily unlearned—it was their anti-heroic stance that indelibly marked them. And it was in Robert Venturi that anti-heroism found its anti-hero.

VENTURI'S BUILDINGS in and around Philadelphia put his doctrine of complexity and contradiction into practice. His first major work, Guild House (1962), managed the hat trick of violating every norm of high modernism—it had a monumental arched entrance, a clear hierarchy of major and minor spaces, ambiguous and multivalent architectural elements—and did so within the context of a modest brick home for aged Quakers. Even the dull brick wall at the rear was radical, an explicit reference to the undistinguished factory architecture of the neighborhood. This was a revolutionary nod to *context*, that most humble of architecture criteria, and one which the International Style, with its universal aspirations, had swept from consideration.

A few years later, Venturi's celebrated Mother's House rehabilitated the gable and the chimney, evoking the great Shingle Style architecture of the nineteenth century, and opening the gates to a deluge of historical references, all playing across the plane of the façade in lively calligraphic animation. In place of the laconic Cartesian order of Mies, here was an architecture that not only spoke to the viewer but did so volubly.

Venturi's book and buildings helped set in motion the movement that came to be known as Postmodernism, although he himself has rejected the term. With its stance of permissive eclecticism, openness to history, and sense of responsibility to make the city more humane and livable, the movement proved enormously attractive. Venturi was soon followed by Charles Moore, Michael Graves, Robert A. M. Stern, and others, the high-spirited doyens of postmodernism. Even Philip Johnson joined in with his AT&T Building in New York, a skyscraper with a broken pediment at the skyline, penance perhaps for the abuse he heaped on Art Deco skyscrapers during his youth. For a brief moment around 1980 it seemed as if postmodernism offered a worthy and viable successor to modernism, which might knit the raveled sleave of history, reconnecting the orphaned present to the great channel of the past. There was a great optimism and idealism about this, and those who were in schools of architecture, here or abroad, at that time will recall the giddy hopes that then blazed up around postmodernism.

ALTHOUGH IT was not immediately apparent, a certain paradox afflicted the Venturi rebellion. On the one hand, it was wonderfully whimsical. Its overflowing bounty of irreverence seemed essential, its laughter the only sure way of deflating the prim custodians of modernism. This was the era of Pop, after all, of "make love not war," and Venturi's aphorisms had the pithy punchiness of protest slogans like "Less is a Bore," "ugly and ordinary," "Main Street is almost all right." After architecture's long afternoon of Teutonic severity, this whimsy came as a much needed tonic. (It is difficult now to imagine how heavy the authoritarian hand rested on schools of architecture. A friend designed a schoolhouse in the 1960s in which each classroom was expressed by a graceful curved bay; her dean drew a large X across them, warning her, "Modern architects do not use curves.")

On the other hand, the movement also invited a certain amount of intellectual pretension. The chimney and roof gable of Venturi's Mother's House, for example, were no mere revival of traditional architectural motifs, no Shingle Style revival, but were primal elements of the house, signs of fire and shelter; they could be read as components of a complex system of signs and symbols, the study of which is semiotics. Through a strange quirk of timing, universities in the 1970s and 1980s were awash in the fashionable study of semiotics, that offshoot of philosophy and linguistics, and it was inevitable that postmodern architecture was studied not so much for its specific cultural content but as a system of language. To many, it seemed, this was as ponderous a philosophical system as the one just toppled, and without the added attraction of imminent utopia.

But while postmodernism turned pretentious in the academy, it turned goofy in the streets. By the mid-1980s it had become a kind of architectural zoot suit (to use Richard Etlin's phrase), distinguished by cut-out windows, red granite stripes, and a liberal share of pastel walls. Many of the examples in Venturi's *Complexity and Contradiction* were drawn from America's anonymous roadside architecture, and now postmodernism returned the favor, bringing the jaunty commercial imagery of the highway strip, of brash billboards and fast-food joints, from the roadside into the very heart of the city, and of civic life.

This process of borrowing motifs from such a diverse range of sources—from Michelangelo to McDonald's—produced a certain leveling, both literally and figuratively. After all, *Complexity and Contradiction* treated architecture in essentially two-dimensional terms, reproducing diagrams of palace and church façades schematically to show their wonderfully complex geometry. The buildings inspired by Venturi's book likewise tended to the two-dimensional and schematic, their façades serving as mere billboards. The act of designing a building came to resemble the work of a graphic designer rather than a sculptor. For commercial buildings, which need to swagger and strut and catch the viewer's eye, this did not matter much, but as complete architecture—fully realized in its tactile, plastic, and sculptural dimensions—it fell short. It is ironic that this movement that faulted modernism for impoverishing architecture did a good bit of impoverishing itself.

As this occurred, and as postmodernism became tainted by its association with the crassness of commerce, it was quickly disavowed by the leading schools of architecture. By the mid-1980s, postmodern buildings were seen as the architectural manifestation of the "decade of greed," of "Ronald Reagan's America," and prominent commercial architects such as Michael Graves and Helmut Jahn were scorned for their frivolity and envied for their success. Their unabashedly commercial practices were contrasted unfavorably with those earlier modernists who had specialized in social housing projects. That it was precisely the disastrous failure of these same social housing projects that had helped bring about postmodernism in the first place was conveniently forgotten.

To some extent, the charge of frivolity was justified. Although postmodernists cheerfully ransacked the past for usable form, much like Palladio of the Wastepaper Basket, they did so without reference to their original meanings, or the historical circumstances of their birth. Their cut-out porticos did not represent, for example, the majesty of Roman law, nor did their great curved atria, such as Charles Moore's Piazza d'Italia, offer a cogent statement of counterreformation theology. (The examples were invariably taken from classicism; Gothic architecture was not included in the general rehabilitation of historical styles, perhaps because the playful sensibility of postmodernism worked better against a strict formal system such as classicism).

IF POSTMODERNISM was playful, it was not insincere, for it never pretended to seek a revival of the historical styles.[2] The

---

2 In fact, within the postmodernist camp only one quixotic band has used classicism with a straight face. There were the new classicists, also known affectionately as the *young fogeys*, including such architects as Thomas

forms it quoted and paraphrased it held at a distance, with the wry detachment of the Pop artist, not recreations but "ironic references." As a foundation on which to revive a style, let alone bring another one into existence, irony is no Gibraltar. But the creation of an authentic new style was never in the cards. The great architectural styles of the past, Roman or Gothic, or modernism for that matter, arose with a new structural principle or new social order—and usually both. Postmodernism offered neither, beyond what modernism had already created. The postmodern revolution tended to touch only the visible surface of the building, the thin cladding atop the steel frame, which exchanged its glass curtain wall for a festive skin of stripes, cutouts, and polished stone panels. For all its lofty rhetoric, it amounted to little more than a thorough-going fashion makeover, giving modernism a new suit of clothes and the fixed knowing wink it has worn ever since.

The ultimate meaning of every building is that conveyed by the society that produces it. Of all the arts, architecture is most fully a social act. The making of a novel, a symphony, or a painting occurs in private, but a building is the product of a complex collaboration between designer, builder and client, involving the expenditure of capital, and insertion of permanent objects in the social space of the community. And whether it represents Communism or Christianity, Roman *civitas* or the Greek *polis*, every building in the end is the concrete manifestation of a belief system. For an architecture without a belief system is but a mechanical art, differing only from plumbing in its complexity and in being subject to certain cyclical oscillations in fashion.

Postmodernism, for all its charms, was not a belief system;

Gordon Smith who made the school of architecture at Notre Dame a center of modern classicism. With the support of Henry Hope Reed and his organization Classical America, they have played an important role in championing classicism as a valuable cultural heritage rather than a set of stuffy, if amusing, forms to make sport of.

modernism, for all its faults, was—and in many ways an attractive one. It certainly had the merit of completeness. It took upon itself the responsibility of providing for everything, its purview reaching from a building's smallest detail to the most spacious aspect of a city. This imperative to transform architecture to meet the demands of the modern world, functional and psychological, gave it an enormous sense of responsibility, which it did not shirk. Nothing like this belief system has emerged in the collapse of modernism, and certainly not the belief system that preceded it: the liberal and modern version of western culture as it emerged from the nineteenth century. Without a confident and self-assured civilization to give it direction from without, architecture was left to fend for itself from within. In place of a comprehensive belief system, it came up with that internal surrogate: theory.

During the 1970s, history made its way back into the academy but now in the form of a professor of history and theory, often of continental (or British) pedigree. It was his task to lend the content-free and relatively straightforward process of teaching students to design a certain *gravitas* (although in some cases, *levitas* might be more to the mark). His was a tall order: to replace the void left by the heroic imperative of modernism, or of belief in western civilization itself, and to do so with nothing more than some speculation about the fundamental ambiguity of signs and symbols. Of course, some theorists have aimed at goals higher than cant. Those who have, like David Leatherbarrow at the University of Pennsylvania and Karsten Harries at Yale, tend to teach architecture from the point of view of decorum, as a cultured art with a long accumulated tradition of rules and customs, with which any aspiring designer must be acquainted. It is by no means the worst approach to teaching young architects: if one does not believe in something, one can at least be literate.

OF COURSE architecture students are not foolish, and they quickly observe that the intellectual and theoretical models in these courses are usually superfluous to the process of learning how to design (although in a pinch they might provide a flashy bit of window dressing in a crit). Those who avidly study theory are typically those who themselves aspire to teach it, who are often foreign students who will later teach in their home countries. Students during the 1990s came to have far more pressing concerns than rarefied continental philosophy, such as the harnessing of the computer and CAD (computer-aided design) in the design process. The architectural student at the end of the century was spending far less time reading treatises and writing essays than his predecessor even a decade earlier.

One of the chief reasons for the indifference to architectural theory is that theory is irrelevant to the element of competition—one might almost say Darwinian struggle—that animates architecture in a capitalist society. It is regrettable that theory has not confronted the fact of competition foursquare, for it is the cauldron of America's most interesting architecture. It is there where new technologies are forged and new forms introduced; these are the most conspicuous buildings, the ones with the largest budgets on the most prominent sites. Of course jostling aggressive competition roils the suburban street as well, where architecture serves the exaggerated descriptive role it always assumes in a nation with an elastic class system. While European architecture has a long tradition as a polite and urbane art, working within a settled social order, the American building invariably seeks to differentiate and distinguish itself. The polite ensemble is not an American strength.

For these reasons, America's bouts of greatest innovation and originality invariably coincide with the most overheated financial booms: the post-Civil War boom produced the aggressive Victorian generation, including Frank Furness and those inventors of the commercial skyscraper, Louis Sullivan and John Wellborn Root; the 1920s boom created the peerless inventor of skyscrapers, Raymond Hood; and even the much lamented 1980s brought Michael Graves and Charles Moore to the fore. The decades of "greed" have been kind to architecture.

WHILE THIS was proceeding apace, one group of architects clung stalwartly to the great modernist cause. These were the Whites, so designated in the early 1970s for their uncompromising quest for purity (in contrast to the omnivorous eclectics of postmodernism, who were termed the Grays). Emulating Le Corbusier's Villa Savoye and Villa Stein, they took as their point of departure the cube, whose sides they unfolded and bent as if held on invisible hinges, in an increasingly complex process of geometric manipulation and axial rotation. Richard Meier and Peter Eisenman are the best known of the Whites, the latter for the emphatically rectilinear houses he built since 1967, which he numbered sequentially (a cheeky act in a field where houses are invariably designated by the names of their clients), indicating that they were part of an experimental series.

The Whites were often congratulated for their "intellectual rigor," as if their whirling axes and colliding grids were the hard-won solution to a vexing mathematical problem. In actuality, the only variable being satisfied was the architect's own eye. At bottom arbitrary, these bent axes and fractured parallelepipeds were not Euclidean proofs but spoofs of them. Clients found all this terribly perplexing but it looked quite earnest, a serious virtue if the alternative was a lighthearted or vacuous commercial architecture. And when a billion-dollar investment was at stake, as the mighty Getty Museum in Los Angeles was, it is easy to see that mock seriousness would trump playful irony—and a modernist like Meier would win the commission.

Several years ago I debated with some colleagues about what our students really ought to know about American history, their own culture. I suggested that an ability to distinguish the War of 1812 from the Spanish-American War (a not uncommon mistake) was essential knowledge. A colleague disagreed, saying the Stonewall Riots were essential knowledge to her. But a more senior colleague was wiser than both of us. Our duty, she said with startling concision, was not to impart a prescribed canon of core knowledge to our students, in the belief that it was necessary for cultural literacy or good citizenship; our duty was *to teach the current hot research topics in graduate programs.*

One appreciates the honesty, but also the insight. In the absence of a collective belief in culture and civilization—in which politics, art, and science are not merely detached and free-floating specializations, but also participants in an over-arching hierarchical structure that relates them to things beyond themselves—no canon is possible. The specialist knows no obligation to a wider structure of things, but merely to the guild-like rules and disciplines of his own conventicle. And something like this has also happened in the past few decades to architecture, whose forms are less likely to refer to the society in which they sit but to architecture it-self—its processes, preoccupations, identity. In short, it has spiraled in upon itself.

This was certainly the path of the Whites. As their geometry grew more intricate, and their axial dissections more obsessive, their buildings soon came apart literally. And per-haps *literarily*, for it was the French philosophical school of deconstruction, with its doctrine about the infinite elasticity of text, that designated the new movement that emerged from the Whites. Here a metaphor about architecture was bor-rowed by philosophy and then returned to architecture, pun-ning on the predilection of Deconstructionist buildings to fragment and disintegrate visibly.

Perhaps the first to do so was Frank Gehry's house in Santa Monica, which conspicuously unpeeled itself in 1978. Even more unruly was Eisenman's Wexner Center for the Visual Arts, in Columbus, Ohio (1983–1989), with its hanging column supporting nothing, a brick arch cleanly sliced in mid-curve, and its flight of stairs leading to a dead end. Here was architecture's irrational dream of itself, as Piranesi might have imagined it, although Piranesi never had the impulse to try to build his fantasies, or the capacity to coax a client into paying for them. And thus the Whites moved inexorably from upholding the ordered rationality of early modernism to a geometry of stupefying irrationality.

If Deconstruction strove mightily to challenge the architectural establishment, it failed. Since weathering the fall of modernism, that establishment has been more or less impervious to shock or scandal. In the schools and in the streets, architects of wildly differing stylistic orientations worked happily alongside one another; nothing was mutually exclusive. Festive postmodern towers rose cheek to jowl beside sleek black cubes with dark tinted windows, much as Gothic and Art Deco skyscrapers huddled gregariously in the 1920s. It was true that there was no single unified style that uniquely expressed the Zeitgeist, but it was not missed. Architecture had settled into an anti-heroic stance, which frowned on absolutes and definitives and endorsed pluralism, grazing omnivorously and pleasantly from the bouquet of offerings to the mild background drone of theory. So architecture ambled on, chartless but content, into the morning of September 11, 2001.

IT IS DIFFICULT to imagine a place in the world less suited for theory than the aching chasm of Ground Zero. Theory by nature is speculative and provisional, and the World Trade Center site needed much stronger medicine than speculation or ironic detachment. And yet in the months following the attacks, as New York began to consider rebuilding the towers of the destroyed World Trade Center, it became clear that contemporary architecture had little else to offer. The rapidly organized exhibition of proposals at Max Protech Gallery in the late fall of 2001 was a warning of things to come, an anarchic pageant of Pop Art gestures in the Claes Oldenburg mode, or mournful earthen mounds.

To the acute embarrassment of the architectural establishment, the attacks of September 11 had an explicit national content. The International Style had effectively abolished national identity as a criterion in architecture, a state of affairs not changed by modernism's failure; certainly postmodernism, which blithely appropriated every symbol without regard for its original context, had no nationalist content. Yet the hijackers who plunged their jets into the World Trade Center towers attacked them not in their architectural or even financial capacity but in their role as emblems of American identity, which they have since become, indelibly, in retrospect.

To replace these towers without taking this into account simply would not do. Here was a commission of clear and unmistakable national importance, perhaps the most in half a century or more. But here, alas, all the factors that had transformed the nature of American architecture since the fall of modernism came into play: the freewheeling and noncommittal eclecticism; the two-tiered system of celebrity architects and mere practitioners; and the abdication by society at large of fundamental questions about the meaning of architecture to the architectural establishment itself—they came into play and converged catastrophically. The result was an incoherent program and the selection of a wildly inappropriate architect.

ONE OF THE unappreciated benefits of having a unified style is that the process of competition and comparison serves as a constant spur to improvement and correction. In the absence of such a yardstick, the intelligent and well-meaning building committee has no recourse but to turn to the architectural establishment for guidance. It is not surprising that the winner was that impeccably credentialed product of the establishment, fifty-seven-year-old Daniel Libeskind.

And Libeskind's credentials were indeed impeccable. His career had been spent largely as a professor of architecture, who only began to receive commissions in the past decade, and almost entirely from institutional clients. His principal work, his Jewish Museum in Berlin, was presumably a qualification for World Trade Center project. After all, until now it was perhaps the world's most visible object consecrated to grief and mourning. This was a Deconstructionist essay, a compressed and bleak procession through a series of irrational and disorienting gestures. In terms of invoking chaos and irrationality, as a mighty spasm of nihilistic despair, it worked well enough. But nihilism is not the proper tone at Ground

Zero, especially when the events set in train on September 11, 2001, are still unfolding turbulently around us.

IT IS A TRUISM in architecture that when the client is weak or divided, the architect fills the void. This is the case at the World Trade Center, where the lease-holder Larry Silverstein was nominally the client, but where his power was offset by the Lower Manhattan Development Corporation, a group finely tuned to public pressure groups. They faced two possible courses of action for Ground Zero, both of them honorable. On the one hand, one might rebuild the towers (or something like them) as quickly as possible as a mighty symbol of defiance and determination. On the other hand, one might plausibly argue that this land had forever been rendered "hallowed ground," akin to the battlefields of Gettysburg or Omaha Beach. To choose between these opposite and irreconcilable options was the responsibility of the client, but this was not done. Instead the decision was relegated to Libeskind, who tried to have it both ways.

Libeskind placed a mantle of commercial buildings, splintered and fractured in his characteristic way, to the north of the site, leaving the pit of Ground Zero open, its rough concrete slurry wall still intact as a visible vestige of the attack and the subsequent heartrending cleaning operation. He was not commissioned to design a formal memorial—for this a separate competition was conducted during the summer of 2003, resulting in the selection of Michael Arad and Peter Walker's project called "Reflecting Absence"—but in fact designed several, including the 1,776-foot tower that was to rise over the site and the so-called "wedge of Light" at the northern edge of the pit, which was to be bathed in sunlight on the anniversary during the precise duration of the attack and collapse of the buildings. The result is a design of tragic incoherence, simultaneously swaggering and weeping, unable to resolve its display of commercial vigor at the skyline and a ghoulish obsession with the yawning pit below.

SHORTLY AFTER Libeskind won the commission, some of his published poetry surfaced, in which nihilism and scatological imagery play a conspicuous part. In his oft-quoted line, "America turns its mass-produced urine antennae toward Caesar's arrogant ganglion, while history is advocated by utopians as a substitute for defecating." This is absurdist, stream-of-consciousness poetry, not to be taken literally. But the train of thought has its own implicit logic. The references to America, to mass-production, and to arrogance, are not random: they are all of a piece, and suggest a vision of his adopted homeland rather different from that of the grateful immigrant.

Under the blaze of public scrutiny, Libeskind's star quickly waned. In the summer of 2003, the actual implementation of his project was put in the hands of David Childs, a competent and seasoned professional who already had several skyscrapers to his credit; Libeskind was relegated to the face-saving role of master planner.

The outcome should have been foreseeable. Anyone casting more than a cursory look into his resume would have noticed that he was fundamentally a philosophical prankster, a creature of the theoretical compound, in which he has thrived, but constitutionally unable to relate that compound to things larger than itself—like America. And when he has tried, as with his memorial tower, the result has been kitsch, the simplistic symbolism of its 1776 exposing his non-Euclidean geometry as simple arithmetic. And with his willingness to plunge into bathos and kitsch, he proved himself another Palladio of the Wastepaper Basket.

After all the fanfare and flourishes, all the giddy hopes and false starts, that marked the course of the World Trade Center competition, the result is a startling letdown, a project bifurcated between an able technician like Childs and an architectural philosopher like Libeskind. But such is the paradox of American architecture today—overwhelming technical prowess and boldness of swagger and gesture, but also a fundamental uncertainty about the ultimate meaning of things.

And this is nothing new. American architecture remains a provincial enterprise, haunted by its psychological dependence on Europe. Although technically unsurpassed and although quivering with commercial vitality, it lacks that natural and unaffected sense of self that characterizes the architectural traditions of Europe. Hence the persistent American willingness to abandon its own lines of development and radically reorient itself almost overnight to European currents. The massive realignment toward European modernism in the 1930s was not a unique event. Something similar happened in the 1890s, when America abandoned the promising direction of its Chicago-style skyscrapers, Richardsonian Romanesque civic buildings, and Shingle Style Houses—each a creation of great originality and merit—and tossed them all overboard in a matter of a few years in a national fad for French classicism, the academic version taught at the Ecole des Beaux Arts in Paris. An entire living architectural culture was displaced in a matter of a few years by the doctrine of Paris. The Beaux-Arts revival produced much that was great, including most of our finest civic buildings, but it had about it a certain cold archaeology. Long-lived Frank Lloyd Wright twice experienced the abrupt and convulsive abandonment of indigenous American lines of architectural development, in his twenties during the 1890s, and in his sixties during the 1940s; it is no wonder that he was so dyspeptic in later years.

SUCH IS THE fragility of the American architectural tradition. The same ability to respond instantly and cleverly to commercial pressures, uninhibited by tradition or academic institutions, is the source of a persistent chronic rootlessness—as Macaulay said of the English constitution: all sail, no anchor. Before Modernism, the meaning of architecture was provided by settled traditions of decorum, custom, and above all belief that architecture was a high and noble art that did more than fill the mundane need for space and shelter, making civilization itself visible in permanent form. Until we can do this again, we cannot reassemble the broken pieces at Ground

Zero, much less restore the void at the center of architecture. We seem able to make objects that proclaim "we suffer," "we mourn," or "we repent"—but not ones that convey the simple assertion "we are good." And a culture that cannot say that will build no pyramids or cathedrals, and in the end not even a very good house.

Tending the Gardens of Music

Jay Nordlinger

A MERICA MAY BE a young country, but it fairly dominated music in the twentieth century. When I say music, I mean classical music, but the statement applies equally to popular music—maybe even with more force. Think of Gershwin, Rodgers, Porter, and the jazz greats, just for starters. It all went wrong in about 1970—you're free to pick your own date—but that is another long, sour essay.

In classical music, America's strength is little short of astonishing. We are talking about a European art form, which the United States embraced with gusto. When the Declaration of Independence was signed, Mozart was already twenty; America had a lot of mud (and political genius and some other things). By the Civil War, we had little to commend us but Louis Moreau Gottschalk. But by the end of World War II, we were rolling.

Of course, Europe helped us immensely, by persecuting—when not trying to kill—so many of its people. America grew to dominance in classical music partly by default, as it did in other areas. Conductors like Reiner, Szell, and Solti may not have chosen to have American careers, but those were the careers they wound up having. Our musical institutions were built on the talent and drive of European émigrés. And those institutions are healthy now, despite clamorous claiming to the contrary. Will they continue to be healthy—even dominant—as the twenty-first century progresses? Probably so, as long as America remains welcoming, ambitious, and free.

To remark the preeminence of America is not to say that Europe is nothing—not at all. Vienna is still a worthy music capital, and Berlin has much to offer, and so does London, not to mention numerous smaller places, such as Oslo. But the United States is still the place where the action is, where big careers are made, where music-making is most predictably excellent—in the orchestral hall, in the opera house, and elsewhere. An acknowledgement of this should have no odor of chauvinism whatever; it is a matter of objectivity. Music is a universal, not a national, enterprise anyway, and people from all over the world come to America to make music, rendering this activity not so much American as human.

The death of classical music is frequently proclaimed, and it has ever been thus. As Charles Rosen once wrote, "The death of classical music is perhaps its oldest tradition." The arguments in favor of death (if you will) are so tired and weak they are hardly worth confronting anymore. But we are usually drawn in. In my experience, some people actually enjoy predicting, or announcing, the death of classical music, because, when they do, others are apt to nod sadly and knowingly. To proclaim the death of classical music marks the proclaimer as a defender of civilization, and a foe of the destroyers.

One who doggedly counters the death idea is Gary Graffman, the pianist and director of the Curtis Institute of Music in Philadelphia. He was even moved to title a recent speech "Dead Again"! He noted that he kept having to give essentially the same speech, because prophecies of doom would not let up. "Disaster is always just around the corner," he said. But "one advantage of having reached the age of pontification"—Graffman is in his mid-seventies—"is that I actually *lived* through experiences identical to those which are now considered unique to our present philistine conditions." He went on to give multiple examples, many of them amusing. Consider this: In 1961, RCA Victor wanted Horowitz to record an album of popular music. His wife, Wanda—the daughter of Toscanini—shouted to an executive, "Better you should open a whorehouse!" RCA canceled the pianist's contract. Somehow, he survived.

When Graffman was coming up, the music business was puny compared with today. In the late 1940s, "there were only two major concert managements, with a total of about 40 pianists between them." In 2001, *Musical America*—a professional bible—listed 624 pianists. "So maybe we should be worrying more about glut than decline." Moreover, at mid-century, "New York had only one large concert hall, and—believe me, because I was there—very few performances were anywhere near sold out." For Horowitz, Rubinstein, and Heifetz? Yes. But for Serkin, Milstein, and Piatigorsky, Carnegie Hall was not even half full. No one thought this condition odd or alarming. Indeed, "a half-empty (or half-full) hall" was "the norm."

Zarin Mehta is eloquent on the subject of glut, as he is on other subjects. (Mehta is the executive director of the New York Philharmonic, and the brother of the conductor Zubin.) "If people think that classical music was healthier in earlier decades," he says, "they should investigate how many seats were available then versus now." The success of classical music in the 1960s and 1970s, when orchestras became full-time instead of part-time, "led to an explosion in every city"—and not just large ones, but simple burbs. Communities wanted their own orchestras. "Many, many more seats became available for classical music." So "if ticket sales are deemed soft today, perhaps it's a question of supply."

I WILL TAKE a little tour of the American music world, looking in on various facets. But here is a basic point: How you think classical music is doing depends, in large measure, on what your expectations are. If you expect classical music to be as popular as popular music, you will be sorely disappointed. As I frequently have cause to say to people, "That's why they call it popular music, you know." There will always be a type that can't stand that the broad public fails to share his concerns, passions, loves. Many such people have an evangelizing, proselytizing spirit—they can hardly sleep at night knowing that their neighbors prefer musical dross to gold. They will not reconcile themselves to the fact that classical music will always be, as it has always been, a minority taste. But the minority—lucky us—has an abundance before it.

The great mezzo-soprano Marilyn Horne said to me, in an interview, "Classical music is under assault in this country." This is an understandable—if strikingly dark—point of view, for in some ways we are slipping. For example, music education in grades K through 12 has all but ceased. And the song recital—a major Horne concern—is dismayingly rare. But in other respects, we are going gangbusters: Chamber music has exploded, for instance. You can hardly walk a block without encountering a chamber-music concert, or festival. As Gary Graffman pointed out to me, there used to be only the Budapest String Quartet, and its most prominent member, Alexander (Sasha) Schneider, liked to recall, "Vee vent by bus." Now there is a comparatively huge number of musicians who make a living in chamber music, and they don't go by bus.

Even in areas where we seem to be distressed, the news is mixed. The recording industry is currently moribund, but why? Because the record stores are groaning with albums already made. Never has so much music been available to so many, and so cheaply. As Zarin Mehta commented, "I started buying records when I was sixteen or seventeen. I don't go to record stores anymore, because I have essentially everything I want. Do I need a fifth recording of the *Ring* cycle?" Furthermore, the Internet is now seen as a great robber of recordings, but it may prove a boon to music in the future. In addition, musicians are making CDs in their own homes or studios, at little expense, and selling them to interested parties.

So the business of music will evolve, as it always has. We may not be able to foresee its forms—but we can count on musical life.

FOR ORCHESTRAS, times have changed dramatically since mid-century. Then, you could hardly make a living as an orchestral musician, even in the best orchestras. "The men," as they were called, had to sell shoes, paint houses, and do other odd jobs in the summer, just to make ends meet. A fifty-two-week contract was only a dream; it is now an entrenched reality. To work in an orchestra is not to take a vow of poverty; pay in one of the big orchestras begins at about $100,000 a year; it soon rises.

Even aside from the top orchestras, there is an embarrassment of riches. Jack McAuliffe, chief operating officer of the American Symphony Orchestra League, reports that there are about 1,800 orchestras in the fifty states. Of these 1,800, about 600 are either youth, conservatory, or collegiate orchestras. They are "important for the development of both orchestras and audiences," says McAuliffe, "but they aren't necessarily a factor in discussing the economics of orchestras today." Of the remaining 1,200 "adult" orchestras, "you have orchestras in which everyone is paid, and, at the other end, orchestras in which no one is paid. Of the 1,200, about 350 fall into the category of professional orchestras, where the majority of members are paid, and participating for professional reasons, not merely for enjoyment."

In the past couple of seasons—since September 11—orchestras have had trouble, as many businesses and other enterprises have. But, as McAuliffe notes, the decade of the 1990s was "probably the best ever for orchestras, with record attendance." About 32 million seats were filled in the 2000–01 season, up 16 percent from ten years before. "During the late '90s," that roaring time, "virtually every orchestra was showing at least a small surplus, with many in the process of building substantial endowments—and the ones that had them already were increasing them."

Since 9/11, we have, again, been in a "much more challenging time." Most orchestras are worrying, but they are succeeding—because they are knuckling down. "Of the 350 professional orchestras," says McAuliffe, "we're aware of eight that haven't made it—that have either ceased operations or filed for bankruptcy. That is a failure rate of three-quarters of 1 percent a year. For most industries, that would be downright enviable." But, if a couple of orchestras stumble, the media tend to play it in death-of-classical-music tones. To be sure, says McAuliffe, the failure of an orchestra is no fun for that orchestra's community, but part of economic life is that some institutions fail—and then, perhaps, recover, get reconstituted, as has happened with many orchestras. In the late 1980s and early 1990s—another difficult period—eight orchestras went under (by coincidence, the same number that would succumb a decade later). In time, however, each of those eight communities gained an orchestra of approximately the same size and scope of the one it lost. For example, the Denver Symphony came back as the Colorado Symphony. The orchestra in Birmingham came back as the Alabama Symphony. Etc. In most such cases, the same basic group plays under a new name, and under different governance.

Quite recently, Pittsburgh suffered a bankruptcy scare. The orchestra there is superb, bearing a storied past. But through the years, the PSO was not supported much by the community at large—that is, with donations—because a few prominent citizens, most of them named Heinz, took care of it. Pittsburghers in general did not have the sense that they needed to contribute in order to have an orchestra. But the prospect of bankruptcy jolted them awake—and they responded with their contributions, utterly unwilling to see their orchestra expire, or even flag.

McAuliffe sums up: "Orchestras are still a robust part of the artistic life of an awful lot of communities. In fact, they are often centerpieces of that artistic life, forming the basis of opera companies, dance companies, music education in schools" (such as it is). Orchestras will never "just work," without effort—"it really takes dedication." But "interest is this art form isn't dying; it's just an expensive form of art to support."

NOT ONLY are today's orchestras robust, they have sturdy homes to live in—in many cases, new ones. Listen to Robert Harth, executive and artistic director of Carnegie Hall: "To those who would sing the swan song of classical music's death, I would point to the fact that the most talked about building on the planet was built for classical music."[1] Harth made that statement in October 2003, and he was speaking of Disney Hall in Los Angeles, designed by Frank Gehry. "It's a magnificent building, a life-changing building, not just for the L.A. Philharmonic, but for that entire city. And that makes a dramatic and positive statement about classical music." Jack McAuliffe would point to Newark, too—yes, Newark: "The New Jersey Performing Arts Center was built in the middle of nothing, and it has spawned all sorts of development. It is now a pleasant experience to go to Newark. I guarantee you that wasn't the case ten years ago." And "the New Jersey Symphony is thriving."

Other new halls include the Kimmel Center in Philadelphia, Benaroya Hall in Seattle, the Max M. Fisher Center in Detroit (nicknamed the Max), the Meyerson Center in Dallas, Bass Hall in Fort Worth, Jacoby Hall in Jacksonville, and the Schuster Center in Dayton. Robert Harth adds, "Atlanta is building a new concert hall, and Toronto just redid theirs. Severance Hall in Cleveland has been completely revamped. This is 'dying'?"

But Marilyn Horne sounds a cautionary note. In Greenville, South Carolina, they built the Peace Center, a fabulous performing-arts complex. (It is named for a philanthropic family named Peace, not for the concept.) The center "has a recital hall, a concert hall, and extraordinary acoustics," says Horne,

> but, as the man responsible told me, "It's easier to raise money than to put a body in a seat." So what did he have to bring in, to put bodies in the seats? *Les Miz, Phantom of the Opera*, and so on. There's nothing wrong with bringing those pieces in, but it's not classical music, and that is worrying.

---

1 Mr. Harth died in January 2004.

It is, indeed: but, in 2003–04, the Peace Center had not only *Les Miz*—and *Seussical*, for that matter—but the Emerson String Quartet (part of this chamber boom I mentioned).

A second cautionary note comes from Sedgwick Clark, editor of *Musical America*. He is concerned about the cost of all this music building. "We must take stock of what we're spending, and control our costs. I look at Disney Hall, and it's an extraordinary thing, but it's going to cost an arm and a leg to maintain." At Disney, "the cheapest seat will be $35. To sit in the orchestra will be $120. For a concert! Maybe I've just gotten old, but the fact of the matter is, $120 for a concert—how many CDs can I buy for that amount? This is a serious problem." Our new orchestral halls are impressive, Clark notes, but "if they're not sold out, or close to sold out, the orchestras have a terrible time." There are those generous salaries to look after, and employee benefits, and pension plans.

Fundraising in music is a special art. Beverly Sills knows quite a bit about it, and about fundraising in general. "I raised $100 million for the March of Dimes," she informs me,

> and hundreds of millions for other charities. Medical causes do better than music. If you have some disease to cure, you're not going to want to fork over millions for another production of *La Bohème*. But I say in all my speeches: "Art is the signature of civilization." We dance for joy, our hearts sing. When we're little children, we take crayons and know immediately how to scribble. When my husband and I moved into a new apartment, the first thing we did, poor as we were, was paint the walls and hang up Mama's pictures. In the car, we want the radio on. We don't want to be in a silent ambiance.

So she tells her audiences that the arts are not a luxury, and they—at least for her, a woman hard to turn down—come through.

MENTION OF Beverly Sills leads us to the opera. It's not easy to be gloomy about this slice of music, no matter how hard you try. Marc Scorca, the president of Opera America, supplies the essential facts: In the second half of the twentieth century, opera in the United States grew enormously—it was practically a boom. Opera America now has 115 member companies; there are companies in all but a handful of states. Aside from these, "there are many smaller, community-based endeavors, and lots of university and conservatory opera programs that put on performances for paying audiences." Of the 115, fully three-quarters have been established since 1960.

Understandably, opera is "the most expensive of the traditional performing arts," as Scorca says. "One of the reasons we see opera-company formation as a relatively recent phenomenon is that the financial and infrastructural requirements of opera are considerable: It takes a long time for a community to have a critical mass of audience members and donors prepared to sustain a company. You can't put on an opera very spontaneously." No, you have to have a chorus and an orchestra; you need technicians, stagehands, a costumer, a stage designer—and that's not even mentioning the soloists. Plus, opera "is traditionally performed in a theater with an orchestra pit, and not every community has one of those. You can put on a play with two characters in a store front. You can have a dance program in a loft, as long as it doesn't have too many pillars." But opera is a formidable undertaking.

Therefore, the public must want it, for these companies to be born and to succeed. Scorca explains that opera is "a multimedia art form in a multimedia world." It includes texts, visual images, drama, often dance—"and these components are very much part of our popular culture." Opera

doesn't ask you to sit and enjoy a purely auditory experience. It involves you in every way that other contemporary entertainments involve you. As people seek a classical-arts experience that is still based on the multimedia sensory experience they have enjoyed in the popular culture, opera is the classical art form they can respond to.

One boost to opera was the advent of titles—supertitles, seatback titles, those lines of words that help an audience member understand what's happening onstage. Says Beverly Sills, "I worked very hard to bring titles into the opera. Jimmy said, 'Over my dead body.'" (That would be James Levine, artistic director of the Metropolitan Opera.) But titles came to the Met, to the satisfaction of most everybody, and with Levine still breathing in the pit. Marc Scorca confirms that titles made for "a huge improvement in reaching out to new audiences." Before, there was always a severe language barrier to overcome. Now people do not sit flummoxed (except by plots and other operatic strangeness). Some traditionalists maintain that titles break an important visual connection to the performer—and they are right—but most of us judge it a sacrifice worth making.

THE REIGNING HOUSE in America, of course—and in the world—is the Met. It has no real rivals, as its general manager, Joseph Volpe, points out (not boasting); it is a unique institution. There are other companies as renowned—La Scala in Milan, Covent Garden in London, the Staatsoper in Vienna—but no one company that does as much. Volpe notes that La Scala puts on seventy or eighty performances a season: "To be general manager there would be a semi-retirement job"! The Met has a full-time orchestra and a full-time chorus, and "it's important that they work"—more or less continuously. In Vienna, "they're known for putting on a production with no rehearsal at all, or just one rehearsal. They're also known for having one leading cast member," with the rest plucked from the company. "We are, and have been historically, noted for having top singers." But, Volpe continues,

as the season expands, this becomes more and more difficult, particularly considering travel. A lot depends on the dollar. Our fees are lower than in the European houses. In Italy, they'll pay $30,000 for a single performance. They'll deny it, but it's true. Our top fee is $15,000. So, what's going to happen is, some singers will spend more time in Europe than in the United States.

Volpe cites Bryn Terfel, the beloved bass-baritone from Wales:

> He has three children, and it's easy for him to jump on a plane and fly to a city in Europe, sing, and go home. To come to the Met is a large commitment. You end up here a long period of time. You can't fly home to be back with the family, as you can in Europe. The days of great singers staying in America are over.

Like everyone else, the Met has taken a financial hit in the post-9/11 environment. Ticket sales and donations are down. But the institution is fundamentally sound. As Volpe observes, a house that survived the Great Depression can survive a lot. You just have to roll with events, and not panic.

A particular concern in recent days has been whether the famous Met radio broadcasts will continue. They began in 1931, and in 1940 came under the sponsorship of Texaco. In 2003, that company—now ChevronTexaco—announced that it would quit sponsoring the broadcasts. This was no small matter to the Met, because, as Volpe points out, radio is responsible for a good deal of its national and international reputation. Three million people listen to the broadcasts in the United States, and seven million listen in forty-one other countries. "That's very important to the Met's image." It takes about $7 million a year to produce these radio broadcasts. At this writing, the Met has not secured permanent sponsorship, but Volpe and Beverly Sills—who is chairman of the Met's board—are confident that they will. There is little reason to doubt them.

About the prospect of making records again, it's hard to be as confident. The recording industry is now stagnant, as I have mentioned. Opera CDs coming out today, says Volpe, tend to be produced in Europe, "with orchestras that are paid a very small fee." Unionized orchestras in the U.S. would have none of that. "What's been happening in our country is that record companies have been saying for years and years and years, 'We can't afford to pay what the musicians demand, and we can't make any money off of classical music.' So business has dried up." And, "frankly, how many *Rosenkavaliers* do you need?" (Back to the glut problem.) Continues Volpe, "The only way the Met will get back into recording is if we produce recordings live, without paying fees, and then have some kind of revenue sharing with our people."

The general manager recounts a conversation with Renée Fleming, the celebrated soprano, who opened the 2003–04 Met season as Violetta. "Renée was unhappy because there was no television for her *Traviata*. I told her that we would broadcast on radio and that maybe, someday, there would be a recording of that." In truth, "that's the real McCoy," the live broadcast, with no touching up, no corrective takes, "and I don't think it's so horrible" to represent the company that way.

Volpe and the Met are often criticized for producing too few new operas—for being a mere "museum," if not a "mausoleum." The GM protests,

> If you look at the last ten years, our track record with contemporary works is probably as good as any opera company's. But understand something: Commissioned works are very, very expensive. We have to fund the commissioning and fund the production. If we can do one every three years, that would be a nice pace. What we can do depends on our financial situation.

Sure, in the good old days, the Met produced one new opera after another. But "do you know what?" asks Volpe. "Composers would come in off the street, shove a manuscript into your hand, and say, 'Here's an opera. Wanna put it on?' They didn't start with, 'First give me $350,000, then . . ?' And remember, we rehearse what we perform: We don't put things onstage unrehearsed." Rehearsal, like time—being time—is money.

The Met seems permanent, unbudgeable, like the U.S. Capitol. Will it be forever? "I think it will be forever," says the GM,

> because there are so many people who love this art form. The question is, What does that mean? The Met in the form of today? Maybe not. Does it mean thirty-two weeks of performances a year? Maybe not. So the question is—I hate the word "evolve." When I first started out, I hated that word. I said, "Don't tell me about 'evolve.' You've got to be in charge and decide things, not just let them evolve!"

But Joe Volpe is more comfortable with that concept now, as one is often forced to become.

A WORD ABOUT the audience—the concertgoers, the operagoers. From time immemorial, people have fretted over the "graying" of the audience, and the relative paucity of the young. This should not be high on any list of worries. As Sedgwick Clark puts it, "You come to appreciate music more when you're older. Also, you tend to have more time and money." Carnegie Hall's Harth says, "If you look at pictures taken during Toscanini's concerts, you will see that the audience is a sea of gray hair. I assume those attendees are now in another realm. But people still come for concerts conducted by Simon Rattle," and these tend also to be grayheaded.

Jack McAuliffe of the Orchestra League notes that the median age of an audience member—for an orchestral concert—is "somewhere in the mid-fifties." And "when you say that, most people think, 'Gee, the concert audience is over fifty-five' or so. But what it really means is that half the people are younger than that, and half are older—sometimes a lot older. What are we supposed to do? Kick people out when they're seventy or eighty? They keep coming." The quest—even lust—for younger people sometimes gets a little comic. They are, for many, a holy grail. Concert presenters want the young, the same as churches do. Experience has shown, however, that people take a while to come to both—that is, to music and to church.

But we should not be overly blithe. McAuliffe stresses a key difference between today and yesterday: "Most young people," now, "have grown up with absolutely no exposure to classical music. People knew something about music a generation or two ago. Even if they didn't want to, they learned something about it. Today, it's easy to avoid, and even if you want to learn about it, it's hard to get." In the past, orchestras were "the provider of the end product," and now they are "the introduction" to it. Orchestras, opera companies, and other institutions are doing what they can to fight musical ignorance, by providing pre-concert lectures, notes on the Internet, and the like.

Zarin Mehta says that it is not only lack of education that gives pause, but "lack of espousal by the media." The larger culture seems unwilling to embrace and instill classical music. Therefore, Mehta wonders whether the gray heads will keep coming, as they always have. Not a few critics maintain that younger people would be attracted by additional contemporary music, as opposed to the standard repertory. Programming is a rich subject, demanding an essay, or a book, unto itself. But suffice it to say that evidence for this claim—newer would attract younger—is thin on the ground. Nor does common sense support it. As Mehta says, "A certain group of young people may go to an avant-garde evening, if it is created in a certain way, but when you talk about a symphony orchestra playing new music, it is as difficult for a young person as it is for an older person." Really, "if someone has not been exposed to much music, do you give him a festival of Beethoven or a festival of Ligeti?"

NOW TO THE DEATH of the recital, or at least its diminishment. This is especially troubling in that a recital is, for many of us, an incomparably satisfying musical experience. Ignat Solzhenitsyn is a pianist and conductor (and son of the great man). Of recitals, he says, "They're going down the tubes. Apparently, they're too boring, they require too much concentration." And the explosion of chamber music has bitten badly into recitals, as presenting organizations "just view them as too risky, economically."

Of course, recitals still abound at Carnegie Hall. Indeed, Carnegie has opened a new hall within its complex—Zankel Hall—that will see a great many recitals. But Robert Harth does not necessarily expect a recital to sell out. He points to one of the best events—in his view, and mine—of the 2002–03 season, an all-unaccompanied recital courtesy of the great Russian violinist Maxim Vengerov. "Let me ask you something," says Harth:

> What's a successful concert? Carnegie Hall has 2,800 seats. For Vengerov, 2,000 were in attendance. I said to my board, "Is it not a success because 800 seats were empty? Or is it a success because 2,000 were filled?" It's absolutely a success, if it's a great concert and those who were there had a wonderful time. It becomes an *unsuccessful* concert when, as an administrator, you budget to sell 2,500. But if you budget to sell 1,500 or 1,800, you'll be happy.

Harth knows that Carnegie Hall will lose money—virtually all classical-music organizations do. He just wants to lose it wisely and enrichingly (in the nonmonetary sense!).

Since 1994, Marilyn Horne has devoted a good bit of her time to the Marilyn Horne Foundation. I have frequently described this organization as a "point of light," to adapt the famous—or once famous—term used by the first President Bush. It is dedicated, in particular, to the perpetuation of the song recital. Is it really true, I ask the great mezzo, that there are fewer recitals now than there used to be? "Oh, my God yes, please. I started going to song recitals when I was a child, and I started singing them in about 1960. From that time on, I could count on doing twenty or thirty recitals a year, depending on my availability. Some years were heavy with concerts [with orchestra] and some years were heavy with opera, but there was no question that the [recital] opportunities were there." The number of "community concerts" has greatly decreased. And those series that remain "seldom take classical singers. They don't take them at all, unless the singer is a big star. So where is the younger singer going to get experience?"

Horne faults the "dumbing down of America" and the tendency to "play to the lowest common denominator." Television, computers, and other innovations play their distracting roles. Opera, the singer concedes, is doing much better than the vocal recital, which is odd, in a way, because recitals are infinitely cheaper to present. "But you have to have people in the seats," regardless of the cost of staging the event. "And opera is much more glamorous, of course," suited to our "very visual age. You can see this is in the way casting is done, and the fact that the stage director and the scene designer have much more power than they used to have. If you read an opera review, you see that seven-eighths of it are about the production." The music is almost an afterthought.

A special shame about the decline of the vocal recital is that there are so many today who do it well. In lieder alone, I might name Michael Schade, Christine Schäfer, Thomas Quasthoff, Marjana Lipovšek, and Thomas Hampson, and I have barely gotten started. I, of course, have heard them, in some cases repeatedly—but I frequent halls in New York and Salzburg. Marilyn Horne has sung in all fifty states—the last of which was Wyoming, where she performed just as her (classical) career was closing. (She now does pop evenings, and marvelously, too.) Whatever the cause for optimism in other areas, it seems clear that the flame of the song recital— and of the recital in general—needs serious tending, which Horne, of course, is laudably engaged in doing.

WE NOW TURN our attention to that "culprit," chamber music. America has progressed far beyond the Budapest String Quartet, the famed four who "vent by bus." There are dozens of string quartets, and other chamber ensembles, making a fine living. As Solzhenitsyn says, "Look at the numbers: The quantity of series and festivals devoted exclusively to chamber music is increasing every year." The Chamber Music Society of Philadelphia, for instance, started off with a handful of concerts, and "now they're doing seventy." Chamber music "has gone from precisely that—a private, intimate affair [in a chamber]—to a major staple of the concert stage."

The leading chamber-music institution in the country is the Chamber Music Society of Lincoln Center. Founded in 1969, it was a mere "niche-filler," to use Solzhenitsyn's term, but it rapidly grew, spawning many imitators. Its artistic director is David Shifrin, who on the side is one of the world's foremost clarinetists. He confirms that presenters find chamber music affordable and even profitable. "You can do it in someone's living room or you can do it in Avery Fisher Hall. Organizations that can't afford to pay stagehands or a high rent can present a chamber ensemble of the highest quality—they can do it in a high-school auditorium." If you have any funds at all, "you have a great shot at getting a world-class performance in great and compelling repertoire." But "as much as I enjoy playing chamber music, these concerts have sort of taken the place of recitals. I wish there were room for both." To be sure, presenters will still engage "the superstar pianists, but not that many violinists or cellists—to say nothing of clarinetists, flutists, or French horn players—have a shot at a recital." So the sonata repertoire, in particular, goes unheard. "Most presenters around the country go for star power, go for box office. If they can't have a famous name, they want more people onstage."

As for the Chamber Music Society of Lincoln Center, Shifrin believes that it will continue to flourish, if "with some bumps here and there," as in most any enterprise. And the festivals keep proliferating. "For a long time, there have been invitations to play really good music, with really good people, in wonderful places from Memorial Day to Labor Day. Now it's even wider. Next year I'm going back to a chamber-music festival in Tucson in March." For a quarter-century, Shifrin has been involved with Chamber Music Northwest, in Portland. That institution now operates year-round, not just in the summer. "They are able to do wonderful things there, in a city of about a million. Arguably the highest-quality cultural institution in Portland is that chamber-music festival."

A wag once said about chamber music, "It's like the cockroach: Try as you might, you'll never stamp it out." An unlovely comparison, perhaps, but clear.

IN THE FIELD of education, the good news is at the top: Conservatories have rarely had it better. Endowments are full, and so are the practice rooms—full to overflowing, actually. Leading conservatories are the Curtis Institute, the Juilliard School, the Peabody Institute, and so on—names that have been renowned for decades. Newer on the block is the Colburn School in Los Angeles; the San Francisco Conservatory is still going strong farther north. Then there are the many music schools in universities, led, probably, by Indiana and Michigan. As Solzhenitsyn observes, there is "an obscene number" of music majors in the United States today—on the order of 100,000 a year. There are not plum jobs for all these aspirers, even if they were equal to them. But those who fall short of their highest goal may teach or otherwise stay close to music.

At Juilliard, applications increase by 10 percent annually. The school admits about 8 percent of those who apply. Joseph Polisi, the president of Juilliard, is adamant that his school provides a better education than it did, say, in 1930: For one thing, "we educate the entire human being, not just the artist." Students are presented with a liberal arts curriculum, and they study every aspect of music, not just their specialty. In addition, says Polisi, "we preach 'the artist as citizen,'" seeking to endow the student with "a sense of responsibility for making sure that the arts flourish in society."

People who tend to look for a dark lining say, "Well, yes, the better music schools are at a peak, but the students aren't

American—they come from overseas, mostly from Asia." True, but, as Zarin Mehta says, "What do you mean by American?" Many of these kids become American in due course, along with the family members who surround them, just as people have done for generations. Polisi reports that 70 percent of the pianists studying at Juilliard come from abroad. The foreign country supplying the most students overall is South Korea, followed by Canada, Taiwan, Communist China, Japan, and then the former Soviet republics. Marilyn Horne reports a similar pattern at the Music Academy of the West (Santa Barbara), where she is voice director. We have gone from a time when Americans went abroad to study music and become musicians, to a time when the world beats a path to the American door.

Joseph Polisi has no doubt about Juilliard's staying-power:

I often get the Chicken Little question: Is the sky falling? Will music survive? Of course it will. I'm surrounded every day by about 800 absolutely motivated, talented, disciplined, energized young people. There's no way in the world they're going to be stopped in music, dance, and drama. They will create audiences, and they will be the leaders of the future. That's what I ask them to be. Yes, the audiences of the New York Philharmonic are grayer than for Pearl Jam [a rock group]. There has never been a large niche for classical music. But it will survive.

We have a glut problem, however. Horne recalls saying fully twenty-five years ago, "We should close all the conservatories for five years," just to give the job market a break. And "now the situation is worse!" For woodwind and brass players, life has always been tricky: Zarin Mehta tells me that, for a recent tuba opening in the Philharmonic, over 120 people applied. One result of all this redundant talent is that players tend to be quite good, everywhere. David Delta Gier, a conductor with wide experience both in America and abroad, says, "You should hear some of the players in Sioux

Falls!" (The orchestra there is the South Dakota Symphony.) The sad part of our cornucopia is that many musicians wind up disappointed. Gier knows many fellow conductors—or would-be conductors—who have not had careers, or satisfying ones, simply because of the number of podiums available (versus all those who want to stand on them). "You get into a great school, you study with a great teacher, you work hard, you do everything right, and you think you ought to be rewarded. But a lot of people have been made to realize that that's not necessarily the case."

It would take a very hard-headed person to state the cold fact that no one asked anyone to pursue a career in music—or in film, or in journalism, or in anything else. But he would not be wrong.

THE DECLINE in music education from kindergarten through high school is a bit of a puzzle. Contrary to what many believe, America's public schools are awash in money. Never has per-pupil expenditure been higher. In some places, it is scandalously high (for what it produces). But music has been downgraded, meaning that it is almost surely a question of priority.

Most people of a certain age—people who love music—can remember with fondness particular music teachers. Marilyn Horne had two of them with whom she kept in touch till the end of their lives. In fact, when she was making a Christmas album (with the Mormon Tabernacle Choir), she remembered a carol from her schooldays, but could not locate the music. So she called the relevant teacher and asked her for it. "All she had was the melody, because we sang without any accompaniment—we only had a pitch pipe." Schools across the country rarely had elaborate facilities. Little Marilyn and her classmates—in Bradford, Pennsylvania—had what was called a "playroom," down in the basement. But there was a sense of caring about music, and the other arts, and nurturing them.

Obviously, there are pockets of excellence—of caring—in primary and secondary schools. As David Shifrin says, "I wouldn't count this country out." It is a big, continental nation, with thousands of school systems. But where music education does exist, it tends to be "aesthetic," according to Joseph Polisi, rather than "performance-based." In aesthetic education, "you just *talk* about the music. You don't play anything. You talk about a symphony or an opera or a piece of chamber music. That's easier to teach, because the teacher doesn't need to be an expert in the oboe, for example. The downside is, that kind of education doesn't stick, in my opinion." Performance-based education is far and away preferable. But we have apparently reached a point where any education at all is a welcome surprise.

As to the recording industry, it is certainly not true that no CDs are coming out—they are. Acres of them. But fewer are being made than in the past, particularly in the U.S. We could live off recordings already made pretty much forever, as almost all the known repertory has been recorded, often many times over. But that would be no fun. First, new music needs to be recorded—and it regularly is, despite the griping of composers and their advocates—and, second, it would be a shame not to capture musicians of today, or of the future, even in the most familiar repertory. Yes, we should have Renée Fleming's Violetta. And we should have Michael Schade's *Schöne Müllerin*, no matter how good Fritz Wunderlich's is.

I will share an anecdote that speaks to the nervous state of recording. It comes from Marilyn Horne, talking about Deborah Voigt, one of the most important sopranos now on the scene. Voigt was scheduled to appear in a gala for Horne's foundation. But she called Horne to say, "I would never do this to you, but I have a chance to record Wagner duets with Domingo, and it would be at the exact same time, and I feel I can't pass it up, because I simply don't get to record." Needless to say, Horne understood, and released her; the recording—a superlative one on EMI—was made.

Horne is incensed at one tactic of the record companies:

They're marketing singers as opera singers who aren't opera singers! Andrea Bocelli, Charlotte Church . . . Whatever else they are—and a person may like them—they're not opera singers. I let out a yell the other day, because I was doing the crossword puzzle, as I do daily, and one clue was "Tune for Bocelli." It turned out to be "aria," and I went, "&*@!" I wish him well, and he has a place, but please don't call him an opera singer.

This would be especially misleading, according to Horne, to those who are new to operatic music or to classical music in general. I could argue that Bocelli and other such "soft" singers are good for music—partly as a starting point for the public, a kind of gateway—but Horne, whose musical standards are rigorous, has a point.

We should also understand that not all companies have flopped with classical CDs. As Benjamin Ivry reported in *The Christian Science Monitor*, "independent" labels such as Naxos, Chandos, and Harmonia Mundi are more than getting by. "Naxos is thriving," said Klaus Heymann, that label's founder, "and other independents who make interesting recordings people want to buy are also doing well. . . . What has been killed, or rather committed suicide [!], are the big-budget, all-star productions which got so expensive that they could never recoup their investment." And Bernard Coutz, founder of Harmonia Mundi, remarked sensibly, "No one killed classical music, which makes up part of the patrimony of humanity." (In 1997, the critic Norman Lebrecht published an incendiary book called *Who Killed Classical Music?*) "Across 2,000 years of history, classical music, like painting or fine cuisine, has not necessarily attracted great crowds . . . but it has always interested people who by luck or talent have learned to love it." That is an attitude of maturity.

A major issue for the first part of our century is, as Robert Harth puts it, "How do you legislate the use of music over the Internet? How do you not overpay, not underpay, not take advantage of musicians?" Harth expects that people will "get their musical fix" from the Internet the way they once did from the radio, and that is already occurring. A site called iClassics is offering "webcasts"—a new word that may become as familiar as "broadcasts"—meaning that people can watch and listen to concerts, over the Internet, for free. How, then, does a company make money? As a representative explained to me, the hope is that those watching and listening for free will come to like the performer, or the music, and thus attend a concert or buy a CD. All involved are still feeling their way around in the new era.

As I mentioned earlier, musicians are beginning to make CDs on their own—without benefit of the big labels—and peddling them themselves. David Shifrin observes that "technology is such that any musician who really wants to be heard, and recorded for posterity, can just go ahead and do it. It costs practically nothing to record and produce CDs, compared to what it used to cost with vinyl." As a result, "you have a proliferation of vanity recordings, plus small labels that have success." The cellist David Finkel makes big-time Deutsche Grammophon recordings with the string quartet of which he is part: the Emerson. But he and his wife—the pianist Wu Han—started www.ArtistLed.com, which they bill as "classical music's first Internet recording company." Other musicians have started similar enterprises. Shifrin notes that "recordings are much easier to find on some websites than they were when you actually had to find a record store, a physical, bricks-and-mortar store. This whole trend is in its infancy."

Here again, we "evolve," to use the word that Joe Volpe has learned to love.

YOU COULD BE sour about the music industry, if you wanted to be. Classical radio stations are dying—even when you can make money in classical, you can make more in pop. But a person can buy Heifetz in the Brahms and Tchaikovsky concertos for seven bucks. And you can listen to the world's best classical stations via the Internet, wherever they are, and wherever you are. It was said, eons ago, that radio would kill concerts, and then that the LP—mass produced and marketed—would. But concerts kept growing in popularity. Sadly, few orchestras now broadcast nationally. But the musicians' union has a lot to answer for. It may have helped to make its members more prosperous, but it has been self-defeating in other ways. Orchestras don't broadcast nation-ally—or record much—because of rigid union rules and, if I may, dumb, fruitless greed.

Some lament that classical musicians are ignored today, kept off the tube and *Time* magazine's cover. The critic and scholar Stuart Isacoff informed me that, when Anton Rubinstein first came to this country, he was greeted with a torchlight parade. And yet this day has its celebrities, ones so big they are known by their first names alone: Itzhak and Yo-Yo; Luciano, Plácido, Renée, Bryn. Some critics shudder at the Three Tenors stadium concerts, those vulgar spectacles—yet these may be the same critics who complain that classical music has no connection to the broader public. It is merely human to want things on one's own terms.

Music-lovers are a terribly nostalgic lot, always going on about golden eras (long past, of course) and cluck-clucking over the present. But there are great and historic musicians in every age—we simply tend not to recognize them when they are before us. The present age, in my view, is a thrilling one for singing. I could give you a list—a long one. And, yes, Heifetz and Milstein are dead. But have you heard Hilary Hahn and Maxim Vengerov? Rostropovich is getting old, but have you heard Han-Na Chang? Rostropovich certainly has: The young lady—girl, really—was the first cellist with whom Slava ever recorded, as conductor. Eventually, these young musicians will teach, and create protégés. Hilary Hahn studied with Jascha Brodsky, who studied with Ysaÿe and Zimbalist. And so it goes.

OUR MUSICAL institutions will survive because people insist that they do—not a vast number of people, as compared with those who love sports or soda, but enough people. As Sedgwick Clark says, "Beethoven, Tchaikovsky, Stravinsky, and the rest will always be performed. Always. There's no doubt about it. And, incidentally, I have no problem viewing orchestras [for example] as museums." This is one of the great sneers: that our institutions have become museums. "They *are* museums, no less than the Metropolitan Museum of Art or the Museum of Modern Art. And there's nothing wrong with that. That doesn't mean that the orchestras don't play contemporary music—they bring it into the museum, and whether it stays on exhibit remains to be seen." I hasten to add that a museum is not a mausoleum. There is great life— throbbing, comforting, provocative, glorious life—in those musical museums of ours.

It pays to remember, too, that people who have been around for a while tend not to sweat the future of classical music. "The pendulum swings back and forth," says Gary Graffman. Already he has lived "through two or three of these round-trip swings"! To obsess over the fate of classical music, notes Graffman, is like obsessing over the fate of the stock market: We should take the long view, and not get carried away by sharp spikes up or sharp spikes down. Echoing our chairman of the Federal Reserve, I might say that both irrational exuberance and irrational gloom are errors to be avoided. And do not, as Gary Graffman says, make the mistake of thinking that "the audience is limitless." Always there will be classical-music fannies in the seats—just don't create a ridiculous excess of them (seats, that is).

And allow me a final repetition: Our institutions will not prosper by themselves. One has to work at them. One has to tend the gardens of music, and they will indeed grow, or if not grow, at least not die, blooming again every year, to one degree or another. America is lucky in its plenitude of gardeners, and the gardens they make. Amidst all the handwringing—some of it justifiable—we should pause, in gratitude, to fold those hands as well.

Expensive Illiterates:
Victimhood & Education

Mark Steyn

A DICTATORSHIP—even a one-man psycho state—can appear surprisingly normal on the surface. For much of Saddam Hussein's long reign, enough brand-name Western enterprises were willing enough to do business with him that parts of downtown Baghdad at first glance have the same multinational blandness as any other capital city. In the outlying towns, the Main Streets have a healthy commercial life, granted that many of them are made up of competing convenience stores lined up side-by-side with the same stacks of the same sweltering soda hot enough to boil a lobster. The residential streets can look quite pleasant, if you don't mind the garbage piled up in the yard—nothing to do with Rumsfeld's destruction of the infrastructure, just a reflection of the relatively low priority municipal services had in Baathist Iraq. The hospitals, despite the alleged humanitarian catastrophe the country's engulfed by (according to the NGOs), are clean, relatively efficient, and uncrowded.

So, when I was driving around western and northern Iraq last year, I made a point in every town I visited of dropping by the local school. A totalitarian state can mimic a free society in much of its civic landscape, but not in the classroom. The first thing you notice is the rectangles of unfaded paint on the walls. This is where the portraits of Saddam once hung. They've all been taken down, freeing up rather more space than anyone knows what to do with. A big pile of frames sat on one principal's desk. "I thought we could re-use these," he told me. "But I don't have anything to put in them."

He was anxious to tell me what I wanted to hear. To get anywhere in Iraq's education system, you had to be a member of the Baath Party, which means that any teacher with experience in Iraq is either someone who joined the party because that was the only way he could fulfill his passionate commitment to the education of Iraq's youth or someone who joined the party because, if you're one of the dimmer Saddamite enforcers, bullying the rest of the staff at some no-account grade school was one of the less demanding jobs. It was hard to discern into which category the various teachers I met fell. Even when they complained that they were no longer allowed to teach the war with Iran and the Gulf War as glorious Iraqi victories, this could have been either ideological bias or mere ignorance (and, in fairness, the Gulf War *was* a glorious Iraqi victory, in the sense that, as many of us came to see, anything that left Saddam in power could not reasonably be defined as a defeat).

Nonetheless, every teacher I ran into had done his or her duty and either torn out Saddam's pictures from the textbooks or put an X across them, in compliance with deBaathification procedures. To give me a sense of what the books used to look like, a nine-year-old boy in Ramadi showed me his "Patriotic Education" reader from the previous year. Like me in my day, he was evidently prone to a little classroom boredom, and the various scenes of Iraqi life were augmented by the usual schoolboy doodles and marginalia. But every page bearing a picture of the great leader remained utterly unblemished: even an absent-minded grade-schooler knows there are some things not to be absent-minded about.

Whatever the nominal subject, in practice it boiled down to the glorification of Saddam. In a first-grade reader, Hassan and Amal—the equivalent of America's Dick and Jane or Britain's Janet and John—hold their portraits and explain the benefits of an Iraqi education:

"O come, Hassan," says Amal. "Let us chant for the homeland and use our pens to write, 'Our beloved Saddam.'"

"I come, Amal," says Hassan. "I come in a hurry to chant, 'O, Saddam, our courageous president, we are all soldiers defending the borders for you, carrying weapons and marching to success.'"

At first, you think this is just a little light propagandist warm-up to kick-start the day. Then you figure, oh, well, it just impacts their take on the Baathist era, Saddam's rise, etc. But pretty soon you realize it infects everything: Iraqis were not allowed to learn that the mighty Saladin was a Kurd because Saddam, as part of his appropriation of Islam's glories, claimed to be his descendant.

And now Iraqi schools are re-joining the real world—or, at any rate, a mildly less unreal world: I noticed the giant picture of a brave Iraqi crushing a soldier from the Zionist Entity underfoot hadn't been taken down. A schoolroom is the place at which the state makes plain the range of its ambitions—either (as in Iraq) to create a bizarre alternative universe in the hopes that its young charges will be unable to see it for the prison it is, or (as in Saudi Arabia and other parts of the Arab world) to disdain education for a toxic ideology of blame and victimhood that renders its graduates incapable of functioning in a modern democratic state.

For example, in 2003 the Alexandria Library opened a manuscript museum, funded by the Egyptian and Italian governments and UNESCO. Its centerpiece is a display of the three holy books of the monotheist religions—i.e., the Torah, the Bible and the Koran. But the museum director, Dr. Yousef Ziedan, decided to display alongside the Torah a copy of *The Protocols of the Elders of Zion*. "When my eyes fell upon the rare copy of this dangerous book, I decided immediately to place it next to the Torah," he told the Egyptian weekly *Al-Usbu*. "Although it is not a monotheistic holy book, it has become one of the sacred [tenets] of the Jews, next to their first constitution, their religious law, [and] their way of life." He then went on to reassure his interviewer that it was not six million Jews but only one million who died in the Holocaust. "In reality," he said, "an analysis of samples from the purported gas chambers has proven that these were sterilization chambers, without a sufficient quantity of cyanide to kill." Whether or not denial is a river in Egypt, Holocaust denial certainly is. And, if we're honest, most of us aren't in the least bit surprised to discover that in Egypt a distinguished man, a scholar, a trustee of the nation's heritage, a teacher of historical truth, is, to use the technical term, nuts.

If you're in an Iraqi school, you learn of Iraq's victory over Iran in their long war. If you're in a Saudi school, you learn that the Jews use the blood of Muslim children for their religious ceremonies. If you're in a Palestinian Authority school, you learn that the most glorious aspiration any child can have is to grow up to be a suicide bomber. If you're in a Syrian school, you study geography from maps which do not show one of your neighboring states.

Now let us return from the Middle East, and visit an American grade school. How about, say, Madison School in Skokie, Illinois? Not for the annual celebrations of Saddam's birthday, but for as close as we get to a local equivalent—say, Thanksgiving, 2003. As *The Chicago Tribune* reported:

> A group of Skokie 1st graders got an unexpected lesson in cultural sensitivity Friday when their principal wouldn't let them dress as American Indians for their annual Thanksgiving celebration.
>
> After a parent complained that the costumes the children had made might be offensive, the principal told the kids to leave their construction-paper headdresses on the classroom shelves.
>
> Those who had opted to be pilgrims fared no better. Their paper black hats and bonnets also were banned, and for the first time in more than two decades, the 1st graders at Madison School commemorated the events of October 1621 in their school clothes.

The children had been preparing their Pilgrim and Indian costumes for a month. But, after receiving the lone parental complaint, the school's principal, Pete Davis, took decisive action. He consulted the American Indian Center and the Native American Educational Services College, and they explained that permitting the children to dress up in "generic Indian outfits" promoted "Hollywood-type stereotypes of American Indians"—which must be news to the kids, because you'd have to be well into late middle-age to remember any "Hollywood-type stereotypes" like poor old Tonto. But Leonard Malatare of the American Indian Center said schools still needed to be alert to the problem. "You let them dress up in feathers and do the little Indian thing, they'll grow up with that image in their head," Mr. Malatare said. "I've had people come up and ask me if I was born in a teepee. We need to start getting away from these stereotypes." His colleague, David Spencer, director of development at the center, agrees. "They are representing Native Americans as one group of people, not a diverse community," he says.

So what did the school do instead? Well, in place of the usual re-enactment of the first Thanksgiving, they booked Mr. Malatare to tell the children about "his culture." He taught them some words in the Oglala Lakota language and led the children in a traditional blessing. A traditional Lakota blessing, I hasten to add. Had he led the children in a traditional Protestant blessing for anything other than the consecration of a gay bishop, the School Board would have been up to its neck in ACLU suits. But a Lakota blessing, you can't go wrong, can you?

Sadly, Keith Liscio, a parent of a child at the school, was somewhat churlish about this cultural enlightenment. "I don't think it had anything to do with Thanksgiving," he grumbled. "It kind of just hijacked the whole purpose of today's program." His daughter and her friend were in tears after being told they couldn't wear their Pilgrim outfits, and he'd found it hard to explain why. "This is a tradition that was changed in the blink of an eyelid because one person complained." But the school was adamant that the "offensive" practice of re-enacting the original Thanksgiving was gone for good, and that the new culturally sensitive program was more appropriate.

Just one question: What have Mr. Malatare and his Oglala Lakota lesson got to do with Thanksgiving?

I hasten to add I have nothing against the Oglala—the first American to win the 10,000 metres at the Olympics was an Oglala Lakota (Billy Mills, Tokyo, 1964); the Pine Ridge Oglala reservation in South Dakota was the first Indian reservation to boast a native-owned and -operated radio station. If Mr. Malatare had time left over, after explaining his feelings at being stereotyped, to impart either of these facts, I'm sure the children appreciated them.

But the Lakota are Plains Indians. They were nowhere near Massachusetts in 1621. They had no contact with the white man until the mid-eighteenth century. The Indians who celebrated the first Thanksgiving were Wampanoags, part of the Eastern Algonquin conference. Did they "dress up in feathers and do the little Indian thing"? Well, their leader, more commonly known as Massasoit, bore the name Usamequin, which means "Yellow Feather." I am indebted for this information to Chief Wilfred "Eagle Heart" Greene, a Wampanoag from the same corner of Rhode Island. His colleague, Three Feathers, is trying to organize a memorial to Massasoit. The Massasoit slide show at their website shows people "dressed up in feathers and doing the little Indian thing."

Was Mr. Malatare born in a teepee? Evidently not, and it must be a nuisance to have to fend off so many enquiries to that effect. But in the Algonquian villages of New England, families lived in small circular wigwams or longhouses shaped like bread loaves and covered with slabs of bark or woven mats. They did not speak Oglala Lakota. Some of them, such as Massasoit's interpreters Tisquantum and Samoset, spoke English. Samoset had picked up the language from white fishermen and Tisquantum, a.k.a. Squanto, had learned English while in, er, England.

So it would seem that the six year olds' unacceptable, offensive, culturally insensitive portrayal of Thanksgiving—feathers, teepees, basic grasp of first-grade English—is broadly historically accurate, while Mr. Malatare's culturally respectful, authentic, ethnic Thanksgiving—no feathers, no teepees, Sioux greetings in the Oglala language—is ahistorical bunk. Which version would you bet will catch on with Illinois school districts?

Insofar as Mr. Malatare has a grievance, it would seem to be not with the six year olds at Madison Elementary but with the Wampanoags and other Algonquin Indians of the Eastern Seaboard. Because they were the first Native Americans encountered by the white man, they established the "Hollywood-type stereotype"—feathers, teepees, the whole "little Indian thing." No doubt many members of the Non-Native American community might complain that all the black hats and bonnets of the Pilgrims—the whole uptight square thing—unfairly stereotypes white people. They might prefer, oh, Hef in his bathrobe relaxing with Joey Bishop and a couple of Bunnies in the grotto at the Playboy Mansion. That would be no more or less inauthentic a Thanksgiving than Mr. Malatare's.

But it's not really about Thanksgiving, is it? On receiving the lone complaint about his school's decades-old holiday celebration, Principal Davis could have done what I did—mooched around in a reference book for ten minutes. Instead, the moment he heard the Sensitivity Police were on his case, he ran to the relevant ethnic-grievance bodies and sub-contracted his pupils' Thanksgiving commemorations to them, even though, as should surely have been clear, Mr. Malatare's approach to the issue is: "But enough about Thanksgiving. Let's talk about me." So now the first graders learn nothing about American history, nothing about that remarkable celebration when the Pilgrims gave thanks for their unlikely survival in this difficult climate with the Indian people who had helped them raise enough food to do so. Instead, they learn about Mr. Malatare's feelings.

Every day small acts of historical vandalism are perpetrated at grade schools across the country by the likes of Principal Davis: something that is true is replaced by something that is "sensitive"—even if, as in this case, "sensitivity" involves being entirely insensitive to historical reality. In diving straight for the refuge of the American Indian Center, Mr. Davis was merely the latest "educator" to embark on the flight from facts to feelings.

AFTER MY RANDOM sampling of Iraqi classrooms, I began to read the foot-of-page-twelve news stories of American schoolhouse loopiness with renewed interest. Considered in the objective sense, is it any crazier to teach that Saddam is descended from Saladin than that the U.S. Constitution was modeled on the forms of government developed by the Iroquois? If anything, the deceptions of the American school system are weirder than those of Saddam's board of education: In Iraq and Saudi Arabia and the Palestinian Authority, the education system exists to indoctrinate its charges in the regime's glories—given the regimes in question, this takes some doing, but at least it has a rough logic of victor's justice about it. In the United States, by contrast, the school system seems dedicated to diminishing if not entirely denigrating American achievement. French education is still, by and large, a celebration of French achievement, which gets harder to pull off with each passing decade. But even Britain and other Anglophone school systems prone to the same cult of self-loathing as America are not quite in the same advanced stage of the disease. No other state education system goes to such comprehensive lengths to portray the founders of the nation only by their flaws—as "racists, murderers of Indians, representatives of class interests," as Allan Bloom wrote in *The Closing of the American Mind*, an emphasis on the feet of clay to the exclusion of all else, "weakening our convictions of the truth or superiority of American principles and our heroes."

That's why so many school Christmas—sorry, holiday—concerts rapidly advanced from banning "Hark, the Herald

Angels Sing" and "O Little Town of Bethlehem" to equally stringent prohibitions on "Rudolph the Red-Nosed Reindeer" and "Frosty the Snowman." It's not about the separation of church and state, so much as the separation of people from other people and, indeed, of all of them from reality. Al Gore somewhat endearingly gave the game away a few years back when he was in Milwaukee giving a speech on diversity: the town's multi-ethnic population, he said, was living proof that, in the words of the Great Seal of the United States, America "can be e pluribus unum—out of one, many." Close enough and, as it happens, a lot more accurate these days than however the old outmoded translation went, which is no doubt why the media gave Al a pass on all those Vice-President-who-can't-speak-Latin cracks they'd buried his predecessor under.

The Gore approach denies the very possibility of a common culture other than the traditional Santa suit filed by the ACLU over the entirely theoretical offense the holly wreath on the town offices gives to Buddhists and Wiccans. As you'll gather from that, the present arrangements are not without their compensations for those of us with a (so to speak) black sense of humor. To be honest, the old-style Christmas concerts were a bit of a bore, with the moppets lurching through the same old seasonal favorites. These days, there's always a thrill of anticipation as one approaches the school gym and prepares for the onslaught of an evening's unseasonal favorites—ancient Swahili Kwanzaa anthems dating all the way back to the early 1970s, New Age drones about the Great Spirit, a token dirge from the Hannukah songbook whose slim pickings testify mainly to the fact that most of America's big-time musical Jews (Irving Berlin, Jule Styne, Sammy Cahn) were too busy writing Christmas songs. My friend emerged from her daughter's kindergarten concert in a rage: not just no Christmas carols, but no "Jingle Bells." The only song she recognized was Lionel Bart's spectacular melisma pile-up from *Oliver!*, "Whe-e-e-ere Is Love?," which is not designed to be sung en masse. "The kids sounded like they were dying," she fumed, before going off to beard the school board, who explained that "Jingle Bells" had been given the heave-ho on the grounds that it might be insensitive to those of a non-jingly persuasion. I'd say maybe 1 percent of us take offense, another 20 percent feel good at having demonstrated the lengths they're prepared to go to to avoid giving offense, another 20 percent feel as steamed as my friend, and the rest of us metaphorically roll our eyes, grin and bear it, and tell ourselves it's basically harmless.

BUT IS IT? My little grade-school chum in Ramadi understood, even at his young age, the relation between state power and personal well-being: several children in his neighborhood had "disappeared" after their parents fell out with the party. He appreciated that, although he could avoid obvious trouble by not succumbing to the temptation to draw twirly bits on the ends of Saddam's moustache, in the end the state's cruelty was, from his perspective, entirely whimsical. But, on the other hand, how would one categorize the judgments of the American school system? As I write, a high school sophomore in Louisiana has fallen afoul of the district's "zero tolerance" drugs policy because she was found to have Advil in her possession. Parkway High expelled Amanda Stiles for a year, her parents went to the school board, but the school board upheld the decision. So the parents, who say they can't afford private school, are now going to have to move to another town. You can turn up stories like this almost every day of the year. Between Iraq and Louisiana, the arbitrariness of the state's viciousness differs in degree. But, even with the important caveat that young Miss Stiles will not be tossed into an underground children's prison, the Louisiana school system seems quite as detached from reality as Baghdad's.

Iraq was a totalitarian killing field, so why wouldn't its education system be insane? Or to put it another way: what's our excuse? Consider the 2002 "Diversity Week" program at Pioneer High School in Ann Arbor, Michigan. For the discussion on "Homosexuality and Religion," school officials hand-picked a panel composed exclusively of pro-gay clergy. When a Catholic student, Betsy Hansen, asked to be allowed to present the Church's traditional teaching on the subject, she was told by the school that her views were "negative" and would "water down" the "positive" message they wanted to convey—that even religious dudes think gay sex is way cool. As we know, "diversity" means homogeneity—even if, as in this case, the homogeneity is utterly at odds with reality.

The issue is not whether this panel is a useful deployment of term time (I spent my formative years at an English boys' school, and those of my friends partial to homosexuality didn't need "positive" messages from the school administration to encourage them to take to it with gusto), or whether homosexual behavior is sinful. What's preposterous are the lengths the school is prepared to go to to deny that there's any difference of opinion on the subject: the Catholic Church and the Baptists and Islam and all kinds of other folks are disapproving of gay sex; even down the Episcopal end of things, one gay bishop in New England has wound up severing American Anglicanism from its brothers around the world. So Pioneer High School's "positive" message is, in fact, false. It's propaganda and, whether or not its propaganda is more "positive" than that of the Baathists, it's not something that a respectable education system should be engaged in.

I'm not plucking apples and oranges here. The reason for examining American education in the light of Iraqi education is a simple one: ever since the coalition victory last spring, the Americans have been in charge of the Iraqi school system. On the face of it, this should be no different from any other sphere of administration under the liberators: British and American soldiers train the new Iraqi army, British and American police train the new Iraqi constabulary, British and American civil servants train the new Iraqi public service. But you'll be relieved to hear the Superintendent of Parkway High and the Principal of Madison Elementary are not on their way to Baghdad. Indeed, no one from the entire American educational establishment seems to have been allowed anywhere

near Iraq's schools. John Agresto, the senior coalition adviser
for higher education, was previously the president of St.
John's College in Santa Fe, a school that specializes in classical
education based on a "great books" curriculum, which sounds
like the sort of thing that would get him blocked by the
Democrats if the President nominated him for U.S. Secretary
of Education. The largest Iraqi education contract has gone to
Creative Associates International, Inc., headed by Charito
Kruvant, whose experience of public education in America is
limited to a spell as an emergency schools trustee in Washington beginning in 1996, when the D.C. financial control board
stripped the elected school board of its powers.

This is very different from the way the British Empire dealt
with the matter in the days when thousands of schoolmarms
from the Welsh valleys and the industrial Midlands were dis-
patched to remote colonial outposts. John Southard of Emory
University has characterized imperial education thus:
"Colonizing governments realize that they gain strength not
necessarily through physical control, but through mental control. This mental control is implemented through a central
intellectual location, the school system." A more benign interpretation of the strategy was made by a great English historian, and at that time a member of the council of the East
India Company, in a famous "Minute on Education": "We
have a fund to be employed as Government shall direct for the
intellectual improvement of the people of this country. The
simple question is, what is the most useful way of employing
it?" wrote Thomas Babington Macaulay in 1835.

It will hardly be disputed, I suppose, that the department of
literature in which the Eastern writers stand highest is poetry.
And I certainly never met with any Orientalist who ventured
to maintain that the Arabic and Sanscrit poetry could be compared to that of the great European nations. But, when we
pass from works of imagination to works in which facts are
recorded and general principles investigated, the superiority of
the Europeans becomes absolutely immeasurable. It is, I

believe, no exaggeration to say, that all the historical information which has been collected from all the books written in the Sanscrit language is less valuable than what may be found in the most paltry abridgements used at preparatory schools in England. In every rank of physical or moral philosophy the relative position of the two nations is nearly the same.

In other words, for Macaulay, to give the people of India a British education was to give them a passport to modernity or, as he put it, "ready access to all the vast intellectual wealth, which all the wisest nations of the earth have created and hoarded in the course of ninety generations." Granted, this was not merely a generous gesture from kindly rulers. The benefit of a vastly expanded and Britannicized school system to the metropolitan power was that, through education, they would create "a class of persons, Indian in blood and color, but English in taste, in opinions, in morals, and in intellect."

THIS SYSTEM did not work everywhere: in Africa especially, the British were too respectful of local chiefs and traditional structures—a prototype deference to "multiculturalism" with consequences that that benighted continent lives with to this day. But in much of Asia, the Pacific, and the Caribbean it worked very well. "American blacks sometimes regard Americans of West Indian origin as uppity and arrogant," writes Colin Powell in his autobiography.

The feeling, I imagine, grows out of an impressive record of accomplishment by West Indians. What explains that success? For one thing, the British ended slavery in the Caribbean in 1833, well over a generation before America did. They told my ancestors that they were now British citizens with all the rights of any subject of the Crown. That was an exaggeration: still, the British did establish good schools and made attendance mandatory. Consequently, West Indians had an opportunity to develop attitudes of independence, self-responsibility, and self-worth.

Which may be one reason that the most prominent black man in American life today is the son of British subjects, raised outside the festering Balkanized grievance culture of the Jesse Jacksified African-American community. But Powell's point is well-taken more generally: A good colonial education system offers short-term advantages to the imperial power but over the long term sows the seeds of its own destruction. Its alumni will eventually be not just "English in taste, in opinions, in morals, and in intellect" but English in the assumption that they are entitled to liberty and responsible government. That's what happened in Colin Powell's Jamaica, as it did in India, Singapore, and Papua New Guinea.

Whether or not you agree with Macaulay's argument or with Professor Southard's characterization of it makes no difference. If education is a critical component of the white man's burden, who's there to take it up? Even if you wanted to teach Iraqis about Washington and Jefferson, New England Town Meetings and the First Amendment, to whom would you entrust the civilizing mission? In the schools of the British Empire, Shakespeare and Wordsworth, Henry V and Sir Isaac Newton were as vivid presences as they were in any classroom in Birmingham or Glasgow. By contrast, George Washington is barely a vivid presence in Washington (too insensitive; he was a slave-holder). Any of those spinster schoolmarms shipped to Tuvalu or Belize could be relied on to teach the exploits of Sir Francis Drake or the Duke of Wellington. If you were to dispatch the likes of Principal Davis to Mosul, Iraqi children would be unlikely to receive any more attractive a view of America than they did under Saddam.

Lest you think that an exaggeration, turn to a 1989 New York State Regents' Report: "African-Americans, Asian-Americans, Puerto Ricans/Latinos and Native Americans have all been the victims of an intellectual and educational oppression that has characterized the culture and institutions of the United States and the European-American world for centuries." Thus the opening sentence of a report on curriculum reform, "A Curriculum of Inclusion."

"The content of the curriculum is distorted, outdated, and completely politicized for the last three decades," said Dr. Ala Alwan. He was talking about Iraq's schools. But re-read that sentence from New York's Regents: it's also distorted and completely politicized, not to mention tediously passé. That's one reason why, despite the fondest hopes of romantics like Niall Ferguson, America can never be an imperial power: the institutions necessary for such a mission not only lack the cultural confidence, they're slumped in what John O'Sullivan calls "counter-tribalism" to such a degree that they reflexively take the other side, no matter who's on it: Oglala Lakota Indians at Thanksgiving; 1960s Afro-Marxists at Christmas; misogynist homophobe fundamentalist mullahs in the war on terror. By the afternoon of September 11, 2001, the social studies teacher had already informed my neighbor's daughter that the allies killed more civilians in the bombing of Dresden. A year later, for the first anniversary on September 11 2002, the National Education Association had prepared a formal series of classroom lessons to discuss the, ah, "tragic events":

Explore the problems inherent in assigning blame to populations or nations of people by looking at contemporary examples of ethnic conflict, discrimination, and stereotyping at home and abroad.

Okay. Any suggestions?

Internment of Japanese Americans after Pearl Harbor and the backlash against Arab Americans during the Gulf War are obvious examples.

I'll say. When our nation comes under attack, some of us turn to our troops, the rest of us retreat to our tropes. It's hard to conceive of an al Qaeda atrocity so horrifying the NEA wouldn't automatically respond by suggesting it provides an excellent opportunity to reflect on the internment of Japanese-Americans and the legacy of slavery. Even America's so-called "cultural hegemony" seems to rest as much on inter-national anti-America blockbusters by Michael Moore and Noam Chomsky or films, TV shows, and pop songs that seem reluctant to promote American virtues other than car chases and meaningless sex. In 2002, I had the bizarre experience of watching the Oscars while in Paris, where Tom Hanks's opening remarks that "when we're at the movies, we're not alone" lost quite a bit in translation. Tom meant that movies bring together the peoples of the world. If that's true, it's mainly so in the sense that decades of exposure to the healing balm of Hanks and Co. have united the world in the cause of anti-Americanism. As I said at the time, right now somewhere in Frankfurt, Rotterdam, or Wolverhampton an Islamist ter-rorist is sitting in a Yankees cap, Disney T-shirt, and Nike sneakers plotting how to blow up the White House. "Cultural imperialism" of this kind is less useful to the mother country than the old-school version.

THE ACTOR Ron Silver, perhaps the least crazy guy in Hol-lywood, recently observed that America was divided into Sep-tember 10th people and September 11th people. Almost all the elites—the arts, the media, the academy, the Episcopal bishops both gay and non-gay—are virtually to a man Sep-tember 10th people. This is a very strange circumstance in which to embark upon a long war. But, in fairness to some of those groups, when they're not in September 10th mode, they can at least do their jobs. I wouldn't want to live in a country run by, say, Paul Newman and Vanessa Redgrave, but I don't dispute their talent as actors. Barbra Streisand's and Tim Robbins's politics are, in that sense, extra-curricular. But in the schoolhouse they are, literally, curricular. The cult of sen-sitivity seeps into every corner: when facts conflict with the "positive" message, junk the facts; when academic rigor risks damaging self-esteem, stick with the self-esteem. The failures of American schoolteachers are uniquely catastrophic, be-cause, unlike Streisand and Robbins, their reflexive cultural cringe has become a substitute for doing their job.

We can plough through the statistics page by page, but in a nutshell it's this: American students are statistically the dumbest in the industrial world. We can flesh this out more politely: in the surveys of twelfth graders in math and science, America scores below pretty well any functioning state—Britain, Australia, New Zealand, Canada, France, Germany, the whole of western Europe, much of eastern Europe, Japan, China, and the Asian tigers; the U.S. comes below Lithuania, which was a Soviet backwater a decade ago, and is only just managing to hold its own with Cyprus. (For those *New Criterion* readers who are American high school graduates, Cyprus is a small island in the Mediterranean; population: 800,000; principal crops: grain, grapes, carobs, citrus fruits, olives.)

That ranking is the culmination of thirteen years in the American system. The upshot of the research is this: the longer American children are exposed to American teachers, the more stupid they get. Kindergarteners can just about compete with their opposite numbers in western Europe. But by middle school, forget it. In a survey of seventeen members of the Organisation for Economic Co-operation and Development, Americans made less progress in mathematics between the fourth and eighth grades than any other nation. Bill Clinton's commitment to ensure that every American child went to college was the logical extension of this system: as I understand his proposal, students would leave college at, oh, twenty-eight, thirty-six, whatever, more or less competitive with Sudanese fourth graders. (For those *New Criterion* readers who are American college graduates, Sudan is a strife-riven East African hellhole; population: 30 million; principal export: Islamist terrorists.)

It would make more sense to quit while you're ahead, or at any rate not yet behind, and institute a mandatory school leaving age of six-and-a-half. Sending every American to college will give the educational establishment yet another excuse to postpone teaching their students anything for a couple more years, so that eventually pupils will be doing as a Bachelor's

Degree what they should have learned in Seventh Grade. The deterioration that begins on Day One of kindergarten should be a source of shame to the NEA. Instead, they pride themselves that, while they have the lowest test scores of any developed country in any measurable discipline, they have the most advanced feelings on issues like the environment. In Allan Bloom's words, "American high school graduates are among the most sensitive illiterates in the world." Perhaps this is true. Or perhaps they're just faking it: shortly before they opened fire at Columbine High School, those two bozos from Littleton, Colorado had managed to ace their anger-management courses. Even the sensitivity regime isn't *that* demanding.

It would be more accurate to say that American high school graduates are the most expensive illiterates in the world. In real terms, education spending has quadrupled in the last four decades to the point where America now lavishes more on its school students than any other country except Switzerland—in 1999, the Swiss spent $9,756 per pupil, the U.S. $8,157, Japan $6,039, Canada $5,981, the United Kingdom $5,608, Spain $4,864, etc. But the Swiss at least have something to show for that ten thousand bucks. By fourth grade, much of the damage done by U.S. teachers becomes irreversible: that's the age at which a competent student stops learning to read and starts reading to learn. According to the National Assessment of Education Progress, in 1998 only 29 percent of American fourth graders achieved such proficiency. The cost to the taxpayer of educating each student to that point was $30,945. Yet, given the 71 percent failure rate, the real cost to taxpayers of producing a proficient fourth grade reader is $30,945 divided by 29 percent or $107,000. In the District of Columbia, it takes almost half a million dollars to produce one proficient fourth grade reader: when you look at it like that, it would be cheaper and more efficient to pluck children at random and send them to boarding school in Switzerland.

It's possible to think the crisis in education is to do with lack of money only if one is as deficient in basic reading and arithmetic as the average D.C. grade schooler. The reductio ad absurdum of the lazy demands for more money and a better pupil/teacher ratio can be found in Bridgehampton, Long Island, whose 153-pupil K-12 public school draws from the deep pockets of an indulgent and partly absentee tax base: It spends $45,090 per student; it has one teacher for every 3.7 pupils; its largest class has twelve students. Yet in math and English its elementary and middle school pupils score below the state averages, which are themselves utterly mediocre. These are sums of money that in other jurisdictions would pay for the most rigorous elite private education. But in the U.S. all you get for $45,000 is vague fluffy feelings about Lakota Indians.

The easy assumption is that this under-performance by comparison with all other industrial countries arises from the fact that America's is a young, rough-and-tumble democracy compared to the older educational traditions of Europe and Japan. But the present abysmal standards are historically unprecedented. Far from being at the bottom of the international leagues, early America had higher standards of literacy than the Continent. In 1818, Noah Webster's spelling book sold five million copies in a population of 20 million. By 1840 over 90 percent of the American population was literate. This was a time before widespread compulsory government schooling, when low-paid rural teachers in one-room multi-grade schoolhouses boarded with neighborhood farmers, and boys especially spent little more than three months a year in class. A century and a half later, the Motorola Corporation was spending $50 million a year teaching seventh grade math and English to its adult factory workers.

AND WHO'S TO SAY the corporations don't do a better job of it than the schools? After all, they could hardly do a worse job—at least to judge by the results of the Commonwealth of Massachusetts's very first basic reading-and-writing test—not for pupils, but for teachers. The legislature passed a bill mandating "standardized examination" for educators in 1985, but, with the insouciance for which the educational establishment is renowned, somehow it took thirteen years for the first test to be administered. Teachers were asked to define what a noun is and spell words like "imminent." When the results came in, 59 percent had failed. Confronted by this unnerving figure, the Massachusetts Board of Education reached an immediate decision: they lowered the bar. Instead of accepting C as a passing grade, the board voted to accept D. That meant that—hey presto!—suddenly only 44 percent had failed. Board members said they'd voted to lower the threshold partly to prevent immanunt—imminnant?—lawsuits from the failed teachers for loss of self-esteem, etc.: as Shaw said, he who can, does; he who cannot, sues.

The Clinton Administration's response was to demand federal funding for "100,000 new teachers." To replace those who failed the Massachusetts test? Perish the thought: it was in addition to those already employed. Because we need to reduce the pupil-teacher ratio. Don't ask me why. One 2003 survey suggests that proximity to Canada is a more accurate predictor of performance than money or class size: low-spending, big-class northern states do better than high-spending small-class southern ones. Yet no one at the NEA is suggesting we need to move the rest of the country up to the 49th parallel. And say what you like about big classes: at least you've improved your odds of finding a pupil who'll be able to tell the teacher how to spell "imminent."

In the 1990s, America got so used to politicians claiming that this or that policy was about "the future of all our children"—war in Kosovo, the highway appropriations bill, the mohair subsidy—that they seemed happy to allow education to be the exception that proves the rule: education is about the future of all our teachers and bureaucrats and administrators; our children will just have to rub along as best they can. It hardly needs stating that the future of all our children is our only future, too. The crisis for most western countries this century is the absence of babies: Japan and Western Europe have collapsed birth rates that will eventually put them out of business entirely and within the next generation impact disastrously on their economic well-being and social order. But education is to America as demographics are to Europe: in Italy, the schoolhouses built in the 1970s in the confident expectation of traditional Catholic birth rates stand empty; in America, we have the raw material but, because of political cravenness, we raise them in an environment of sappy propaganda so inadequate to preparing them for what lies ahead it verges on child abuse.

People will be in short supply in the western world in 2050, and educated people will be at a premium. It would be a tragedy for the U.S. to throw away its demographic advantage for a stale self-victimization fetish. But at some point the deteriorating education system will threaten America's future. It goes wrong from Day One and that's where it has to be fixed—at the kindergarten end, rather than college. If American children receive an effective, challenging grade-school education, there's a limit to the damage high school and even Ivy League professors can do. So how to go about it? The unions and bureaucrats are too entrenched at state and municipal level to make it likely it can ever be fixed on a school-by-school basis. But, looked at in political terms, I'm struck by one of the real changes since 9/11. If Ron Silver is correct in his division of America into September 11th and September 10th people, then it seems clear that, with one exception, all this year's Democratic candidates have fallen into the latter camp. That's one reason why Mr. Silver, a Democrat, is now a Bush supporter: if you're a September 11th person, if you think the "war on terror" is a war and not just a matter of closer cooperation between the Department of Justice and Interpol or of more discussions with the French, then it's awfully hard to be a Democrat. Mr. Silver is representative of a small but significant sliver of the citizenry for whom the pieties of multilateralism no longer fly.

Would it not be possible to extend this post-9/11 clarity to the domestic scene and the pieties of multiculturalism? Transformational presidents seize the opportunities presented by extreme events, as FDR did in the Depression. After September 11, George W. Bush had his own opportunity to reverse the most malign tide in the civilized world—the multiculti gloop in which all cultures are accorded equal "respect" and "tolerance," even the intolerant ones that are trying to kill us. The President could have stated the obvious—that western self-loathing is a psychosis we can no longer afford; that it's fraudulent and damaging, especially when it's presented to American children as a religious faith whose orthodoxies all have to sign on to, and which in the name of "inclusivity" excludes everything, from Paul Revere to "Frosty the Snowman."

When Cromwell instructed his portraitist to paint him "warts and all," he meant both halves of the equation: unless you see "all," you cannot honestly evaluate the "warts"; to understand the blemishes on the record, you first have to understand the record. To teach the warts alone is a morbid fetish. Mr. Bush should take the lead in a campaign against the debilitating equivalence of multiculturalism, but parents must play their part, too: every little first-grade Thanksgiving that gets hijacked by the grievance culture is an act of violence against truth and history. In the Nineties, urban police departments came to realize that if you failed to deal with small, trivial crimes they led to more and bigger ones. We need a cultural equivalent of that "broken window" policy. If you let a craven principal take the Pilgrims and Algonquins out of Thanksgiving, you kick away one of the small steps on which a child climbs to informed adulthood.

The enemy understands this. What is the principal weapon of militant Islamism? The schoolhouse. Toxic Wahhabist madrasahs are found not just where you'd expect them to be—Saudi Arabia, Yemen, Sudan—but around the world—Pakistan, Indonesia, Chechnya, the Balkans, Berlin, Amsterdam, Virginia, Oregon. The Islamists have set up an education system that at the very least radicalizes hitherto moderate Muslim populations and at the worst serves as an active recruiting mill for terrorists. For young Muslims in the West, the attraction is obvious: radical Islamism provides all the cultural confidence the state of which they're nominally citizens goes out of the way to avoid. From Russian Communism to Japanese militarism, many of the most murderous ideologies in a murderous century arose in societies which were aware of their material inferiority (vis à vis other countries) but convinced of their cultural superiority. By inverting the formula, the perverse philosophy of Western education—that our society is materially superior but culturally inferior—seems almost to invite the obvious response: the radical madrasahs merely answered the call. If all you teach is that everyone else is the victim of the "intellectual and educational oppression that has characterized the culture and institutions of the United States and the European-American world for centuries," people will eventually take you at your word. If you trumpet how much you despise yourself, it would be churlish for everyone else not to despise you also.

THOMAS MACAULAY, pondering the Indian education system, was no admirer of the madrasahs, which he would have abolished if he could. "We are to teach false history, false astronomy, false medicine because we find them in company with a false religion," he remarked, somewhat insensitively. But today, increasingly, we teach false history, false astronomy, false medicine because of the false religion of sensitivity. Macaulay's critique of Muslim and Hindu education is as pertinent to our schools today: too much is excluded or distorted or ignored because it conflicts with the articles of faith. Was he a racist? No. Looking back to the fifteenth and sixteenth centuries, he wrote, "At that time almost everything worth reading was contained in the writings of the Greeks and Romans. Had our ancestors neglected the language of Thucydides and Plato, of Cicero and Tacitus, would England ever have been what she is now?" Cultures don't become dominant only through plunder and oppression, whatever the New York State Regents say. To deprive students of a full appreciation of the cultural inheritance of the last half-millennium is to deprive them of an understanding of literature, medicine, science, art, and their own historical inheritance.

Macaulay advocated the teaching of Greek and Latin and English as part of the seamless robe of history.

Charles Grant, the first advocate of modernizing education in India, put it simply: "The true cure of darkness is the introduction of light." If a progressive education is truly enlightened, it's curious that it depends so much on keeping people in the dark. When President Bush visited London in 2003, he gave an interesting speech, in the course of which he paid tribute to the Royal Navy for its role in ending the slave trade. Well said. It's true. The agency that did more to abolish slaving than anybody else was the military force of the dominant white Anglo-Saxon power of the day. But, for all the self-flagellation about slavery in American schools, how many pupils are ever exposed to that fact? Like Saladin's ethnicity in the classrooms of Tikrit, it's a fact that doesn't fit the propaganda. This new faith of sensitivity must be a very delicate bloom if it cannot be exposed to the light of one contrary shaft: How many of our teachers understand this and are ashamed at what they do, as some of those teachers I met in Iraq were? Or do they truly believe, like the Baathist apparatchiks, that they're engaged on a great project that will enable their young charges to be model citizens of a remade society? I confess that, in America as in Iraq, I can't tell which is which, and have come to the conclusion it doesn't matter either way. Grant is right: our schools are dark places of irrationality and superstition; let there be light.

Religion in America:
Ancient & Modern
David B. Hart

All culture arises out of religion. When religious faith decays, culture must decline, though often seeming to flourish for a space after the religion which has nourished it has sunk into disbelief . . . no cultured person should remain indifferent to erosion of apprehension of the transcendent.
—Russell Kirk, *Eliot and His Age*

T HE HERDSMAN who comes to Pentheus from Mount Cithaeron, in *The Bacchae*, tells how the Theban women possessed by Dionysus take up serpents without being bitten and fire without being burned. It is not unlikely, given how common such phenomena are in "enthusiast" and "ecstatic" religion, that here and elsewhere Euripides grants us some glimpse of the actual Dionysiac orgy, even long after its migration into Greece from Thrace, when the cult had been assumed into the soberer mysteries of the Olympians.

And other features of the rite, reported in various sources, follow the familiar enthusiast pattern. At the height of their devotions, the maenads were seized by violent raptures, to which they surrendered entirely; absorbed in the formless beauty of the god, and tormented by fitful intimations of his presence, they worshipped him with cries of longing and delight, desperate invocations, wild dithyrambs, delirious dance, inebriation, and the throbbing din of corybantic music; abandoning all sense of themselves, they suffered visions and uttered prophecies, fell ravished and writhing to the earth, or sank into insensibility. In short, it was all very—in a word—American.

AT LEAST, that is what I have been disposed to think ever since an epiphany visited itself upon me nearly twenty years ago, as I stood amid the pestilential squalor of an English railway station, awaiting my train, and deliberating on whether I should risk the ordeal of a British Rail sandwich.

Generally one might prefer grander settings for one's moments of illumination—Wordsworth's lakes, Amiel's azure peaks—but it was, in this instance, the very dreariness of my surroundings that occasioned my awakening. The station's oblong pillars were blackly begrimed; shreds of posters in garish hues hung limply from the walls; in shallow depressions of the concrete floor opaque pools of oleaginous water glistened with a sinister opalescence; an astringent chemical odor of antiseptics vying with various organic purulences suffused the damp air; a scattering of gaunt torsos farther along the platform bore eloquent witness to the malaise of Britain's post-war gene pool; and nothing was out of the ordinary. But, all at once, two thoughts occurred to me simultaneously, and their wholly fortuitous conjunction amounted to a revelation. One was something like "Boredom is the death of civilization"; and the other something like "America has never been this modern."

Not that this place was conspicuously worse than—or even as wretched as—countless stops along the way in the United States, but anyone who has lived in Britain for some time should understand how such a place might, in a moment of calm clarity, seem like the gray glacial heart of a gray and glaciated universe. Somehow this place was adequate to its age—to that pervasive social atmosphere of resignation at which modern Britain is all but unsurpassed; it was disenchantment made palpable, the material manifestation of a national soul unstirred by extravagant expectations or exorbitant hopes. Admittedly, contemporary England's epic drabness makes everything seem worse; in the Mediterranean sun, culture's decay can be intoxicatingly charming (and Catholic decadence is so much richer than Protestant decadence).

But really, anywhere throughout the autumnal world of old and dying Christendom, there are instants (however fleeting) when one cannot help but feel (however imprecisely) that something vital has perished, a cultural confidence or a spiritual aspiration, and it is obviously something inseparable from the faith that shaped and animated European civilization for nearly two millennia. Hence the almost prophetic "fittingness" of that rail station: once religious imagination and yearning have departed from a culture, the lowest, grimmest, most tedious level of material existence becomes not just one of reality's unpleasant aspects, but in some sense the limit that marks out the "truth" of things.

This is an inexcusably impressionistic way of thinking, I know, but it seems to me at least to suggest a larger cause for the remarkable willful infertility of the native European peoples: not simply general affluence, high taxes, sybaritism, working women, or historical exhaustion, but a vast metaphysical boredom. This is not to say that the American birthrate overall is particularly robust, hovering as it is just at or below "replacement level," but it has not sunk to the European continental average of only 1.4 children per woman (so reports the UN), let alone to that of such extreme individual cases as Spain (1.07), Germany (1.3), or Italy (1.2). Britain, at almost 1.7 children per woman, is positively philoprogenitive by European standards. And the most important reason for the greater—though not spectacular—fecundity of the United States appears to be the relatively high rate of birth among its most religious families (the godless being also usually the most likely to be childless).

It is fairly obvious that there is some direct, indissoluble bond between faith and the will to a future, or between the desire for a future and the imagination of eternity. And I think this is why post-Christian Europe seems to lack not only the moral and imaginative resources for sustaining its civilization, but even any good reason for continuing to reproduce. There are of course those few idealists who harbor some kind of unnatural attachment to that misbegotten abomination, the European Union—that grand project for forging an identity for post-Christian civilization out of the meager provisions of heroic humanism or liberal utopianism or ethical sincerity—but, apart from a bureaucratic superstate, providently and tenderly totalitarian, one cannot say what there is to expect from that quarter: certainly nothing on the order of some great cultural renewal that might inspire a new zeal for having children.

Unless one grants credence to the small but fashionable set that has of late been predicting a reviviscence of Christianity in Europe (in gay defiance of all tangible evidence), it seems certain that Europe will continue to sink into its demographic twilight and increasingly to look like the land of the "last men" that Nietzsche prophesied would follow the "death of God": a realm of sanctimony, petty sensualisms, pettier rationalisms, and a vaguely euthanasiac addiction to comfort. For, stated simply, against the withering boredom that descends upon a culture no longer invaded by visions of eternal order, no civilization can endure.

As I SAY, however, this absolute degree of modernity has never quite reached America's shores. Obviously, in any number of ways, America is late modernity's avant-garde; in popular culture, especially, so prolific are we in forms of brutal vapidity and intellectual poverty that less enterprising savages can only marvel in impotent envy. Nevertheless, here alone among Western nations the total victory of the modern is not indubitable; there are whole regions of the country—geographical and social—where the sea of faith's melancholy, long, withdrawing roar is scarcely audible. There is in America something that, while not "Christendom," is not simply "post-Christian" either; it is (for want of a better term) a "new antiquity." In many ways, one might go so far as to say, the great difference between Europeans and Americans is that the former are moderns and the latter ancients (if sometimes of a still rather barbarous sort); and the reasons for this are religious.

Though really it would be truer to say that, as Americans, we know the extremes of both antiquity and modernity; what we have never yet possessed is the middle term—a native civilization, with religion as a staid and stable institution uniformly supporting the integrity of the greater culture—that might have allowed for a transition from the one to the other. Thus it is the tension between the two that makes America exceptional, and that lends a certain credibility both to those who contemn her for being so menacingly religious and to those who despise her for being so aggressively godless. In part because the United States broke from the old world at a fateful moment in history, in part because its immense geography preserves the restive peculiarities of various regions and social classes relatively inviolate and so allows even the most exotic expressions of religious devotion to survive and flourish, it has never lost the impress of much of the seventeenth-century Protestantism—evangelistic, ecclesially deracinated, congregationalist, separatist—that provided it with its initial spiritual impulse. Hence Christendom could never die from within for us, as it has for the rest of the West; we fled from it long ago into an apocalyptic future and so never quite suffered Europe's total descent into the penury of the present.

Instead, the United States, to the consternation of bien pensants here and abroad, is saturated in religion as no other developed nation is. Not only do 40 percent of its citizens claim to attend worship weekly, and 60 percent at least monthly (though those numbers have been disputed), but apparently—staggeringly—fewer than 5 percent are willing to call themselves atheists or even agnostics. And an extraordinary number of the devout (at least in certain classes) are not merely pious, but God-haunted, apocalyptic, chiliastic, vulgarly religiose, and always living in the end times.

Moreover, for most of us (even if we refuse to admit it), America itself is a kind of evangelical faith, a transcendent truth beyond the reach of historical contingency. Even our native secularism tends towards the fanatical. We remain believers. To some, of course, this American religiousness is simply an exasperatingly persistent residue of something obsolete, an alloy of which modernity has not yet entirely purged itself, and perhaps history will prove them right. But it is likely that such persons do not quite grasp the scale, potency, or creativity of the "ancient" aspect of America and have little sense of its deepest wellsprings. Which brings me back to the maenads of Dionysus.

In his account of Appalachian snake handling, *Salvation on Sand Mountain* (1995), Dennis Covington tells of worshippers taking up serpents without being bitten and fire without being burned; of a woman, seized by raptures, emitting ecstatic cries of pain and pleasure, which Covington himself involuntarily accompanies with a tambourine; of the "anointed" losing themselves in what could only be called an erotic torment; of wild clamors of glossolalia, fervent invocation, and the throbbing din of Pentecostalist music; of the faithful suffering visions and uttering prophecies; even of his own experience of handling a snake, and of his sense of world and self, in that moment, disappearing into an abyss of light. Nor is it unusual in many "Holiness" congregations for worshippers to fall to the ground writhing and "rolling" or— "slain in the Spirit"—to lapse into insensibility.

Not that such forms of devotion are unknown in other parts of the developed world, but only here have they been so profuse, spontaneous, and genuinely indigenous. One might, for instance, adduce the 1801 week-long revival at Cane Ridge, whose orgiastic rites were celebrated by as many as twenty-five thousand worshippers, or the 1906 "new outpouring" of the scriptural "gifts" or "charisms" of the Holy Spirit—prophecy, speaking in tongues, miraculous healings, the casting out of demons, and so forth—upon the Azusa Street Mission in Los Angeles, which gave birth to the "Pentecostalist" or "charismatic" spirituality that has spread throughout the global South more rapidly than any other form of Christianity in the modern world. Examples are abundant.

And this is why I say Americans are "ancients:" not simply because, throughout the breadth of their continental empire, as in the world of late antiquity, there exists a vague civic piety ramifying into a vast diversity of religious expressions, even of the most mysterious and disturbing kind; but because here there are those to whom the god—or rather God or his angel—still appears. That sort of religion is immune to disillusion, as it has never coalesced into an "illusion"; it moves at the level of vision. In a country where such things are possible, and even somewhat ordinary, the future cannot be predicted with any certitude.

ONE MUST at least say of the old Christendom that, if indeed it has died, it has nonetheless left behind plentiful and glorious evidence of its vanished majesty: its millennial growths of etherealized granite and filigreed marble, its exquisitely wrought silver, its vaults of gold: in all the arts miracles of immensity and delicacy. And the very desuetude of these remnants imbues them with a special charm. Just as the exuviae of cicadas acquire their milky translucence and poignant fragility only in being evacuated of anything living, so the misty, haunting glamour of the churches of France might be invisible but for the desolation in their pews. Similarly, countless traces of the old social accommodations—laws, institutions, customs, traditions of education, public calendars, moral prejudices, in short all those complex "mediating structures" by which the old religion united, permeated, shaped, and preserved a Christian civilization—linger on, ruined, barren, but very lovely.

There is nothing in the least majestic, poignant, or "exuvial" about American religion, and not only because it possessed very little by way of mediating structures to begin with. If the vestigial Christianity of the old world presents one with the pathetic spectacle of shape without energy, the quite robust Christianity of the new world often presents one with the disturbing spectacle of energy without shape. It is not particularly original to observe that, in the dissolution of

Christendom, Europe retained the body while America inherited the spirit, but one sometimes wonders whether for "spirit" it would not be better to say "poltergeist." It is true that the majority of observant Christians and Jews in the United States are fairly conventional in their practices and observances, and the "mainstream" denominations are nothing if not reserved. But, at its most unrestrained and disembodied, the American religious imagination drifts with astonishing ease towards the fantastical and mantic, the messianic and hermetic. We are occasionally given shocking reminders of this—when a communitarian separatist sect in Guyana or a cult of comet-gazing castrati commits mass suicide, or when an encampment of deviant Adventists is incinerated by an inept Attorney General—but these are merely acute manifestations of a chronic condition. The special genius of American religion (if that is what it is) is an inchoate, irrepressibly fissiparous force, a peregrine spirit of beginnings and endings (always re-founding the church and preparing for Armageddon), without any middle in which to come to rest.

In part, this is explicable simply in light of colonial history. The founding myth of the English settlements, after all, was in large part that of an evangelical adventure (as can be confirmed from the first Charter of Virginia, or the Mayflower Compact, or the Fundamental Orders of Connecticut), marked indelibly by covenantal Puritanism. Even the Anglican establishments in the Deep South, Virginia, and Maryland (a criminal imposition, in this last case, upon an aboriginal Catholicism) were deeply influenced by Puritan piety, as were perhaps even the Presbyterian churches. Quakerism, principally in Pennsylvania, New Jersey, and Rhode Island, infused a mystical noncomformism into the colonies, while later immigrations of German Anabaptists—Mennonites, the Amish, Hutterites—imported a "free church" discipline of somewhat more rigorist variety, and perhaps something of radical Anabaptism's apocalyptic utopianism (it would be difficult, at any rate, to be unimpressed by the similarities between the tragic history of the 1535 "Kingdom of Münster" and that of the compound at Waco). In time even small Pietist communities added their distinctive colorations. And so on.

Though the churches of the magisterial reformation, the Church of England, and Catholicism found America fertile soil (as every religion does), the atmosphere in which they flourished was one permeated by a religious consciousness little bound to tradition, creed, hierarchy, or historical memory, but certain of its spiritual liberty and special election.

Which is why one could argue that American religion found its first genuinely native expression during the great age of revivalism. The two Great Awakenings, early and late in the eighteenth century, the spread of evangelical Christianity throughout the southern states, the sporadic but powerful western revivals—all of these contributed to the larger synthesis by which contemporary American religion was fashioned. And from the revivalist impulse followed not only the broad main currents of American evangelical Protestantism, but also innumerable more heterodox and inventive forms of Christianity: millenarian sects like the Adventists or Jehovah's Witnesses, spiritual or enthusiast movements like Pentecostalism, perhaps even (in a way) "transcendentalist" schools like the quasi-Swedenborgian Christian Scientists. Nor, indeed, are the differences in sensibility as great as one might imagine between all of mainstream evangelicalism and its more outlandish offshoots (one need only consider the huge success of the ghastly *Left Behind* novels to realize that an appetite for luridly absurd chiliastic fantasies is by no means confined to marginal sects).

Certainly it is only in regard to this revivalist milieu that one might legitimately speak of "*the* American religion," as Harold Bloom did in his 1992 book of that title. Bloom, it should be noted, was scarcely the first to call it a "gnostic" religion, nor is his treatment of the matter exemplary in analytic precision, but he must be given credit for having grasped how deeply constitutive of America's normal religious temper the gnostic impulse is. If the pathos of ancient Gnosticism lay in a sense of cosmic alienation—in an intuition of the self's exile in a strange world, called in its loneliness to an identity and a salvation experienced only within the self's inmost core, and that by the agencies of a special spiritual election and knowledge that elevate the self above the ignorance of the derelict—then it is a pathos readily discernible in any number of distinctively American religious movements and moments. One finds it at its most speculatively refined and eloquent in Emerson and in the transcendentalism to which he gave voice; at its most risible and grotesque in Scientology and similar "schools." As Bloom notes, nothing more perfectly fits the classic pattern of gnostic religion—fabulous mythologies, jealously guarded cryptadia, a collapse of the distinction between the divine and the human—than Mormonism. But it requires somewhat greater perspicacity to recognize this same pathos at work under more conventional guises.

Most of us, for instance, rarely have cause to reflect that some of the variants of America's indigenous evangelical Christianity, especially of the "fundamentalist" sort, would have to be reckoned—if judged in the full light of Christian history—positively bizarre. Yet many of its dominant and most reputable churches have—quite naturally and without any apparent attempt at novelty—evolved a Christianity so peculiar as to be practically without precedent: an entire theological and spiritual world, internally consistent, deeply satisfying to many, and nearly impossible to ground in the scriptural texts its inhabitants incessantly invoke. And Bloom deserves some (reluctant) praise for having seen this and having seen why it should be: the American myth of salvation, at its purest, is a myth of genuinely personal redemption, the escape of the soul from everything that might confine and repress it—sin, the world, and the devil, but also authority, tradition, and community—into an eternal, immediate, and indefectible relation with God, and it is to this myth, much more than the teachings of the New Testament, that some forms of American evangelical Christianity, especially fundamentalism, adhere.

This is obvious if one merely considers the central (and some might say only) spiritual event of fundamentalist faith and practice, that of being "born again." In the third chapter of John's Gospel, where this phrase is originally found, its context is mystagogical and clearly refers to baptism, but so far removed has it become from its original significance in many evangelical circles that it is now taken to mean a purely private conversion experience, occurring in that one un-repeatable authentic instant in which one accepts Jesus as one's "personal" lord and savior. Some fundamentalists even profess a doctrine of "perpetual security," which says that this conversion experience, if genuine (and therefrom hangs, for some, an agonizing uncertainty), is irreversible; like the in-itiation ceremonies of the ancient mystery cults, it is a magic threshold, across which—once it has been passed—one can never again retreat, no matter how wicked one may become. One could scarcely conceive of a more "gnostic" concept of redemption: liberation through private illumination, a spiritual security won only in the deepest soundings of the soul, a moment of awakening that lifts the soul above the darkness of this world into a realm of spiritual liberty beyond even the reach of the moral law, and an immediate intimacy with the divine whose medium is one of purest subjectivity.

THIS, AT ANY RATE, is one very plausible way of approaching the matter of religion in America: to consider it primarily in its most distinctive of autochthonous forms, as a new gnostic adventure allied to a new eschatological mythology, which has transformed the original Puritan impulse of the upper English colonies into something like a genuinely new version of Christianity, a Christianity whose moderate expressions are, in the long historical view, amiably aberrant, but whose extreme expressions are frequently apocalyptic, enthusiast, and even—again—Dionysiac. One could argue, though, that it is an ap-proach that, while not exactly unjust, is a mite perverse. After all, the exceptional nature of American piety consists not only in the opulence and prodigality of its innovations and deviations, but also in the extraordinary tenacity (as compared, at least, to the situation in other developed nations) with which the more established and traditional communities hold on to their own, generation after generation, and in some cases attract new converts: Roman Catholicism, Lutheranism, Methodism, Presbyterianism, Eastern Orthodoxy, not to mention the various kinds of synagogical Judaism.

And surely one should note that—however widespread and dynamic the (by no means uniform) phenomenon of evangelical Christianity may be—the Roman Catholic Church constitutes the single largest denomination in the United States and is growing at an impressive pace (in large part, obviously, because of Hispanic immigration). If fifty years hence, as demographic trends adumbrate, there are approximately 400 million Americans, fully a quarter may be Hispanic. Of these, one must immediately note, as many as a third may be evangelicals, but it seems clear that Catholicism will continue to increase not only in absolute numbers, but also relative to other Christian denominations. And, despite Harold Bloom's quaint asseveration that "most" American Catholics are gnostics (rather than, as is true, "very many"), this might perhaps mean that the more extreme species of revivalist individualism may actually relinquish some slight measure of its dominance of the American religious consciousness.

And, then again, perhaps not. The institutional reality of American Christianity has always been too diverse for simple characterizations, but at present this much is certain: the churches most likely to prosper greatly are those that make an appeal to—and an attempt to adopt the style of—an emotive individualism. Whether this means seeking to provide a sort of chaplaincy for small communities of earnest, socially conscientious liberals (as do many mainstream Protestant parishes and many Catholic parishes that might as well be mainstream Protestant), or promoting a more traditional—if largely undemanding—popular moralism, or promising more extreme forms of spiritual experience, or supplying a sort of light spiritual therapy, what is ultimately important is that institutional authority and creedal tradition not interpose themselves between the believer and his God. And as a general, moderate, and respectable Christian piety has gradually lost its hold on the center of American society, this spiritual individualism has become more pronounced.

Nothing is more suggestive of the immense institutional transformations that may lie ahead for American Christianity than the growth of the so-called "mega-churches," enormous urban "parishes" built more or less on the model of suburban shopping malls, accommodating sometimes more than 20,000 congregants, and often featuring such amenities as bookstores, weight rooms, food courts, playing fields, coffee houses, even hostelries and credit unions. Worship in such churches often takes the form of mass entertainments—popular music, video spectaculars, sermons of a distinctly theatrical nature—and constitutes only one among a host of available services. Obviously, the scale of such enterprises is possible only because the spiritual life to which they give refuge is essentially private: each worshipper alone amid a crowd of other worshippers, finding Christ in the emotional release that only so generously shared a solitude permits. When Christ is one's personal savior, sacramental mediation is unnecessary and pastoral authority nugatory; convenience, however, and social support remain vital.

I do not mean to ridicule these churches, incidentally: I am not competent to say whether they represent merely a final disintegration of American Christianity into an absurd variety of consumerism, or whether they might be taken as—within the constraints of contemporary culture—a kind of new medievalism, an attempt to gather small cities into the precincts of the church and to retreat into them from a world increasingly inimical to spiritual longing. For me they do, however, occasion three reflections: first, that no other developed nation could produce such churches, because no other developed nation suffers from so unrelenting a hunger for God; second, that the social medium, the "middle," that I have claimed American religion has always largely lacked is perhaps more profoundly absent now than it has ever been, so much so that many Christians find themselves forced to create alternative societies to shelter their faith; and, third, that evangelical individualism may in fact be becoming even more thoroughly the standard form of American Christianity.

Prognostication is of course always perilous, especially when one is considering a matter as thronged with imponderables as America's religious future. My tendency, though, is to assume that for some years to come America will continue to be abnormally devout for an industrialized society; in fact I suspect (for reasons that will presently become clear) that it might even become a great deal more devout. But there is also that "other America" that could scarcely be more energetically post-Christian, and it requires only a generation or two for a society to go from being generally pious to being all but ubiquitously infidel; in the age of mass communication and inescapable "information," when an idea or habit of thought or fashionable depravity does not have to crawl from pen to pen or printing press to printing press, these cultural metabolisms occur far more quickly than they used to do. The ease with which an ever more flamboyant and temerarious sexual antinomianism has migrated through the general culture is instructive, at the very least, of how pliant even the most redoubtable of moral prejudices can prove before the blandishments of modern ideas when those ideas are conveyed, principally, by television.

There is no reason to be confident that the rising and succeeding generations of Catholics and evangelicals, Hispanic or "Anglo," will not progressively yield to the attractions (whatever they are) of secularist modernity. Some estimates of the decline in church attendance over just the past dozen years put it as high as 20 percent (though neither the accuracy nor the meaning of that number is certain). And the young of college age profess markedly less faith than their elders, say some surveys (though this, if true, may be little more than callow defiance of parents or the affectation of intellectual and moral autonomy). The American habit of faith will probably run many of the new unbelievers to earth, of course, but the great age of disenchantment may yet dawn here as it has in other technologically and economically advanced societies.

What, however, I suspect will be the case is that—however playfully or balefully heathen the circumambient culture may continue to become—religion in America will remain at least as vigorous as it is now for at least a few decades. The two most influential and vital forms of Christianity, almost certainly, will be evangelical Protestantism and Roman Catholicism (between which even now, however irreconcilable their ecclesiological principles, one can observe certain areas of intellectual and cultural rapprochement taking shape). Pentecostalism, moreover, is growing everywhere in the Christian world, and it is reasonable to suppose that more "charismatic" forms of both Catholicism and Protestantism will increasingly flourish here as well.

Around these two massive realities, smaller Protestant denominations of a markedly conservative complexion may remain relatively stable, I would imagine, so long as they remain conservative. Eastern Orthodoxy—along with the other ancient Eastern Churches, the most intransigently immune of Christian communities to the lure of change—has enjoyed something of a golden age of conversions over the past three decades, especially from Protestant denominations. Though it has long been seen as a predominantly "ethnic preserve" for Greeks, Russians, Serbs, Arabs, etc., Orthodoxy will probably continue to grow from outside its "natural" constituency, and may in a few generations come to be dominated in this country by communicants with no ethnic ties to the tradition.

Faiths other than Christianity will in all likelihood, even as their total numbers increase, decline in their percentage of the population (with the possible exception of Mormonism). The cultural and even religious influence of Judaism on America society will persist, one assumes, but in this regard it will be practically unique. Certainly nothing like the constant and volatile growth of Islam in Europe is likely here in the near term; despite occasional claims to the contrary, there are probably fewer than two million American Muslims; the majority of American Arabs are Christian, and our immigrants come principally from cultures where Islam is a small presence at best.

Where, among Christian congregations, it seems obvious to me that there will be no conspicuous growth, and indeed a great deal of diminution, is among the more liberal of the mainstream Protestant denominations. As much attention as is given in the press to the "lively" debates underway in many of the Protestant churches over such things as sexual morality, or to the New Hampshire Episcopal church's elevation of the adulterous and actively homosexual Gene Robinson to its episcopacy, these remain matters of concern to communities so minuscule by comparison to the larger religious realities of American culture, and so clearly destined for further fragmentation and tabescence, that it is inconceivable that they could be very relevant to the future shape of American religion.

Things like the Gene Robinson affair may, of course, be genuinely instructive regarding certain shifts in the larger society, especially in certain regions of the country. But, when one considers the most liberal forms of mainstream American Protestantism, it is not even obvious that one is any longer dealing with religion at all, except in a formal sense. Certainly they exhibit very few recognizable features of living faiths (such as a reluctance to make up their beliefs as they go along), and it is difficult to see many of their "bolder" gestures of accommodation as amounting to anything more than judicious preparations for a final obsolescence. The future of American religion in the main, whatever it is, lies almost certainly elsewhere.

In saying this, I am not, I hasten to add, attempting to be either cavalier or contemptuous. My judgments are prompted simply by two immense sets of statistical fact: those concerning birthrates and those concerning immigration. As for the former, I merely observe that theologically and morally conservative believers tend to have more children. Conservative

American Christians reproduce at a far greater rate than their liberal brethren and at an enormously higher rate than secularized America; the extraordinary growth of traditionalist Christian communities in recent decades is something that has been accomplished not only by indefatigable evangelization, but by the ancient and infallible methods of lawful conjugation and due fruition.

More importantly, though, the form that American religion will take in coming years is increasingly dictated by the demographic influx from Latin America, Asia, and Africa. In his indispensable book *The Next Christendom* (2002), Philip Jenkins remarks that the effect of mass immigration from the global South and Pacific East to the United States in recent years has been, in fact, to make America a more Christian nation. And the Christianity that is being imported from these parts of the world is, to a great extent, very conservative in its most basic moral precepts and metaphysical presuppositions. And, throughout the developing world, the Christianity that is growing most exuberantly (with, as Jenkins demonstrates, a rapidity that beggars the imagination) is in many cases marked by the New Testament charisms: prophecy, exorcisms, glossolalia, visions, miraculous healings. These are not things, one must make clear, confined only to small, sectarian communities. A Ugandan Catholic priest of my acquaintance has claimed to me—with obviously some hyperbole—that all African Christianity is charismatic to one degree or another. And the effect of Pentecostalism's success on the worship of Catholic congregations in places like the Philippines and Brazil is well documented.

All of which tends to make rather hilarious a figure like John Spong, the quondam Episcopal bishop of Newark. It was Spong who, in 1998, produced an hysterical screed of a book, pompously entitled *Why Christianity Must Change or Die*, that—in arguing for a "new Christianity," unburdened by such cumbrous appurtenances as, for instance, God—succeeded only in making audible the protracted death rattle of a moribund church. It was Spong also who, that same year, appalled that African bishops at the Lambeth Conference were about to defeat movements towards an official Anglican approbation of homosexuality, delivered himself of a fiercely petulant diatribe almost touching in its unreflective racism; these Africans, he declared (all of whom were far better scholars and linguists than he, as it happens), had only recently slouched their way out of animism, and so were susceptible to "religious extremism" and "very superstitious" forms of Christianity.

Now, admittedly, Spong is a notorious simpleton, whose special combination of emotional instability and intellectual fatuity leaves him in a condition rather like chronic *delirium tremens*; so it is not surprising that, on being somewhat unceremoniously roused from the parochial midden on which he had been contentedly reclining, his reaction should be puerile and vicious; but his perplexity and rage were genuine and understandable. Many within the languishing denominations of the affluent North, until they are similarly shaken from the slumber of their ignorance, are simply unprepared for the truth that, in the century ahead, Christianity will not only expand mightily, but will also increasingly be dominated by believers whose understanding of engagement with the non-Christian or post-Christian world is likely to be one not of accommodation, compromise, or even necessarily coexistence, but of spiritual warfare. This is, in many ways, an "ancient" Christianity. As immigration from the developing world continues, it will almost certainly find itself most at home in "ancient" America. (But this suggests that my earlier approach to my topic was better after all.)

THE IRONY that attaches to these reflections is that many of the forms of Christianity entering America from the developing world are in a sense merely coming home. The Christian movements that have had the most prodigious success in Asia and the global South are arguably those that were born here and then sent abroad: revivalist evangelicalism, Pentecostalism, even the charismatic movement within Catholicism and certain of the mainstream Protestant churches. Indeed, when one considers the influence American Christianity has had on the evolution of Christianity in the wider world, and considers also the effect of America's popular culture on the evolution of secular culture everywhere, one might almost conclude that America's great central and defining tension—between, as I have said, extreme forms of antiquity and modernity—has somehow reached out to draw the world into itself.

And it is a tension that—for want of that precious medium, civilization—looks likely to increase, for our extremes are becoming very extreme indeed: a modernity drained of any of the bright refinements and moral ambitions of Enlightenment reason or humanist idealism, reduced to a "high" culture of insipid ethical authoritarianism and a low culture consisting in dreary hedonism (without a hint of healthy Rabelaisian festivity), ever more explicit and repetitive celebrations of violence, sartorial and sexual slovenliness, atrocious music, and an idyllic emancipation from the fetters of literacy or (in fact) articulacy; and an antiquity of real and dynamic power, but largely uncontrolled by any mediating forces of order, stability, unity, or calm. To the dispassionate observer, there might be something exhilarating in the spectacle: the grand titanic struggle—within the very heart of their homeland—between a secular culture of militant vanity and incorruptible coarseness and a Christian culture of often purely experientialist ardor.

More prosaically speaking, though, a genuine civil religious struggle may well mark the coming decades, and how it will play out is hard to say. For the demographic reasons to which I have already adverted, as much as the social history of the United States, America is the one place in the Western world where one could conceivably see the inexorable advance of late modernity somewhat falter, or even the cultural power of the Christian global South establish something of a Northern redoubt. Ultimately, however, our strident secularity may triumph, and with it all the pathologies of cultural exhaustion.

Perhaps not only will the courts, and educational establishment, and ACLU, and all the other leal servants of a constitutional principle that does not actually exist, succeed in purging the last traces of Christian belief from our licit social grammar, but we may all finally, by forces of persuasion impossible to foresee, be conducted out of the darkness of our immemorial superstitions, nationalisms, moral prejudices, and retrograde loyalties into the radiant and pure universe of the International Criminal Court, reproductive choice, and the Turner Prize. Or some kind of uncomfortable but equable balance might continue to be struck between our extremes, under the sheltering pavilion of material satisfaction and narcissist individualism. But I prefer to think otherwise, and not only because "spiritual warfare" is more interesting to write about than bland social concord.

A CULTURE—a civilization—is only as great as the religious ideas that animate it; the magnitude of a people's cultural achievements is determined by the height of its spiritual aspirations. One need only turn one's gaze back to the frozen mires and fetid marshes of modern Europe, where once the greatest of human civilizations resided, to grasp how devastating and omnivorous a power metaphysical boredom is. The eye of faith presumes to see something miraculous within the ordinariness of the moment, mysterious hints of an intelligible order calling out for translation into artifacts, institutions, ideas, and great deeds, but boredom's disenchantment renders the imagination inert and desire torpid.

This claim is of course completely at variance with the Enlightenment mythology of modern secularism: that faith confined mankind within an incurious intellectual infancy, from which it has only lately been liberated to pursue the adult adventure of self-perfection; that the lineaments of all reality are clear and precise, and available to disinterested rationality and its powers of representation; that moral truth is not only something upon which all reasonable persons can agree, but also something that, in being grasped, is immediately compelling; that human nature, when measured only by itself, will of course advance towards higher expressions of life rather than retreat into the insipid self-indulgence of the last men or into mere brutish lawlessness; that reason can order society best only when all supernaturalism has been banished from its deliberations; and so on (and, in Wellington's words, if you believe that, you will believe anything).

Even if, however, one does not share my view that this entire mythology is an immense banality, and that modernity as a whole has resulted not in man's emergence into maturity, but in a degrading descent into a second childhood, still one must acknowledge that all the colossal creativity of modern culture taken together is manifestly unable to rise above a certain level of aesthetic or spiritual accomplishment (despite the greatness of certain individual achievements). And even if one has so little acquaintance with religious phenomena as to imagine that there are no moments of revelation, and that behind the surface of things there move no massive shapes that the religious consciousness dimly descries and imperfectly limns, and that in short religion is nothing but a gigantic feat of willful imagination, one must still grant that it is an engagement of, precisely, will and imagination, from which springs a magnificent profusion of cultural forms.

Europe may now be its own mausoleum, but once, under the golden canopy of an infinite aspiration—the God-man— the noblest of human worlds took shape: Hagia Sophia, Chartres, Rouen, and il Duomo; Giotto and Michelangelo; Palestrina and Bach; Dante and Shakespeare; Ronsard and Herbert; institutions that endured, economies that prospered, laws that worked justice, hypocrisies but also a cultural conscience that never forgot to hate them; and the elevation of charity above all other virtues.

As an unapologetic Christian reactionary, suffering from a romantic devotion to the vanished Christian order, and to all the marvels that flowed from its glorious synthesis of Judaic and Hellenic genius, I confess I often detest American religion (no doubt superciliously) as something formless, vulgar, saccharine, idolatrous, or—to intrude theology—heretical; I continue to delude myself that Europe's spiritual patrimony need not have been squandered had it been more duly cherished and reverently guarded. At the same time, as something of an American chauvinist, I cannot help but see in our often absurd and sometimes barbarous spiritual and social ferment something infinitely preferable to the defatigation of vision, wisdom, and moral fortitude that is the evident condition of the post-Christian West. There may not be much hope that anything worth dignifying with the term "civilization" will ever emerge from American culture—but, then again, where religious life persists there are always possibilities.

And, if nothing else, there is such a thing as moral civilization, and that, I often think, is nowhere more advanced than among the sort of persons whose beliefs will always be a scandal to the John Spongs of the world. American religion is poor in palpable splendors, true, but it is often difficult not to be amazed at, say, the virtues that southern evangelical culture is able to instill and preserve amid the wreck of modern civility and conscience: the graciousness of true hospitality; the spontaneous generosity that prompts evangelicals (even those of small substance) to donate so great a portion of their wealth to charitable relief for the developing world; the haunting consciousness of sin, righteousness, and redemption that often even the most brutal of men cannot escape and that can ennoble their lives with the dignity of repentance; a moral imagination capable of a belief in real "rebirth" (not merely "reform") and the power frequently to bring it to pass. A culture capable of such things—and of the surrender of faith necessary to sustain them—is something rare and delightful, which cannot be recovered once it is lost.

If indeed American religion was born out of the exhaustion of one set of mediating cultural and institutional structures and has yet to find any to take their place; and if American secularism was born out of the decadence of European civilization and has so far succeeded only at producing a new kind of savagery; and if the two are destined to continue to struggle for the soul of the nation, it is obvious where the sympathies of anyone anxious about the survival or even recrudescence of Western civilization should lie. I am not always entirely convinced that irreligious cultural conservatives have an unquestioned right to lament the general decline around them, as in ungenerous moments I tend to see them as its tacit accomplices, whose devotion to the past I suspect of having more the character of nostalgia than commitment; but I should think such persons would not be indifferent to religion.

For, if we succumb to post-Christian modernity, and the limits of its vision, what then? Most of us will surrender to a passive decay of will and aspiration, perhaps, find fewer reasons to resist as government insinuates itself into the little liberties of the family, continue to seek out hitherto unsuspected insensitivities to denounce and prejudices to extirpate, allow morality to give way to sentimentality; the impetuous among us will attempt to enjoy Balzac, or take up herb gardening, or discover "issues"; a few dilettantish amoralists will ascertain that everything is permitted and dabble in bestiality or cannibalism; the rest of us will mostly watch television; crime rates will rise more steeply and birth rates fall more precipitously; being the "last men," we shall think ourselves at the end of history; an occasional sense of the pointlessness of it all will induce in us a certain morose feeling of impotence (but what can one do?); and, in short, we shall become Europeans (but without the vestiges of the old civilization ranged about us to soothe our despondency).

Surely we can hope for a nobler fate. Better the world of Appalachian snake handlers, mass revivals, Hispanic Pentecostals, charismatic Catholics, and millenarian evangelicals (even the gnostics among them); better a disembodied, violent, and even Dionysiac hunger for God than a dispirited and eviscerate capitulation before material reality; and much better a general atmosphere of earnest, if sometimes unsophisticated, faith.

My "epiphany" of twenty years ago, on the rail platform in

England, was undoubtedly lacking in a certain balance, but the intuition that lay behind it was correct: that material circumstances (unless they are absolutely crushing) possess only such gravity or levity as one's interpretation of them; and how one interprets them is determined not merely by one's personal psychology, but by the cultural element in which they subsist. The almost luxuriant squalor of that railway station, had I found myself confronted by it in some corner of America, might have seemed a bleak disfigurement of the greater world in which I lived; it might even have struck me as depressingly emblematic of the profound hideousness of late industrial society and its inevitable utilitarian minimalism, but I do not believe it would have seemed to me the dark mystical epitome of a nation's soul.

Allowing for all the peculiarities of personal temperament, and for the special pathos that homesickness can induce, my reaction to my miserable surroundings was a real—if inevitably subjective—awakening to a larger cultural and spiritual truth. Either the material order is the whole of being, wherein all transcendence is an illusion, or it is the phenomenal surface—mysterious, beautiful, terrible, harsh, and haunting—of a world of living spirits. That the former view is philosophically incoherent is something of which I am convinced; even if one cannot share that conviction, however, one should still be able to recognize that it is only the latter view that has ever had the power—over centuries and in every realm of human accomplishment—to summon desire beyond the boring limits marked by mortality, to endow the will with constancy and purpose, and to shape imagination towards ends that should not be possible within the narrow economies of the flesh.

In any event, whatever one makes of American religion—its genially odd individualism, or its often ponderous stolidity, or its lunatic extremism, or its prodigies of kitsch, or its sometimes unseemly servility to a national mythology, or simply its unostentatious pertinacity—it is as well to realize that it is far more in harmony with the general condition of humanity throughout history than are the preposterous superstitions of secular reason or the vile ephemeralities of post-Christian popular culture. It is something alive and striving, which has the power to shelter innumerable natural virtues under its promises of supernatural grace. Most importantly, its strength and vitality portend something that might just survive the self-consuming culture of disenchantment; for, while it is possible that modernity may not have very much of a future, antiquity may very well prove deathless.

Of Lapdogs & Loners:
American Poetry Today

Eric Ormsby

W HEN I WAS eight years old, and living with my grandmother near Miami, I received a copy of Walter Scott's
book-length poem *Marmion* for my birthday. Perhaps my
grandmother, English-born and raised in Victorian times,
remembered the custom she and her sisters had of reading
poetry aloud on winter evenings in those distant days when
poetry was written to give pleasure; perhaps she even hoped
that the book would persuade me to introduce my scruffy pals
to the joys of verse. Not likely: this wasn't a gift calculated to
thrill a boy already addicted to the pleasures of snake- and
turtle-hunting in the Everglades, and tactfully I shunted it to
the side. One day not long after, however, perhaps disappointed in my quarry, I picked the book up and began to read,
drawn initially by the old steel engravings and the strange
ticklish scent of the stiffly glazed pages. To my own considerable surprise I was hooked like one of my own terrapins
after a stanza or two and read the verse-saga through from
beginning to end. The forceful rhythms of the lines held me at
first as much as the stirring tale:

> The guards their morrice-pikes advanced,
>   The trumpets flourished brave,
> The cannon from the ramparts glanced,
>   And thundering welcome gave.

A blithe salute, in martial sort,
  The minstrels well might sound,
For, as Lord Marmion crossed the court,
  He scattered angels round.

Powerful stuff, this, for an eight-year-old (even now, I confess, quaint and outmoded though Scott's manner may be, the verses can tingle my blood). For weeks I perched on our balcony in the blazing sun and declaimed whole stanzas to indifferent mockingbirds. I was drunk on the language which struck me then as valorous and charged in a way I couldn't comprehend. Tennyson, Wordsworth, Keats, and Shakespeare, and others, followed soon after, but I have never forgotten that first impression which Scott's poem made on my childish sensibility. This experience was what I think of as my "*Marmion* moment," and it doesn't matter that the poem which inspired it no longer seems to me especially good or even memorable. I was infected, deliciously so, by the poetry bug, and to this day I haven't recovered from its bite.

I mention this because I believe that it is from such early encounters with the magic of words that a sense not merely of the intoxicating effects of language but of the secret power of poetry itself takes root; and furthermore, that the encounter is replicated and repeated in a thousand different guises when we read poetry later in life. It is a sense of privileged intimacy, of delectable secrecy, which everyone who loves to read seeks to recover and prolong. In my own, no doubt partial, view, the experience occurs and recurs in its most concentrated form in the encounter with poetry.

Anyone who comes to love poetry from childhood as a pleasure in itself and who tries later, however hesitantly, to write it—who tries, that is, to recreate that pleasure in others which one received oneself as a reader—knows the strange almost trance-like sense of interior expansiveness which the effort can induce. How harsh then and unsettling the encounter with what is commonly called "the world of poetry" later proves to be! By "world of poetry" I mean the entire edifice of poetry as transaction: the magazines and publishing houses, the foundations, academies, and societies, the prizes and awards and fellowships, the workshops, the conferences, the colloquia, the cabals, and the covens. "The world of poetry is so *tiny!*" a distinguished editor once exclaimed to me. Not tiny enough, I thought. She meant, of course, that the networks, affiliations, lines of patronage, and so forth, were so closely and jealously monitored by those involved that the faintest ripple of repute in one corner would almost instantaneously produce a bulge of envy in another.

THE INSTITUTIONS in North America that seek to sustain and promote poetry strive mainly to buoy up this factitious but not insignificant "world," however tiny it might be. And the shadows that they cast, while ever lengthening, are neither healing nor apostolic but thin and chill. By this I do not mean that foundations such as the Guggenheim or prizes such as the Pulitzer or any of the sundry emoluments, accolades, or entitlements which they confer are intrinsically, or even wholly, malign; but rather, that they exist to serve poetry as a purely exterior endeavor. They exist principally not to encourage or inspire the composition of great poems but mainly, and unashamedly, to further careers. (I cannot think of a single example of a grant or an award or a prize leading to the creation of a poem, or book of poems, that promises to have lasting value.) There is of course nothing wrong with poetry as a career, except that it rarely has anything to do with poetry as such, in its innermost essence. Poetry that has a chance of lasting arises from a sense of vocation. While a genuine vocation may coincide with a career, and often has (think of Edna St. Vincent Millay or Elizabeth Bishop), it is something quite different from, and fundamentally incompatible with, that "world of poetry" which institutions sustain.

The continuing institutionalization of poetry in North America with its concomitant proliferation of writing workshops, professorial positions, validating agencies, and award-giving bodies, not to mention such pointless offices as that of

Poet Laureate, has had a stultifying effect on the creation of good poetry over the last few decades that has often been noted, sometimes by poets themselves. This isn't very surprising. After all, if you're writing in the hope of winning an award, you are liable to tailor your composition to prevailing tastes. This may account at least in part for the weird sameness of tone of so many contemporary poems. If I had to choose a single term to characterize this tone, I would be compelled to identify earnestness as its overriding trait.

Earnestness is a splendid virtue; while essential to social workers and scoutmasters, it is, however, of limited value to poets who usually prove to be better writers when they are shifty, unscrupulous, and shamelessly insincere—in matters, that is, unconnected with their craft. Earnestness, by contrast, deadens; it homogenizes the sentiments; it may flirt with irony but never dangerously so; it subordinates magic to agenda; it seeks to please rather than to charm; it hankers after acceptance and respectability, however much it may squawk the opposite—and was any great or good poem ever truly respectable?

It would be easy enough to pack this essay with examples of earnestness in current American verse. When Marilyn Hacker, a fine translator and sometimes quite fine sonneteer, writes, "I need transmission fluid for the brain," we are in the Land of Dreadful Earnestness. When the former Poet Laureate Robert Hass can begin a poem by writing

> You think you've grown up in various ways
> and then the elevator door opens and you're standing inside
> reaming out your nose

we feel a clammy pall of sincerity settling over our hapless shoulders. Even though Hass wants to be coyly self-deprecating ("What, me, a *laureate*, picking his nose in public?"), the earnestness bores through. When I read this and similar stuff, I long for the frivolous days of Ogden Nash and Dorothy Parker who were as adroit as they were malicious, and funny to boot. If I limit myself to a few such representative instances of poetic asininity, it is not solely to poke fun (though I see nothing wrong with that). Earnestness has other more damaging consequences—a vitiation of language, a renunciation of playfulness, a tinny solemnity—that do not bode well for the future of our verse. "Ogden, thou should'st be living at this hour!"

THE POET LAUREATESHIP of the United States—recently rechristened the Poet Laureate/Consultant for some reason—represents earnestness incarnate. The pay is modest, the duties undefined; even so, there seems to be any number of eager aspirants to this quaintly archaic position, as if the official honor paid to poetry stood in inverse ratio to its actual importance in the world today. We might as well, I suppose, have an official lutenist while we're at it for all the significance poetry possesses for the U.S. Congress (to whom the laureate is answerable).

Equally puzzling is the ambition recent poets laureate have nourished to evangelize poetry among the populace. With grim determination, like Nurse Ratchets killing with kindness, they have sought to spoon the tonic of poesy down the reluctant throats of the public. One of the kookiest proposals—surely this was not made seriously?—was to distribute collections of poetry to hotels and motels across the land in place of the good old Gideon Bibles. Another was to make books of poems available near the check-out counters of supermarkets and department stores. Now be honest: When faced with the choice between Rita Dove's *On the Bus with Rosa Parks* or the latest issue of *The Star* with its screaming headline "Bat Child Found Living in Cave," which would you go for?

At least in England, where the laureateship means something, the Queen provides the laureate with a goodly stock of wine once a year; a case of Jim Beam might do wonders for our own laureates, if only to loosen them up a bit. There is something inherently foolish about a kept bard; a court jester without the jokes (or the court). Of course, we cannot expect that our laureates will soon be penning triumphal odes on the entry of the U.S. Army into Baghdad; though minions of the Administration, they are more likely to be picketing their own offices. But couldn't they at least grind out a villanelle or two for the First Lady's birthday or finesse a limerick for the Speaker of the House? Instead, our laureates seem bent on proving their entrepreneurship in the deluded hope of making poetry genuinely popular. Beyond the implausibility of this project, it strikes me as fundamentally misguided. I find myself, somewhat improbably, in agreement with the poet Richard Howard who noted in a talk, later published as "The Ghettoization of Poetry," that the reading of poetry is essentially a private and intimate experience. Public events, such as the tiresome "Poetry Month" (April really is the cruellest month), offer little more than lip-service to an art that has no genuine significance in the lives of most Americans.

GIVEN THAT we're stuck with this odd office, and now that the jocular Billy Collins has been succeeded by the lugubrious Louise Glück, perhaps a more radical approach is finally in order. How astonishing, and genuinely exemplary, it would be, for instance, if the poet laureate were to sit firmly in her office, sustained by her stipend and the uncountable resources of the Library of Congress, and—write poetry? Wouldn't one good poem, or even a single slim book of good poems resulting from a year of subsidized toil, make it all worthwhile and serve as a better example than the ponderous readings and twittering tea parties and marketing campaigns now so much in vogue?

A bizarre corollary of the laureateship is the delusional sense of self-importance the position appears to confer on certain of its occupiers, often long after they have left office. The former laureate Rita Dove offers a cautionary instance of this tendency. Originally a poet of modest promise, whose best collection is still probably *Thomas and Beulah* (1987), she now produces this kind of stuff:

Joe takes after Mama.
Joe's Mr. Magoo.
Joe
thinks, half
dreaming, if he ever finds
a place where he can think,
he'd stop clowning
and drinking and then that wife
of his would quit
sending prayers through the chimney.

One consequence of her protracted laureateship has been Dove's exalted view of herself as a "role model" for others. This is a responsibility she claims to take with the utmost earnestness. Thus, in an interview she gave in 2002 to one Earl G. Ingersoll, she remarked:

> How does it feel to be a role model? That one's difficult because I have to build in disclaimers about what people consider role models to be and how I define a role model. Newspapers don't want to hear it; but the fact is, I think one's role models should be everyday people, the people you see living life minute-by-minute, because that's how you live your life. You don't live your life in the limelight; you don't live your life in sound bites or a brief interview. But that's what's seen when you look at the role models kids have today.

These are reasonable comments but are belied by Dove's incessant self-publicity. By her own relentless puffery, and that of others (Helen Vendler in particular), Rita Dove has been transmogrified into a kind of monstrous caricature of a poet. Like La Fontaine's frog that longed to turn into an ox and ended up by exploding, Dove has been expanding relentlessly until she has reached the limits of what a single fragile human ego can possibly contain. The poetry in the meantime has ended up as the tinsel on the float. Sad to say, the whole ghastly process has been doggedly documented by her own husband, the obscure German novelist Fred Viebahn, who every year issues his notorious *Dove–Viebahn Newsletter.* "Fred's Annual Letter," as he fondly dubs it on the masthead, is one of those embarrassing circular letters self-infatuated families love to send out at Christmas to stupefied friends ("Estelle is starting harp lessons in the fall"), but it is, if I may say so, the Mother of all Holiday Letters.

A MONUMENT TO what another of its ardent fans terms "gloating self-regard," the newsletter, replete with publicity photos and side-bars, positively brims with braggadocio, not solely about Rita and Fred but about their strenuously over-achieving daughter, Aviva. Significantly, the many pages of self-praise never turn on poetry which is rarely mentioned except as the occasion for some accolade, however minor. Instead, the names of celebrities, or would-be ones, are dropped with dogged abandon, as when Rita is summoned—"yet again!"—to trip the cha-cha with "Bill" on the presidential patio. ("'Well,' a Washington establishment lady at the next table said to Rita with ill-concealed cattiness, 'I guess you must be somebody!'" For once the intrepid Fred fails to get her name. *Quandoque bonus dormitat Viebahnus!*) At the same time, no distinction is too trifling to escape mention. Thus, Rita is inducted into the American Academy of Achievement, whatever that is, or attends the "Poetry Africa" festival "in the province of KwaZulu-Natal on the Indian Ocean," and still manages to fit in "a splendid Argentinean tango-paso doble combination at the local medal ball." Wherever he travels, Fred is like a celebrity-seeking missile and rarely hits a name he cannot drop. Viebahn may know the German proverb *Selbstlob stinkt* ("Self-praise stinks") but clearly he doesn't subscribe to it.

I'm all for poets tripping the light fantastic, even at the White House (and have been known to foot a mean cha-cha myself, albeit in less august surroundings), and I don't in the slightest begrudge this merry couple their social whirl. Nevertheless, the obsessive detail and wide distribution of the newsletter—it is sent not solely to family and friends but to literary magazines nationwide—say something alarming about what a very visible poet considers important in the end. How does this square with Dove's commitment to poetry, to which she presumably still pays lip-service, and how can it be reconciled with her solemn sense of herself as a role model? I have a pretty good idea of what "the kids" for whom she professes such concern will think when they witness the disparity between her formal pronouncements and "Fred's Annual Letter." In the end, the newsletter is not merely a laughable if unwitting exposé of the perils of self-importance, it also illustrates, better than anything I could invent, that externalized, transactional "world of poetry" which is the diametric opposite of everything genuine that poetry, and an authentic life in poetry, stands for.

Herbert Morris was not, thank God, a celebrity; the dust jackets of his four books of poetry carry neither photo nor biography. Whether this is from modesty or reclusiveness I have no idea, and yet he has written some of the best work to emerge in North America in recent decades. His most recent collection, *What Was Lost* (Counterpoint), contains fifteen poems, every one of which merits reading and re-reading. I have admired his work since *Peru*, his first book, appeared in 1983, and while not all his books are of equal strength, he remains one of the subtlest and most original of poets. Though he favors the dramatic or interior monologue, Morris is difficult to categorize. Eschewing rhyme and metaphor, his verse gives an unadorned impression; at the same time, it is musical and densely textured. His true Penelope, we might say, is Henry James, and, like James, he accumulates clauses within clauses, like some sly lasso virtuoso, to achieve his unusual effects, at once Ciceronian and Prufrockian. Overlapping repetitions, variations on phrases, spilling rivulets of hesitancy and asseveration, lend serpentine momentum to his lines. The result is a kind of verbal impasto which, fused with an uncanny ear for cadences, creates an incantatory, rather mesmerizing pattern.

In *What Was Lost*, there are at least two masterpieces, the opening poem, "House of Words," in Henry James's voice, and "To Baden," a long, strange, hypnotic poem in thirty-eight strict five-line stanzas. The first of these traces what the speaker calls "intimations of extreme dislocation," arising from a dreamed visit to James at Lamb House, his residence in Rye, by the "handsome, stylish" portrait photographer Alvin Landon Coburn (one of whose beautiful prints adorns the dust jacket). These intimations are of words not spoken or spoken wrongly, of gestures too ambiguous or hesitant, of vacillations and second-thoughts, of what-might-have-been or still-might-be, that whole restless penumbra of an exquisitely questioning and baffled consciousness which James himself was so skilled at adumbrating. The poem is full of what James termed "glimmerings," as in the following passage:

> I, who had always held himself apart,
> had cause to hold himself apart, from crowds,
> others en masse, I who had found himself
> never less than reluctant to plunge in,
> to brave the onslaught of that tide, that wave,
> more than hesitant to immerse oneself
> in currents likely to sweep one far out,
> that turbulence which raged past one's control,
> that chaos from which there seems no way back;
> I, finder of refuge, maker of refuge,
> in words, whose life, indeed, was spun of words,
> spun and respun, spun once more, then respun,
> a life which has itself become a refuge
> (words, in a world bordered by blood, on one side,
> by the tumult of passion on the other;
> the thinness, yes, the thinness of one's life:
> what has one built if not a house of words?;
> what can one's life have been said to have come to?).

Morris's qualities cannot be captured in excerpts, but this one does at least demonstrate how accurately he catches James's

voice, as well as the cumulative force his variations weave. For
all its understatement, the poem is piercing and vastly sad.

"To Baden" is quite another matter. In contradistinction to
"House of Words" with its anguished, almost paralyzed
meditation, this is a racehorse of a poem and never stops
(*Marmion* certainly never hit these speeds). Drawn from a
whimsical subject—the nineteenth-century aristocratic habit
of sending servants out at night on horseback to bring back
Spanischbrotli, a "butter-rich pastry," from Baden—the poem
proceeds at a breathless and terrifying gallop from start to
finish. Here's how it begins:

> Into the dark to Baden, then, if need be,
> now, or the moment just before, but hurry,
> lest mood shift, need diminish, alteration
> insinuate its presence, light change, time pass,
> education, somewhere, at last, begin,
>
> never looking back, never asking why—and to what avail, what,
> > to look, to ask,
> to know, or hope to know, initiate
> an approach to some fixed, ultimate knowledge,
> hard-won, if won at all, of what it was.

THERE IS SOMETHING at once ludicrous and desperate in this
urge for pastry at midnight, but it gives the poem its compelling drive:

> Marta, time, it is time, such longing flays us
> as one cannot depict, and all for pastry;
>
> but be warned, take fair caution: each step, misstep,
> skirts disaster, ground shifts, the route meanders,
> footing turns treacherous, in due course, worse,
> and the delicate, hand-turned crusts, their perfume
> carrying through the depths of unmapped woods,
>
> break at a touch, less than that, crumble, shatter.

Anyone who has ever yearned to live next to an all-night *Konditerei* will savor this poem which is, of course, about much more than *Spanischbrotli*, those "infinite kneadings, rich drenched butterings" (though, to Morris's credit, it is very much about them too). The poem is about seizing an instant, or an impulse (already forever lost); it is about seizing life itself, at the apogee of its intensity, as opposed to "the long, slow settling in, the making do."

Morris has the rare knack of making a *tour de force* such as "To Baden" more than a mere display of ingenuity; its absurd momentum grips us even as we acknowledge the absurdity, for it is the momentum of all our longings.

IN HIS POETICS, Aristotle identified a gift for metaphor as the defining mark of a poet of genius. But metaphor demands a certain playfulness, and for the over-earnest, the ludic is a mode to be strenuously avoided. Nevertheless, when such figures do crop up in contemporary American poetry, they are often manhandled for lack of exactitude. A successful metaphor works or flops in accord with the precision of its affinity. This is not to invoke some hidebound set of rules. It's simply how metaphor operates. Two entities are brought into unexpected but just collocation on the basis of a quality, hidden or unsuspected, which they share. When Shakespeare writes "bare ruined choirs where late the sweet birds sang," we respond to it because of a hitherto unnoticed common element—the famous *tertium quid*, or "third thing" of the rhetoricians—between winter trees and devastated chapels; call it songlessness or what you will.

Of course, a metaphor may consciously subvert its purpose. When André Breton says of his wife (in "L'Union libre")

Ma femme au sexe de placer et d'ornithorynque
(My wife with the sex of a placer mine and a platypus)

we will not expect to find monotreme anatomy—or explosives—under Mme. Breton's svelte Chanel *tailleur*. That is the point: The *tertium quid* has been deliberately abolished to confound and startle our expectations. Such effects once seemed daring but have by now (I hope) run their course.

What I have in mind is something different and which seems alarmingly like a tendency: The proliferation not simply of bad images but of pseudo-metaphors, metaphors that through carelessness or imprecision miss the mark. My card-file runneth over, but I have space for two examples of such misfired metaphor. The first is, again, by Robert Hass, whose debut collection, *Field Guide*, still in print and still much admired, has exerted considerable influence since its publication in 1973. In a poem to his wife from that collection, Hass attempts a rare apostrophe that strains to be at once earnest and erotic (a combination without a future, I'd say). He exclaims, "O spider cunt, O raw devourer!" Now the phrase "spider cunt" does have a certain phonic piquancy with that long i arrested abruptly by the blunt u of "cunt." (We can ignore "O raw devourer" as a bit of sheer pubic persiflage.) But consider the comparison that is implicitly being made. Is there anything in common between a vagina and an arachnid? Eight legs? Multiple eyes? Are we witnessing here the rebirth of the long-discredited *vagina dentata*? Is his wife what the comic books call "a webslinger?" The verbal combination initially startles but ultimately fails because there is no affinity, however covert, between the two items brought into conjunction.

Another example of inaccuracy in metaphoric language occurs in the work of the much-ballyhooed Anne Carson, a poet whose figurative imprecision is virtually the signature of her work. Whenever I try out the "Larkin Test" on her admirers, I always receive the same response. (The Larkin Test refers to the occasion when Margaret Thatcher told Philip Larkin how much she admired his verse and he responded, "Can you quote three lines?" She couldn't, but then the Iron Lady had other things on her mind.) Two examples are regularly adduced to illustrate Carson's lyric brilliance; one of these is the poem in which she repeats the word "river," and nothing else, some fifteen times—at least that's where I stopped counting—and the other is, without fail, "Praguing the eye." The use of a proper name in a verbal mode is nothing new in English poetry, of course, but it still elicits a mild surprise. What though does the phrase mean? Does it refer to the golden towers of the Prague skyline and the fabled splendor of an ancient city which illumines the gaze? Could it allude to the ubiquitous air pollution of Prague that stings the eye of every visitor? The answer, I suspect, is that it refers to all of these and to none of them. It's an ersatz metaphor without a third referent, not because the poet, in Surrealist fashion, wishes to jostle our expectations but, instead, because she means only to gauze them in shallow and gratuitous vagueness. It is both an ugly phrase to the ear and one that can denote anything you want while meaning nothing at all. When I asked a sophisticated friend what he made of it, he responded by asking, "What is *progging*?"

EARNESTNESS can run amok at times and give way to zealotry. *Poets Against the War* (Thunder Mouth Press) may not be the worst collection of poems I have ever read—competitors abound—but it's definitely a top contender. It is edited by Sam Hamill, the poet, publisher, and translator who was instrumental last year in torpedoing a White House symposium, sponsored by the First Lady, to which a sampling of American poets had been invited. Hamill declined his invitation, patterning himself on Robert Lowell who refused to attend a similar White House event during the Vietnam War. Hamill's reasoning seems to have been that if he cannot hope to write like Robert Lowell, he can at least behave as badly. Lowell's refusal took no great courage and Hamill's took none. In a gratuitously churlish note he dedicates his anthology "For Laura Bush."

The present confection is a perfect illustration of André Gide's dictum that "it is with fine sentiments that bad literature is made." The collection offers not a single worthwhile poem; the only poems that stick in the mind do so because they are too fatuous to forget. But this is not merely bad poetry. It is bad poetry that positively suppurates self-righteousness. Worse, it is a deeply dishonest book.

Hamill affects a specious populism in his selections. The bulk of the anthology consists of work by unknown poets from all regions of the country. Hamill tells us that his website was deluged with 13,000 poems from 11,000 poets (ghastly statistic: I didn't know there were that many poets in world history, let alone in the U.S.). Out of these he selected just under 200; nevertheless, as he assures us, "there are, no doubt, innumerable jewels still to be found in the vaults of poetsagainstthewar.org." His reluctance to explore "the vaults" further is understandable, given what he has dragged out so far.

Each poet is furnished with a prefatory blurb indicating what part of America he or she hails from; the age of many is given, for reasons that escape me. Should we overlook the lame lines and spavined stanzas of Patricia Ikeda, forty-nine years old, and "a socially engaged Buddhist activist in the Bay Area" because she is over the hill? Or the appalling ear of William Irwin Thompson, a "semi-finalist for the National Book Award in 1972" (what is a "semi-finalist" anyway?), because he has reached the threshold of his dotage at sixty-seven? At least the seven-year-old second-grader Wilden McIntosh-Round can write a serviceable, if banal, declarative sentence: "Our earth was created for us to live in peace on," but who would call it poetry?

There are plenty of well-known names too, most of whom contribute utterly egregious twaddle (and all of whom withhold their ages). Thus, Robert Bly writes:

We will have to call especially to reach
Our angels, who are hard of hearing.

I suspect that at Bly's approach the "angels" switch off their hearing aids. Rita Dove treats us to lamely jogging doggerel: "One lay slathered in garlands, one left only a smear." Tess Gallagher maunders on for three long pages, mostly about attending a parade when she was in pigtails, and offers this trenchant quibble:

> What about a manual exhorting the patriotic
> Duty of pushing doll buggies?

Even worse is Lucille Clifton, who can perpetrate the Technicolor lines:

> Our ears bleed
> Red white and blue

The level of passion in these poems is so low as to be insulting. There is a lot of rant but no real feeling here. Their words betray the poets; even the outrage is recycled, drawing on mildewed slogans tucked in some mental attic since Vietnam. If I were an Iraqi, I wouldn't be comforted by the poem by Pamela Hale, "35 years old" from Houston, that begins with less pathos than a Hallmark card:

> I'm sorry that your mom was killed
> When a missile struck your home.

The editor himself chimes in with "Sheepherder's Coffee," though what it has to do with the war eludes me (do we get coffee—or sheep—from Iraq?); one line stands out, because it manages to be both asinine and untrue in equal measure:

> There are fewer names for coffee
> Than for love.

Hamill provides an introduction that is nonpareil for sheer boastfulness. Thus, he writes that "never before in recorded history have so many poets spoken in a single chorus; never before has a single-theme anthology of this proportion been assembled." It is daunting when you think about it: a chorus of 13,000 poets all chanting in unison. Shipped to Baghdad and set asinging, their combined verses would reduce the most hardened Baathist to gibbering capitulation.

Of course, such a book is all too easy to ridicule, but there is a deeper moral that I feel obliged to note, which is the patent dishonesty of the whole endeavor. Not once in this wretched assemblage is there any hint that Iraqi Kurds or Shi'ites or Chaldean Christians ever suffered the least harm under Saddam Hussein, nor is that brute once mentioned. But even Hamill cannot completely hide the truth. In the note to a poem by an Iraqi poet named Salam al-Asadi, who died in 1994, we are told that he was "an eyewitness to the bombing of his hometown in southern Iraq." If Salam died in 1994, it must have been under the savage reprisals set loose by Saddam Hussein against the Shi'ites of the south, and the bombing he witnessed must have been at the hands of the regime. This is left unmentioned. It is misleading, if not downright mendacious, to oppose the war in Iraq without at least hinting that there may have been plausible and defensible reasons for it.

Lovers of verse at its worst, and whose grimed copies of *The Stuffed Owl* are collapsing at the seams, will find much to rejoice in here. If truth, in the old adage, is the first casualty of war, poetry, on the evidence of this farrago, must be the second.

Poets often complain that good critics of poetry are essential to the furtherance of good poetry but that nowadays such critics are dangerously rare, and the names of Randall Jarrell and R. P. Blackmur, among others, are usually invoked in this lament. I doubt the truth both of the proposition and of the supposed scarcity. Most of the outstanding critics we still read, from Aristotle and Longinus to Johnson, Hazlitt, Coleridge and the rest, have at best a retrospective value as arbiters; their marvelous prose is of course another matter. Their judgments on their contemporaries were often dead wrong, sometimes spectacularly so. And we do have brilliant critics at work today, such as Christopher Ricks or the indispensable poet and critic William Logan (who, of course, writes regularly for these pages). When poets utter this complaint, what they really mean is that there are no influential critics who support *their* work, and while this may be understandable, it is blinkered.

The problem that does arise, however, is not that we lack good critics but that we have a profusion of gatekeepers. The gatekeeper is not interested in winnowing out what is good from what is bad in contemporary poetry; the gatekeeper is at once a shill and a bouncer, admitting those he or she favors while excluding or ejecting others who can do nothing for the gatekeeper's own interests.

Our two most prominent gatekeepers are Harold Bloom and Helen Vendler, both of whom exercise their self-conferred prerogatives with freewheeling abandon. By dint of vociferous patronage and bullying admonishment, these two professors of literature, pontificating *ex cathedra* from Yale and Harvard, respectively, are reputed to "make or break" the reputations of aspiring poets. The fact that neither professor displays any notable fund of either taste or judgment whenever they stray from their well-demarcated areas of expertise apparently makes no difference to the influence they wield.

Bloom need not detain us unduly. When he is not churning out another fat door-stopper on some well-trodden topic, he is furiously composing blurbs for books by cronies and colleagues; in this compulsive endeavor he is rivaled only by Richard Howard, another blurboholic whose puffery at least has the virtue of being largely unintelligible and, so, harmless. There is also, I must admit, something faintly endearing in Bloom's literary buffoonery; the same cannot be said, alas, of Professor Vendler, who brandishes her laurels, and her secateurs, with appalling earnestness.

No poet I have ever met takes Professor Vendler's judgments seriously, but by the same token, no poet I know will venture to challenge her in print. The usual demurral I hear is that "she's good on Shakespeare." And it is true: Point her in the right direction, towards such established poets as Keats or

Shakespeare or Wallace Stevens, and she does have, on occasion, interesting and perceptive comments; left to her own devices, however, she goes sadly, and often embarrassingly, astray. Her enthusiastic espousal of such nugatory poets as Rita Dove or Jorie Graham—at best, poets of only passing interest; at worst, boring and unreadable—confounds even her most craven acolytes.

I never considered Professor Vendler's opinions of any great moment, except as flagrant instances of the captious taste that reigns in the academy, until I read an article by Dinitia Smith in *The New York Times* of November 22, 1997, entitled "A Woman of Power in the Ivory Tower." There I learned, for the first time, and to my considerable amazement, that other people heeded her pronouncements and, in fact, that poets in particular cowered before her like eunuchs at the court of some unstable potentate. After reading the article I began to notice that whenever Professor Vendler's name came up in conversation with other poets, the chat grew conspicuously guarded; though all agreed, when pressed, that she was fundamentally clueless, not one would deliver an opinion that was not evasive in the end.

The most astonishing comment in the *Times* article came from a poet who wanted to say "something nice" about Professor Vendler but was fearful that she might misconstrue his praise and punish him for it later. A textual authority on Shakespeare's *Sonnets* might misinterpret a word of praise? Extraordinary. Of course, this says more about the cowardice of poets than about Professor Vendler, and yet, how did such a grotesque state of affairs arise in the first place? Have our poets been reduced to the status of curs who flinch in anticipation of a blow? Even allowing for the sort of mischievous exaggeration that *The New York Times*, for all its own overweening earnestness, occasionally indulges in, the situation as described would be comical if it were not so pitiful.

Despite my early reading, I'm no Marmion "whose steady heart and eye/ Ne'er changed in worst extremity," and so I won't risk Professor Vendler's ire by saying "something nice" about her critical endeavors. On matters relating to contemporary poetry, though I agree with some of her opinions and respect her passion in advancing them, I believe that she is more often wrong than not; this wouldn't matter much if she were not a gatekeeper of such influence. Like some self-elected dog-catcher she strews the tainted kibble of her patronage in every direction in the hope of luring new lap-dogs to her gilded kennels; never mind if they later turn out to be sidewalk terriers rather than pedigreed hounds, Professor Vendler will champion them at every show in town. And, to be honest, who wouldn't be tempted? Pulitzer Prizes, MacArthur Awards, tenured jobs at Harvard, fulsome reviews in widely read magazines—all these, if Dinitia Smith is to be believed, flow from her favor.

OF JORIE GRAHAM, her most fervently championed protégé, Vendler can write, with regard to such lank and gelatinous lines as the following,

> the start of a story, the mind trying to fasten
> and fasten, the mind feeling it like a sickness this wanting
> to snag, catch hold, begin, the mind crawling out to the
> edge of the cliff
> and feeling the body as if for the first time—how it cannot
> follow, cannot love.

"the dizzying extension of the mind, as it crawls out to the edge of the cliff of the conceptual, presses Graham to her long lines and to their 'outrides'—small piece-lines dropping down at the right margin of their precursor-line." In my view, Graham long since fell over the edge of the cliff, but never mind; does this sentence say anything that can be meaningfully elucidated or even parsed? Again, from the same passage: "Graham redefines the human aim of verse as an earthly, terrain-oriented lateral search (which can reach even the epic dimensions of the Columbian voyage) rather than a vertical Signorelli-like descent into depth." Come again? What is or could be a "terrain-oriented lateral search"? Is there any other kind of descent than "into depth"? Is Vendler writing about a poem or about spelunking? And earlier in the same volume (her 1995 study of Hopkins, Heaney, and Graham entitled *The Breaking of Style*), she confides that she found Graham's early poems "so seductive that one's heart, reproducing those poems, almost found a new way to beat," a symptom that would send most of us to the nearest cardiac unit.

Well, leaving aside the pretentious and vapid prose and the misplaced praise, what is really wrong with all this? Though it may seem a *volte-face*, I would say, not much. Though I disagree with Vendler's patronage of Graham and her other sycophants, though I wish she would lend her support to the many worthier poets who might benefit from it, I believe that she is doing exactly what she has been paid to do, that is, pressing her advocacy, with whatever means are at her disposal, to further what she so earnestly believes is good and castigate, with equal earnestness, what she thinks is bad. True, nothing is more galling or more redolent of injustice than to see the dimly gifted or the patently fraudulent hyped out of all proportion to their true merits, but this is how the "world of poetry" functions, after all; you or I, given her opportunities, would be tempted to do the same, though (we like to hope) with happier results.

THE PROBLEM LIES, alas, not with Professor Vendler or Professor Bloom or any other panjandrum of contemporary verse, nor does it lie, I believe, with a dearth of good critics, but rather, with poets themselves. "The fault, dear Brutus . . ." Why do so few poets, and especially those with some reputation, shrink from speaking up? Why does no one (with the admirable exception of William Logan) challenge Professor Vendler and her cronies by rebutting their judgments and questioning their taste? Most urgently, why is there almost no critical discourse worthy of the name in the current "world of poetry?" In my exasperation I am forced back on *Marmion* (indulge me!):

Thus oft it haps, that when within
They shrink at sense of secret sin,
   A feather daunts the brave;
A fool's wild speech confounds the wise,
And proudest princes veil their eyes
   Before their meanest slave.

There are, of course, poets whose work I admire as much as Professor Vendler does, and particularly, Seamus Heaney and Charles Wright, to name but these. In fact, the Tennessee-born Charles Wright strikes me as one of the most original and profoundly impressive American poets now active. He is also one of the most ambitious, though his ambition is directed to the growing body of his work rather than to the ephemera drifting from the world of poetry. His *Negative Blue* (Farrar Straus and Giroux, 2000), which gathers up the last of his three sets of trilogies, composed over many years, does not constitute an epic—or if so, only in the sense that Hart Crane's *The Bridge* is one—but is a persuasive sequence of lyrics in which all the finest qualities of a master poet are conspicuous: a gift for metaphor, an intense musicality, a sense of form uniquely his own, and a kind of unmistakable suavity of voice capable of evoking tenderness as well as rage, despair as well as a credible ecstasy.

Wright would be easy to parody, the sure sign of a strong style; there are far too many poems that bear titles such as "After Reading Chuang Tzu I Step out on the Veranda to Eat a Bowl of Weetabix and Contemplate Orion." But this is a minor fault, if fault it is, as opposed to idiosyncracy. His is also a forcefully spiritual poetry in a very American mode; there is a constant awareness of the holy as manifested in the natural world (an awareness without any of the gush of such worshipful contemporaries of his as, say, Mary Oliver). Drawn by this mystical bent he often resorts to abstractions but these are always counterfoiled by the touched, the smelled, the seen, as well as nuanced by his wry sense of himself as an imperfect observer. Notice how in the first section of "Apologia Pro Vita

Sua" (from *Black Zodiac* of 1997) Wright begins with a grand abstraction which he then narrows relentlessly down to the tiniest actualities:

> Time is the source of all good,
> > time the engenderer
> Of entropy and decay,
> Time the destroyer, our only-begetter and advocate.
>
> For instance, my fingernail,
> > so pink, so amplified,
> > In the half-dark, for instance,
> These force-fed dogwood blossoms, green-leafed, defused,
> > limp on their long branches.
>
> St. Stone, say a little prayer for me,
> > grackles and jay in the black gum,
> Drowse of the peony head,
> Dandelion globes luminous in the last light, more work to be done.

But Wright can be quite directly religious in an uncommon way and some of his poems read like prayers—prayers mediated, it must be said, not only through Dante but through Montale and Paul Celan—as in his variation on the old *Salve Regina* in "Winter-Worship:"

> Mother of Darkness, Our Lady,
> Suffer our supplications,
> > our hurts come unto you.
> Hear us from absence your dwelling place,
> Whose ear we plead for.
> > End us our outstay.

Wright is also a sensible and edifying commenter on poetry, his own and that of others; from his interviews, moreover, it is clear that he is quite aware of what he himself is trying to accomplish, though, thankfully, not overly so. Hence he can remark, "Mostly, it has to do with the 'music' of poems, whatever that is. Everyone hears it differently, of course. I tend to work in stress groups. I am, like most people who write poems, inordinately fond of my own ear, and trust my ear maybe more than I should. As Woody Allen says, 'It's my second favorite organ.' I'm a primitive poet, I think. I trust my ear, I trust my instincts." Every practiced poet will recognize the truth of this; where the critic spots calculation and intentionality, always after the fact, the poet proceeds by instinct and by ear.

THOUGH WRIGHT is anything but a "confessional" poet, his poems constitute a kind of diary of his sensibility over a span of decades; the record is rarely self-indulgent, however, because each lyric in the several sequences is guided by a shaping will. All his poems, and not only the threefold trilogy that culminates in *Negative Blue*, possess a densely layered texture woven of the spontaneous and the recollected; if some, or even much, of it appears inconsequential—those small, personal, quotidian details of life as it is lived, day after day—the successive force of the ensemble has an irresistible power. It is the magical, in nature and in history, in words, in the individual consciousness, that Wright incessantly seeks and listens for, and it is astonishing how often he succeeds in summoning intimations of pure magic from the most improbable provocations, not only the "wonderful in the ordinary" (tired trope!), but the odd, unfolding wonder of being here and now, at this time and in this place, wherever it may be, Italy or the Appalachians or under the night sky of Charlottesville. "What I remember redeems me," he writes, but also:

> My life, like others' lives, has been circumscribed by stars.
> *O vaghe stelle dell'orso,*
> > Beautiful stars of the Bear,
> I took, one time, from a book.
> Tonight, I take it again, that I, like Leopardi, might
> One day immerse myself in its cold, Lethean shine.

In her earlier, longer version of "Poetry," Marianne Moore wrote, "there are things that are important beyond all this fiddle." By "this fiddle" she meant all the trappings that surround the writing of verse, the hoopla as well as the exaggerated hush. Against this she invoked "the raw material of poetry in/ all its rawness" and "that which is on the other hand/ genuine." Her own fastidious reluctance to publish, her drastic later revisions, her extreme scrupulosity with words, her fidelity to the factual, bear witness to the justice of her "perfect contempt" for poetry, a contempt which was her ultimate integrity. Such a posture with respect to what mattered most to her kept her sense of the genuine intact and alive, but it isn't a posture likely to bring down the usual rewards on its holder's head from the various institutions that take an interest in poetry. I'd argue, however, that it is an essential posture. After all, it is from life that poetry draws its importance, and not the other way around, that is, from what Henry James once called "felt life," and certainly not from workshops or MFA programs or foundations or academies, however useful these may be along the way.

When I read poems that move me by virtue of their authenticity of word and image and music, I'm not "transported to a better world," but returned to this one with enhanced senses, to a world, that is, which is infinitely more particular, more specific, more once-and-for-all-time than my habitual world. I was lucky, I think, to experience it as a kid in however clumsy a form in the stanzas of *Marmion*, a poem I now find pretty much unreadable. What remained wasn't the shape or sound of the lines themselves but a sensation of unlimited and unanticipated possibility confined to a discrete but strangely malleable instant of time. To recover that instant— call it one of enchantment or imaginative liberation or sudden vision, whatever you will—is what counts for both the poet who writes and the lover of poetry who reads. "*Et tout le reste est littérature,*" as Verlaine said; or, in other words, the rest is pure gravy.

Olympians on the March: the Courts & the Culture Wars

Robert H. Bork

[T]o be "reactionary" means nothing more than to believe that in some of its aspects, however secondary, the past was better than the present.
—Leszek Kolakowski

Everything has been said before, but since nobody listens we have to keep going back and beginning all over again.
—André Gide

WALTER BAGEHOT said of the English constitution, "[I]n the full activity of an historical constitution, its subjects repeat phrases true in the time of their fathers, and inculcated by those fathers, but now no longer true." So it is with us. Though they have a mystical veneration for the document, very few Americans have even the slightest idea of what is in the Constitution, how it was understood by the ratifiers who made it law, or what time and the Supreme Court have done to it. We are living with a vision of a Constitution that no longer exists. The reason is apparent. The Constitution, which is, for all practical purposes, the Supreme Court, follows the elite culture. Thus it is that the liberal transformation of the Constitution over the past fifty years has been accomplished by Courts with heavy majorities appointed by Republican presidents (the current count is seven to two).

As cultural dominance passes from one elite to the next, so

does the Supreme Court's law change to reflect the views of the new elite. New values are added and old ones abandoned. Not all values, however, can find even remotely plausible support in the historical Constitution. When vagabond values are to be implemented, the Court's declarations that various executive or legislative acts are unconstitutional are often not even colorably related to the charter supposedly being applied. Disregard for text, legislative purpose, and history confers enormous freedom, so that the Court, employing some primitive and often sophomoric version of moral philosophy or natural law, is at liberty to enforce what it chooses.

It is not to be expected that lives devoted to lawyers' arts would, upon the donning of black robes, suddenly produce philosophers. We are then governed not by law but by the moods of an unelected, unrepresentative, and unaccountable committee of nine lawyers. What they decide is often law only in the sense that we will obey their ukases, even when they split five to four and the four have by far the better arguments. What they decide is not law, however, in the sense that it has its origin, its root, in any legal materials and that the result falls within a range that would be regarded as acceptable by most judges, past, present, and future. Moods shift; the range of fair readings does not.

THE PROGRESSION is clear on the record. In the last third of the nineteenth century and the first third of the twentieth, the dominant culture was that of the business class, and the Court frequently responded with the invention of constitutional rights favorable to that class, striking down reform legislation which, however unwise, was clearly within the constitutional powers of state and federal legislatures.

The Court invented, for example, a right to enter into contracts that is nowhere to be found in the Constitution. *Lochner* v. *New York*, a 1905 decision, is the classic example. The Court, dividing six to three, struck down a state statute setting maximum hours for bakers as violative of the (nonexistent) right to make contracts. Early New Deal economic regulations were routinely invalidated until a series of retirements and deaths enabled Franklin Roosevelt to remake the Court. The cultural dominance of the business class having been ended by the Great Depression, the new Court freely approved economic regulations and began to prepare the ground for the creation of new rights. An even more momentous shift came with the Court headed by Earl Warren.

The New Deal Court had been philosophically riven. Arthur Schlesinger, Jr., has described the Court as it stood in 1947. The wing occupied by Justices Black and Douglas was "concerned with settling particular cases in accordance with their own social preconceptions," a version of "value jurisprudence" identified largely with the Yale law school. Its dominant theme was equality, as shown by its heavy reliance upon the Equal Protection Clause. Schlesinger, Jr. wrote that "Black and Douglas vote less regularly for doctrines than for interests—for the trade union against the employer, for the government against the large taxpayer, for the administrative agency against the business, for the injured workman, for the unprotected defendant, against the patent holder—so that in the phrase of Professor Thomas Reed Powell 'the less favored in life will be the more favored in law.'" This was, of course, a flat contradiction of the judicial oath to "administer justice without respect to persons and do equal right to the poor and to the rich." It was as well an expression of the socialist impulse which, significantly, became the regnant outlook of the Court at a time when the American intelligentsia was socialist. As a consequence of the Warren Court's preference for equal results rather than equal justice, it politicized every branch of the law, statutes as well as the Constitution. Ironically, the Court's favored constitutional implement was the clause of the Fourteenth Amendment promising "equal protection of the laws."

Socialism, however, was then discredited. In practice it produced impoverishment and tyranny so that not even intellectuals could cling to its dream, or at least most of them could not do so publicly. Radicalism took the form of the New Left of the 1960s, which gradually grew more interested in personal freedom unrestricted by law, morals, or even the rules of self-preservation (drugs and filthy living conditions were often considered signs of "authenticity"). The New Left practiced a politics of expression and self-absorption. A vision of radical individual autonomy thus lay at the heart of their world view. There was a good deal of that in their intellectual class elders and now it is the dominant mood of the intelligentsia.

IT IS NOT too surprising, then, that a mood of radical autonomy or, if you will, moral relativism began to appear in the jurisprudence of the Supreme Court. The Court, in step with the intellectual class, has dropped the socialist drive of the Warren Court. The difference between the two Courts is shown by the differing fates of the two fields I know best, antitrust and constitutional law. The death of the socialist illusion made possible the use of basic economics to return antitrust to rationality. But the rise of moral relativism—perhaps a better term would be moral chaos—drove constitutional law in a new but no more respectable or rational direction.

Today, a lawyer who appears before the Court in a case involving antitrust, taxation, labor law, or a similar question will find his case is typically dealt with in a straightforward, lawyerly manner. But when the Court is presented with a cultural issue in a constitutional context, the Court majority usually departs from the Constitution, often indeed from any conceivable meaning of the Constitution, in order to enact an item on the modern liberal agenda, generally resulting in the enshrinement of radical individual autonomy as part of the Bill of Rights. That is signified by the Court's heavy use of the Due Process Clause's guarantee of liberty. To some considerable degree, therefore, it seems valid to say that the current Court is dominated by a gentrified form of Sixties radicalism. I do not know how otherwise to account for the absolute mess of our current jurisprudence of individual rights from abortion to pornography to homosexuality to radical feminism to ratifying the suppression of political speech, and more.

Though the justices are properly criticized for abandoning the proper judicial function in order to follow intellectual class fecklessness, responsibility for the health of the legal order does not, of course, depend entirely upon judges or even upon a reckless and rootless intellectual class. Responsibility rests as well with the practicing bar, the law schools, and, ultimately, with the public that elects or delegates to representatives the election of judges. None of these is performing well or even tolerably. The problems, not all of which may be soluble, lie in the nature of legal practice, the way law is taught, the modern conception of legal scholarship, the ideological direction of the courts, the enormously enlarged area of authority and competence appropriated by those courts, the eagerness of factions to circumvent democracy by litigation, and, finally, public incomprehension of what is and is not in our Constitution and so the public's inability to judge the judges. I have had some experience as a practitioner, professor, government lawyer before the Supreme Court, and judge; doubtless my views are colored by that fact.

WHEN COLLEGE GRADUATION approached and I was trying to decide on a career, law still recruited the young with prettified images of Holmes and Brandeis. It was Holmes who said that it was possible to live greatly in the law, a rather obscure remark that seemed meaningful at the time. A life in the law seemed to promise battle, require devotion, and reward learning—and what idealistic young man would not choose to be warrior, priest, and scholar? The reality proved to be rather different. Economic pressures have made law less of a profession and more of a business, drastically limiting the role the bar can play in maintaining the integrity of the law. Such concerns necessarily give way to an absorption with billable hours. Though it is not quite true, as a British barrister put it, that success in law depends on the ability to eat sawdust without butter, quite a bit of sawdust-munching is required.

Firms have, moreover, entered an era of giantism. When I

joined the largest law firm in Chicago, it had fifty-three lawyers with fewer than a dozen more in a Washington branch. Today the firm has over 450 lawyers in Chicago and well over 900 nationwide, and it is by no means the largest in either category. A firm of fifty-three lawyers would today be considered practically a boutique operation. Giantism produces an atmosphere more like a corporate headquarters than a partnership of the old style. Corporations are not renowned for a selfless devotion to sound public policy, nor, it turns out, is the practicing bar. That is not a criticism of either business or the bar, but merely a fact that cannot be altered.

At one time we were reconciled to the democratic unaccountability of courts by the promise that their powers would be kept within tolerable limits by the informed criticism of the bar. That has not been borne out. Practitioners have provided very little in-depth analyses of major constitutional doctrines; the organized bar has offered none. Attorneys, by and large, have not the time and energy left over from busy practices to study the fields in which the courts operate or to engage in sustained critiques. My practice was primarily in antitrust, but while it was apparent that the law was a doctrinal hodgepodge, there was no time to study it as a field; the problems present themselves case by case so that connecting links are not obvious, nor is it in either the client's or the firm's interest to have lawyers spending time on theoretical inquiries that, in any event, a busy judge is more likely to find irritating than persuasive. It is probably for that reason that the reform of antitrust law, when it occurred, came from the academy rather than from the practicing bar. Fields such as constitutional law, which rarely arise in ordinary practice, go almost entirely unexamined. Only ideological litigants, like the ACLU which is devoted to distorting constitutional law in the service of cultural leftism, have any occasion to spend a great deal of time on the subject. Moreover, since their success depends on judges, very few lawyers are willing to risk criticizing them. Bar politicians, leaders of the American Bar Association, for example, find it congenial to hobnob with judges and defend them from criticism. (The ABA, while it engages in professional training to some extent, is increasingly a culturally liberal political organization rather than a professional one, passing resolutions favoring a right to abortion, racial preferences, a universal right to food, AIDS needle-exchange programs, campaign finance reform, and opposing laws regulating sexual conduct between adults.) Its presidents make statements favoring judicial activism. So far sunk is the ABA in court idolatry that one of its presidents could actually say, "An attack on activist judges is an attack on our Constitution. It is an attack on our tripartite system of government"— thus demonstrating that he had no idea who was attacking the Constitution or what the different functions of the three branches were intended to be. Rather than providing an informed critique of the courts' performance, the ABA is a cheerleader for some of the worst tendencies of modern jurisprudence.

The exigencies of law practice discourage inquiries that have no immediate practical use. The last thing an advocate wants to tell a judge is that the case at bar presents a profound, or even a moderately interesting, question. That would suggest the case could be decided either way. His case, the lawyer must say, with every appearance of sincerity, is clear, so simple that it is hardly worth discussing, and must obviously be decided in favor of his client. The cases he cites are controlling whereas those mistakenly, and perhaps disingenuously, relied upon by his opponent are wide of the mark. So, too, with respect to policy arguments and hypothetical instances, both relied upon to show that only beneficial results will follow from accepting his position while his adversary's contentions would plunge the law into chaos and black night. It can be an exhilarating game, but some lawyers eventually find its repetition turns into drudgery. If they are lucky, they find alternatives.

While the time had come to leave the practice, I did not regret in the slightest the eight years I spent there. There was a great deal of satisfaction in winning, the excitement of the contest, the tactical maneuvering, and the camaraderie of a team working on high-stakes and difficult cases. There was the night of the "lost chord" when at 4 A.M. a colleague at last found the perfect precedent for our side and slapped the book triumphantly back on the shelf. We went down the hall for a celebratory coffee, only to discover, upon returning to the library, that we never could find that case again. Or the night in the conference room when I looked up from drafting a difficult paragraph, found that my colleague had disappeared, and finally located him sleeping on the floor underneath the table. There was the romanticism (I don't know how else to put it) of leaving the office in the first gray light before dawn, the old stone buildings of Chicago just beginning to emerge from the blackness beyond the reach of the street lamps, catching a rare cab on Michigan Boulevard to go home to Hyde Park, shower, shave, put on fresh clothes, and, my wife and children still asleep, return downtown for another day's work.

ULTIMATELY, however, that was not the intellectual life the law had seemed to promise. Litigation is a plastic art; only those who were involved remember it at all. Like working a crossword puzzle, it is absorbing while you are doing it, but, when it is done, there is nothing left. In the days and nights, for weeks on end, that a friend and I spent writing and endlessly rewriting a brief about a now-forgotten trust estate worth many millions, we could have produced, I flatter myself, a book of some worth. In the long run, however, the real value of practice to me was that I learned how the court system works. Too many students and professors are inclined to view judges, particularly Supreme Court justices, as philosopher kings. Some experience trying to persuade real-life judges would disabuse the professors, and hence their students, of that notion.

In seeking an academic position, I discovered that eight years of practice made me highly suspect. Some professors apparently thought former practitioners would tell war stories about their cases and teach students how to schmooze with the court clerk. Yale, however, with whatever reservations, appointed me to its law faculty, for which I will always be grateful. The first five years, until the student radicals arrived, were the best years of my professional life. The students were bright and argumentative. Ward Bowman, an economist, provided invaluable discussions about antitrust. Alexander Bickel—whom I count as the best friend I ever had—was equally important to my development of a theory of constitutional interpretation, though we disagreed about it. Together, we taught a seminar in Constitutional Theory. Influenced by John Stuart Mill and extrapolating from *Griswold* v. *Connecticut*, the original right of privacy case, I made the preposterous argument that the only harm government should be permitted to prevent was physical injury. Bickel said, "What if I engage in indecent exposure?" I replied that the law already had a doctrine to deal with that. "What doctrine?," Bickel asked. "De minimis non curat lex—the law does not take cognizance of trifles." That was the only time in a long relationship that he was silenced for a minute.

Bickel emphasized tradition as the only effective curb on courts. His judicial philosophy, I told our class on the First Amendment, was a combination of Edmund Burke and *Fiddler on the Roof.* That one he liked. He recognized, however, that the Warren Court had shattered whatever tradition there was left to lean upon. I, in contrast, was searching for a firm theory of when government was permitted to coerce and when it was not. Both of us, I now think, were wrong. The tradition, such as it was, is now gone forever, and I came to realize that Lord Patrick Devlin was right: "it is not possible to set theoretical limits to the power of the State to legislate against immorality."

Teaching is the best way to learn an entire field of law. Practitioners drill deeply into narrow areas in preparing a case. Academics teach across an entire field though necessarily superficially, discussing, for the most part, only the leading Supreme Court cases. Each has advantages, and, when combined, they nourish each other. When not combined, there is in each the danger of sterility. It is unfortunate that these two branches of the profession view each other with suspicion. It is even more unfortunate that sometimes the suspicion on both sides is justified. The aversion of many professors to those who practiced what the professors were supposedly teaching was astonishing. When I spoke at an appointments committee meeting against hiring young men and women just out of school or clerkships, I was met with stony expressions; nobody on the committee and few on the faculty had more than trivial experience with the day-to-day operation of the law. One exceptionally able student, urged to join the faculty, said he would like two or three years of experience first. He was told not to waste his time.

The insularity of legal academia has become a major problem. Many articles published in major law reviews are of no use to practitioners or judges but consist of philosophical exercises (at which law professors are not, to put it gently, very good), often on the trilogy familiar in the humanities—race, sex, and class. Some prestigious law schools actually award tenure to those who write stories bereft of any legal analysis about the anguish of living in an oppressive society. It may be tempting to view such follies as no more than raw material for another *Lucky Jim*, but the situation is serious. Many law students are ill-prepared for their careers and potentially dangerous to their clients; they must be socialized and in some cases educated by the law firms that hire them. Should they eventually become judges, they are all too likely to imagine that their job is to engage in the liberal philosophizing they learned in law school and for which the professoriate will applaud them.

Working in tandem with this distrust of professionalism is the strong liberal bias of law faculties. One professor said to another, with the intent that I should overhear, that it was the "shame of the law school" that it had two Republicans when no other department at Yale had any. Two out of about thirty-five was, in his view, too many by two, but he was wrong about the rest of the university: aside from the two excrescences in the law school, there was one other admitted Republican on Yale's faculty of two thousand. There surely must have been more, but they had the sense to keep their heads down.

I would not overstate the matter. There were professors who offered professional training and maintained good relationships with the practicing bar. Nor do I do wish to give the impression that I was in any way ill-treated. That was a time when liberalism was still good-humored and tolerant. Most of the faculty, if somewhat bemused by finding a conservative in their midst, were friendly and willing to hear, if not to adopt, nonliberal views. The problem was that ideas and attitudes were clustered at one end of the spectrum. Students were not exposed to the full range of opinion about law. The addition of former student radicals to faculties, moralistic men and women with harder ideological edges, seems at many schools to have made the few conservatives actually beleaguered. That is particularly true, though not exclusively so, of the tenured radicals who teach and write about constitutional law.

MY TENURE at Yale was interrupted by service as solicitor general of the United States. The solicitor general must approve any government appeals from adverse decisions in any court, federal, state, or local, and also, along with members of a relatively small staff, argue government cases in the Supreme Court. Contrary to what might be supposed, the Supreme Court is the most enjoyable court to argue before. The justices are prepared and engage in lively questioning. Not all courts are like that. There are few more disheartening experiences than arguing for half an hour or more to a judge who has not read the briefs and who sits silent and impassive throughout.

Oral argument ranks low as a spectator sport, though it can be engrossing for the direct participants, judges and lawyers who are intimately familiar with the state of play. The third party observer rarely knows the intricacies of the case, the legal terrain over which it is fought, the danger points for the advocates, the skill or lack thereof with which the lawyer finesses the difficulties and attempts to turn the case his way, and finally, as an anticlimax, the court reserves judgement and leaves the room without announcing a winner. For that reason, the memorable oral arguments are usually the disastrous ones. A single example, the argument in *Cantwell* v. *Connecticut* (1940), once a legend in the New Haven bar which I heard thirty-five years ago, may suffice. Cantwell, a Jehovah's Witness, played a phonograph record highly offensive to Catholics in a Catholic section of New Haven. A threatening crowd gathered and, after some explicit warnings, Cantwell picked up his machine and left. He was subsequently arrested and convicted of inciting a breach of the peace. When the case reached the Supreme Court, New Haven was represented by a very large and loud police court prosecutor, perhaps as a reward for his years of putting away petty criminals. As he launched into his argument, Justice Owen Roberts interrupted, as justices routinely do to clarify issues. "Counsel," he said, "I have a question." Courtroom etiquette as well as prudence dictates that the advocate stop to deal with the question. Instead, New Haven's champion is alleged to have held up his massive hand in a gesture of dismissal. "I'll come to you later." At that, Chief Justice Charles Evans Hughes intervened. "Counsel, I want to ask you a favor." "For you, anything." "Would you please answer Justice Roberts' question?" "All right." Turning to Roberts, "What's your question?" "Is it your position that the police of New Haven can arrest anyone who walks the streets of the city preaching unpopular doctrine?" "That's my position." "Are you aware that Jesus of Nazareth walked the streets of Jerusalem preaching unpopular doctrine?" "Yeah, and the cops took care of him."

The solicitor general necessarily comes to know the justices' tendencies and abilities very well. There was then, as there is today, a wide range in both characteristics. Justice Byron White was perhaps the quickest intellectually, often seeing the point well before the advocate got to it. At the other end of that spectrum was Justice Harry Blackmun. He frequently told the story, including the internal politics of the Court, of how he came to write the opinion in *Roe* v. *Wade*, by common estimation, even by those who hail the result, as one of the worst reasoned opinions of the twentieth century: in just over 51 pages of the official reports, no legal argument puts in an appearance. Blackmun, however, regarded it as the crowning glory of his judicial career and himself something of a martyr in a great cause because of the abuse he endured. I once asked him where in the Constitution he could find any support for a right to abortion. His only reply, which he seemed to regard as conclusive, was to produce a letter from a man who said he was sitting in an anteroom while his wife had an abortion and who expressed profound gratitude to Blackmun and his colleagues for making the operation legal.

Though I have no desire to pick on Blackmun in particular, he was an extreme example of one powerful tendency on the Court—the determination to reach results that cannot be even plausibly related to the Constitution. This produced, and continues to produce, vapid essays that cannot withstand even the most cursory and sympathetic analysis. A. Bartlett Giamatti, a professor of literature who became president of Yale, said to a professor of constitutional law that their endeavors were quite similar: both were engaged in discerning the meaning of ancient documents. The law professor said, "Yes, but you read Dante and I read Harry Blackmun."

Law is inescapably centered on courts. Studying what they do and say is of far more practical importance than studying the underlying subject matter, which is one reason that for the past half century the more interesting writing about the Constitution has been produced by political scientists and historians rather than lawyers. If you wanted, for example, to know the actual meaning of the religion clauses of the First Amendment, you would read such scholars as Walter Berns and Philip Hamburger, a political scientist and a legal historian, respectively, rather than the anti-historical opinions of the Court. That is why it is increasingly difficult to take law seriously as an intellectual pursuit. Intellectual development requires reading material above one's own level, not below.

The most ideological justice was probably William J. Brennan, Jr., who was also the most charming and friendly member, though his view of the judicial function was as different from my own as could be. He was the real leader of the Court in its adoption of deplorable tendencies. An affable man, his compelling attractiveness undoubtedly accounted for much of his influence with other justices. It seems likely that Brennan played a major role in converting Earl Warren, whose strong point was not conceptual thinking, from a moderate conservative into a judicial radical.

Looking back on those years, 1973 to 1977, it appears that the Court was in transition, as were the American elites to which the justices belonged and responded. Though it was still possible to win some important constitutional cases for the government—perhaps more so that it is today—the Court was moving from a sort of cultural socialism with its stress on equality of results toward a new emphasis on individual autonomy. The one thing that did not change, however, was the Court's frequent willingness to go beyond its constitutional authority to bring more aspects of American domestic policies within its control. That tendency seems to have accelerated in recent years. Robert Nisbet, a particularly insightful observer, stated the ideological situation in the law schools and the judiciary somewhat dramatically but with considerable accuracy:

> The crusading and coercing roles of the Supreme Court and the federal judiciary . . . have created a new and important model for all those whose primary aim is the wholesale reconstruction of American society. . . . There are more and more judges, more and more lawyers, and more and more law students and professors who have entered easily into a state of mind that sees in the Supreme Court precisely what Rousseau saw in his archetypical legislators and Bentham in his omnipotent magistrate: sovereign forces for permanent revolution.

The ideological movement of constitutional law can be gauged by the changes in the casebooks used in the law schools. When I began teaching the subject in 1964, most of the casebooks concerned the structural features of the Constitution—separation of powers, federalism, the scope of Congress's and the President's powers, the legitimacy and rationale of judicial supremacy, and so on. Cases involving the Bill of Rights took up less than half the book. Indeed, to a modern reader, it is amazing that in Joseph Story's *Commentaries on the Constitution of the United States*, written in 1833, the discussion of the first ten amendments, the Bill of Rights, occupies about one-fiftieth of the pages. In truth, the Bill of Rights, supplemented after the Civil War by the Fourteenth Amendment guaranteeing due process of law and the equal protection of the laws against incursions by state government, did not generate many cases until well into the twentieth century. The pace picked up with the Warren Court and has not slackened since. In the 1997 edition of a leading constitutional law casebook, Bill of Rights cases took up almost four times the space given to the structural Constitution, signifying an enormous shift from interest in the processes of government to the rights of individuals. The Bill of Rights took up about 2 percent of Story's *Commentaries* and about 73 percent of the casebook. The American public has come to regard constitutional law as little more than a list of individual rights, and they may be correct.

The reasons for this shift are no doubt various, including the multiplying confrontations of an increasingly pluralistic society, to which the judicial response has been to multiply rights. The most important reason for present purposes, however, was the 1954 discovery by the Supreme Court that it could order massive social change (the end of government racial discrimination in *Brown* v. *Board of Education*) unrelated, so the Court thought, to the meaning of the Constitution, and could prevail over strong resistance. I have argued elsewhere that *Brown* could have been justified on constitutional principles, but the crucial fact is that the Court did not think so. Encouraged to improve society further, it went on to ordain other major changes in governmental processes and in cultural and moral matters that were clearly not within the Court's constitutional authority. Thus, as Lino Graglia puts it, "The first and foremost thing to know about constitutional law . . . is that it has very little to do with the Constitution." The unpalatable truth is that the Court is making up the Constitution and has been doing so for many years.

COURTS BELOW the Supreme Court have less freedom to legislate large new principles, but judges at any level can be consciously influenced by political considerations and personal predilections. In a case with large political implications, our court clearly lacked jurisdiction, but one judge, while privately admitting that to be so, placed his decision on factual grounds because that would leave him free to decide a future case, as a ruling of lack of jurisdiction would not. "You never know," he said, "what may come down the pike next." That was lawlessness. A number of other examples come to mind. I have no doubt that my views and temperament influenced my judging, but that is inevitable, and the influence was never conscious, and a number of my colleagues on the bench could honestly say the same thing. There is a great difference between judges who, knowing it impossible to succeed entirely, do their best to eliminate views that have no proper role in reaching decisions and those who actively enforce their prejudices.

Judges belong to the class that John O'Sullivan first identified as "Olympians." The political philosopher Kenneth Minogue described the outlook of this class:

> Olympianism is the project of an intellectual elite that believes that it enjoys superior enlightenment and that its business is to spread this benefit to those living on the lower slopes of human achievement. . . . Olympianism burrowed like a parasite into the most powerful institution of the emerging knowledge economy—the universities.

From there the infection spread to other culture-shaping institutions, most notably the Supreme Court which was accused, justly in my opinion, with reasoning backwards from desired results to spurious rationales. "[T]hat is a reality," Alexander Bickel wrote, "if it be true, on which we cannot allow the edifice of judicial review to be based, for if that is all judges do, then their authority over us is totally intolerable and totally irreconcilable with the theory and practice of political democracy." Yet that is the reality upon which judicial review rests today.

The Court's dominant theme is now radical personal autonomy or moral relativism, signified by its emphasis on the liberty mentioned in the Due Process Clauses. That reliance, though repeated scores of times, is utterly illegitimate. Those clauses were clearly meant to guarantee that no one be deprived of liberty without a fair process; it has nothing to say about a fair substance of the law. History as well as the constitutional text proves that. As John Hart Ely wrote, "there is simply no avoiding the fact that the word that follows 'due' is 'process.' . . . [W]e apparently need periodic reminding that 'substantive due process' is a contradiction in terms—sort of like 'green pastel redness.'" Unfortunately, periodic reminding does no good. The Court continues on its way, judging the substance of laws according to the justices' personal opinions of what liberties we should or should not enjoy. There could be no clearer demonstration that the Court regularly and frequently orders our lives changed with a power it has no legitimate claim to wield.

THE QUESTION arises, why is the movement of judge-made constitutional law in the direction of extreme personal autonomy? It is, of course, the world view of the Olympians, but it has also come to be a feature of popular culture. Look where you will, rampant autonomy erodes discipline everywhere. Religion is a field in many ways very much like law, and both have heresies that threaten to overcome orthodoxy. The phenomenon of "cafeteria Catholics" is well known: despite the Church's doctrine, Catholic rates of contraceptive use and abortion are about the same as those of Protestants and Jews. When the Episcopal Church ordained a practicing homosexual as a bishop, appeals to scripture were brushed aside with amused disdain. A United Methodist lesbian minister was acquitted in a church trial of the charge that lesbianism was incompatible with Christianity, though it clearly is. The restraints of public decency have been abandoned on cable TV and are losing force on over-the-air TV and radio. No small part of these developments is due to the Court's advocacy of unrestrained freedom in cultural matters and its protection of obscenity and its marginalization of religion. But, equally, no small part of the Court's behavior is due to the culture in which it operates. The real doctrines of the Constitution have no more chance to control the Court than do the real doctrines of the churches to control the behavior of their clergy and parishioners.

And why are legal arguments—in law schools as much as in courts—frequently invested with so much anger, an anger that also suffuses and distorts our politics? Law is unlikely, after all, to develop an intense emotional temperature unrelated to the wider world of political and social discourse. To say that the anger is due to the culture war is accurate but hardly an explanation. An explanation that I find eminently plausible is that there is always a segment of the population, usually the intellectuals, that requires meaning in life. The decline of religion, the loss of its redemptive vision, required a new transcendent principle. The obvious, the only, candidate was, for a time, socialism.

Conservatism offers no comparable utopian goal. As Charles Krauthammer points out, the collapse of the socialist ideal has left Olympians with nothing except anger. Anger at the existing state of society was, of course, always an active ingredient in socialism. Some compensation for the loss of socialism is sought by various angry radicals in the extreme versions of feminism, environmentalism, animal rights, racial and gender preferences, homosexual rights, international control of American actions, and other causes. That anger characterizes the Democratic party, which is the party of the Olympians, and the activist groups that are what's left of socialism.

The debate within the Supreme Court is usually, though not invariably, more genteel, but the same urge to reconstruct a highly imperfect society is apparent. The Supreme Court is enacting a program of radical personal autonomy, indeed moral chaos, piece by piece, creating new and hitherto unsuspected constitutional rights: rights to abortion, homosexual sodomy (and, coming soon, homosexual marriage), freedom from religion in the public square, racial and sexual preferences. None of these is justified by the actual Bill of Rights.

I could easily multiply examples. But the underlying philosophy of the Olympians—if it deserves so dignified a name as "philosophy"—is wonderfully summed up in the famous "mystery passage" that Justice Anthony Kennedy first articulated in an opinion reaffirming the made-up constitutional right to abortion. "These matters," Justice Kennedy wrote for the Court,

> involving the most intimate and personal choices a person may make in a lifetime [abortion, etc.], choices central to personal dignity and autonomy, are central to the liberty protected by the Fourteenth Amendment. *At the heart of liberty is the right to define one's own concept of existence, of meaning, of the universe, and of the mystery of human life.* Beliefs about these matters could not define the attributes of personhood were they formed under compulsion of the State. [emphasis added]

Although this passage instantly attracted some measure of the ridicule it deserved, Justice Kennedy chose to repeat it in the majority opinion in *Lawrence* v. *Texas* (2003), which pretends to discover a constitutional right to homosexual sodomy. What other practices, we may wonder, are now "at the heart of liberty"? Kennedy's aria about "the right to define one's own concept of existence, of meaning," etc., is not simply laughable intellectually; it also tells us something grim about our future, the Court, and a people that supinely accepts such judicial diktats.

Kennedy's rhetoric is loaded with legal and cultural messages. First, and most obviously, the "mystery passage" demonstrates once again that today's Bill of Rights jurisprudence has almost nothing to do with the Bill of Rights. Once more the procedural meaning of the Due Process Clause has been transformed into an unconfined substantive judgment by a majority of the justices. When new rights are not invented out of whole cloth, as in *Lawrence*, real rights are expanded beyond all recognition. The Court is now the Olympians' heavy artillery and panzer divisions in the culture war. The "mystery passage," in particular, and the opinions on social and cultural issues, generally, demonstrate that a majority of the Court is willing to make decisions for which it can offer no intelligible argument. There is thus a sharp decline in intellectual honesty and the integrity of constitutional law. Constitutional law is no longer an intellectual discipline but a series of political impulses. I sometimes feel sorry for the editors of casebooks who accompany each opinion with a series of questions and observations about the doctrines the Court is laying down, modifying, refining, and abandoning. Doctrines don't matter; politics do.

The sanctity of these decisions is a litmus test for judicial nominees but they have become articles of faith among Democratic politicians. One of the more dismaying sights of the year was all seven candidates for the Democratic presidential nomination standing before a feminist organization obsequiously pledging undying fealty to *Roe* v. *Wade*. The Senate Democrats, along with a few Northeastern Republicans, will not confirm any nominee to the Supreme Court, and very few to any federal court, who does not express wholehearted support for that ghastly decision. To almost all Democratic senators, virtually unrestrained judicial activism in the service of the cultural Left has become the "mainstream."

IN THE HANDS of the Court, radical individualism approaches judicial nihilism. Since each individual must be permitted to define meaning for himself, it must follow that there is no allowable truth, legal or moral. Yet, as Lord Devlin observed, "What makes a society of any sort is community of ideas, not only political ideas but also ideas about the way its members should behave and govern their lives; these latter ideas are its morals." Partly as a consequence of the Supreme Court's extra-constitutional adventures, we are losing our community of ideas about moral behavior. The result is a species of legal triumphalism: When law has disintegrated the bonds of society, its common moral assumptions, there will be nothing left but law to sustain us, and law alone cannot bear that weight.

Thus, the sense of the sacred is now a mocked and withered virtue. This is no small matter. As Leszek Kolakowski put it, "Culture, when it loses its sacred sense, loses all sense." The idea of the sacred limits the sphere of the profane, which supposes that "there are no limits to the changes human life can undergo, that society is in 'in principle' an endlessly flexible thing, and that to deny this flexibility and this perfectibility is to deny man's total autonomy and thus to deny man himself." Kolakowski labels that "one of the most dangerous illusions of our civilization" because "the bottom line . . . of the ideal of total liberation is the sanctioning of force and violence and thereby, finally, of despotism and the destruction of culture." He did not perhaps take into account a judiciary like ours which has no need of force and violence to edge toward a form of despotism because its commands are obeyed on the belief that the Court is the custodian and voice of our sacred document. The irony is that that document is increasingly read as denying that anything else is sacred, and that society is, indeed, an endlessly flexible thing.

Today's justices seem to have taken their inspiration from the radically libertarian John Stuart Mill of *On Liberty*—from the Mill, that is, who endorsed the view that "society has no business *as* society to decide anything to be wrong which concerns only the individual." *This* Mill would have applauded the sentiment if not the logic of Kennedy's "mystery passage." As Gerturde Himmelfarb has pointed out, however, there was another, more sober Mill, a Mill who acknowledged that

> In all political societies which have had a durable existence, there has been some fixed point; something which men agreed in holding sacred; which it might or might not be lawful to contest in theory, but which no one could either fear or hope to see shaken in practice. . . . But when the questioning of these fundamental principles is (not an occasional disease but) the habitual condition of the body politic . . . the state is virtually in a position of civil war; and can never long remain free from it in act and fact.

That describes our culture war to a T. Examples of the denigration of the formerly sacred are numerous: the symbol of the American flag, patriotism, the idea of public decency, the centrality of religion, and even traditional marriage—all are clearly threatened if not, indeed, mortally damaged. Of all the institutions of society, perhaps only the judiciary and, most especially, the Supreme Court, as the keeper of the Constitution, is still regarded as sacred. Certainly, a majority of the justices think of the Court that way, and three of them have been explicit about the sacrosanct nature of their office. In *Planned Parenthood* v. *Casey* (1992), three of the five justices who voted to retain a right to abortion wrote of Americans who would be "tested" by following the Court's decision:

> [The American people's] belief in themselves as [a] people [who aspire to live according to the rule of law] is not readily separable from their understanding of the Court invested with the authority to decide their constitutional cases and speak before all others for their constitutional ideals. If the Court's legitimacy should be undermined, then so would the country be in its very ability to see itself through its constitutional ideals.

That the people are "tested" by their willingness to follow the puerile moralizing of judges and that their "belief in themselves" is inextricably bound to their obedience to the Court is a piece of hubris that might have been expected to produce a backlash of outrage. That it did not is worth pondering.

HAVING ESTABLISHED virtually unquestioned authority on the domestic front, judges, also without any warrant in the Constitution, appear to be contemplating roles as international statesmen. Justice Stevens, writing for four members of the Court in 1988, relied upon "the views that have been expressed by respected professional organizations, by other nations that share our Anglo-American heritage, and by leading members of the Western European community" to hold it a forbidden cruel and unusual punishment to execute a person for a capital crime committed when he was fifteen years of age. There have been other instances of reliance upon foreign decisions and statutes in interpreting the Constitution of the United States, but perhaps the most intriguing was Justice Steven Breyer's statement in 1999 that he found "useful" decisions concerning allowable delays in executions by the Privy Council of Jamaica, the Supreme Court of India, and the Supreme Court of Zimbabwe. It is puzzling how decisions handed down by obscure foreign courts in the late twentieth century shed light on the meaning of an American document written in the late eighteenth century.

The citation of foreign decisions in American constitutional opinions may be irritating, but it may also be only window-dressing: the Court would probably reach the same results without the aid of the Supreme Court of Zimbabwe. Still, Justice Sandra Day O'Connor suggests the justices will go further. She said in a recent speech that decisions by the courts of other countries could be persuasive authority in American courts. At a time, she said, when 30 percent of the United States's gross national product is internationally derived, "No institution of government can afford to ignore the rest of the world." It might seem that the one institution of government that *should* ignore the rest of the world is the one that derives its sole authority from a purely domestic source, the United States Constitution. It got worse. Justice O'Connor said the Court had found persuasive an amicus brief submitted by American diplomats saying that their jobs in foreign countries were made difficult by the practice of capital punishment in the United States. Rather than representing us to foreign nations, the diplomats were representing foreign countries in our Court. This internationalizing trend is so delightful to Olympians—though they might draw the line at Zimbabwe—that Linda Greenhouse could write with apparent approval in *The New York Times* that "it is not surprising that the justices have begun to see themselves as participants in a worldwide constitutional conversation." It would be more accurate to say that they are participants in a worldwide constitutional convention.

Perhaps we should have seen this coming. For as Minogue pointed out, "We may define Olympianism as a vision of human betterment to be achieved on a global scale by forging the peoples of the world into a single community based on the universal enjoyment of appropriate human rights. . . . Olympians instruct people, they do not obey them." And Olympians require constitutional courts to make certain their instructions stick. They may succeed. The idea of international law is catnip to some people, particularly to the intelligentsia. They may sell the notion to much of the public because it is often supposed that removing disputes from the arenas of diplomacy and force is to substitute high principle for the clash of crass interests. Those who make and ratify our treaties ought not to place authority in international courts without considering what we know about judges. Added to the usual tendency of courts with vague charters to enlarge their powers beyond anything anticipated by the law writers, there is the additional, and insoluble, problem of conflicting national interests and animosities, particularly animosity to the West in general and to the United States in particular. Nevertheless, the process of internationalizing law is taking place in our and in foreign courts without the consent of representative institutions.

In short, what we are witnessing is the homogenization of the constitutional laws of the nations of the West. And, since constitutional law is increasingly made by judges without reference to the actual constitutions they purport to be applying, there is developing an international constitutional common law. That is made possible by the fact that judges in almost all Western nations share Olympian values. Thus, we tend to see indifference or hostility to religion, the embrace of sexual permissiveness, the normalization of homosexuality, the creation of abortion rights, the classification of pornography and extreme vulgarity as protected free speech, hostility to traditional authorities, and special rights for favored ethnic minorities and, often, for women. All this leads to the Balkanization of society and the weakening of social discipline based upon a shared morality. It is difficult to say what the next developments in the judicial reconstruction of society will be. No one could have foreseen many of the developments just listed early in the twentieth century: many were not anticipated even ten or fifteen years ago. Who even a decade ago could have concluded that "homosexual marriage" was a right guaranteed by the Massachusetts state constitution (a document written by John Adams)? Or that the United States Supreme Court would appear to be on the verge of making such marriage a right nationally.

It sometimes seems that there is nothing left for judges to invent. But then one recalls the cautionary tale of the patent office commissioner who resigned in the nineteenth century because he believed all significant inventions had already been made. We may rely upon the apparently endless creativity of judges to continue to find new socially disintegrating rights in various federal, state, and foreign constitutions.

THOUGH IT MAY seem a matter for wonder that the public and its elected representatives accept all this with so little resistance, they are in fact almost completely helpless. Those who devised and ratified the Constitution had no idea what courts could become and so they built no safeguards against imperialistic judges. The framers carefully provided means for Congress to check the President and for the President to restrain Congress, but they provided no means for either of those branches to check the judiciary. Impeachment is utterly impracticable. The Jeffersonians tried that in order to replace the Federalist Supreme Court and failed. Impeachment is almost never successful unless bribery is involved. Some commentators suggest reliance on the congressional power under the Constitution to make exceptions to the Supreme Court's appellate jurisdiction. But even if the Court would accept the subtraction of its authority over a class of cases—and it is by no means certain that it would—the Constitution also provides that jurisdiction over federal constitutional questions lodges in state courts, many of which are at least as activist as the U.S. Court, and neither Congress nor state legislatures could remove it.

Only a draconian response to unconstitutional court decisions remains. The Massachusetts Supreme Judicial Court has ordered the state's legislature to amend its statutory law to permit homosexual marriage. It is, or should seem, extraordinary that a court should order a legislature to amend and enact laws. The underlying decision is so self-evidently an act of judicial usurpation of the legislative function, and so wrong as a matter of constitutional interpretation, that it might seem that any self-respecting legislature would simply refuse to comply, and if it did comply, that the governor would veto the bill. So accustomed have we become to judicial supremacy, however, that such a course sounds revolutionary. Yet there must be some means of standing up to a court that itself is behaving unconstitutionally in very serious matters.

The classic hypothetical supposes that in 1860 the southern states had claimed a constitutional right to secede (they would have had a plausible argument) and that the Court, most of whose members were southerners, had agreed and ordered Lincoln to let the states go peacefully. Should Lincoln have obediently removed federal troops from Fort Sumter and ordered the armed forces not to interfere with the secession? The question answers itself. Some issues are too important for courts to determine national policy. We may disagree about which issues are that crucial, but that there must be a line beyond which courts must not go and demand obedience seems incontrovertible. At present, we have no criteria for drawing such lines. The Court has employed the political question doctrine to discipline itself, but that doctrine rests with the discretion of the Court.

It is understandable that no legislature or governor has taken such action in the past. (Lincoln provides an exception. During the Civil War he suspended the writ of habeas corpus before Congress, which alone had the authority to do so, acted to ratify what he had done.) We have become so used to the supremacy of the courts that it might be politically dangerous for legislators to stand against judges. Defying a court's constitutional ruling, moreover, might set a dangerous precedent. The power of courts rests entirely upon moral authority granted by the perception that they stand on principle. Our sense of their fragility and fear of harming their capacity to do good restrains us. Thus the vulnerability of courts paradoxically renders them almost invulnerable. But what has happened in Massachusetts, and is likely to happen nationally, is so outrageous that a stand against an imperialistic court might be popular, and it would certainly be wise, because it would be a last-stand defense of the constitutional order.

The problems with all efforts to rein in runaway courts, including the appointment of restrained judges, are manifold, but two require mention. The first is that there is a large and powerful constituency for activist courts. The Olympians, who control virtually all the means of opinion formation, are also powerful in the Senate and will resist by any means available, including, as they are now demonstrating, the filibuster, to stop any effort to attempt to restrict courts to their proper constitutional function. In that they will be supported by a large portion of the non-Olympian public, which simply does not know what is in the Constitution. The judiciary, and most especially the Supreme Court, is held in higher esteem, with the possible exception of the churches and the military, than any other institution, public or private. And this seems true in all Western nations where judges have acquired the power of judicial review.

One reason, oddly enough, is that the Court is held in high esteem precisely because it is unelected, unrepresentative, and unaccountable—which is to say that the justices are not seen as politicians. To survive and to get anything done, politicians have to make expedient compromises. Judges, or so it is mistakenly believed, are not politicians but men and women of principle, untarnished by compromise. The public does not stop to consider that compromise gives all the players some of what they want while judicial principle usually turns out to be a zero-sum game, and, moreover that the non-elite majority is usually the loser in ideological litigation. The preference for judges over legislators seems to signify a weariness with and distrust of democracy. If so, that is an ominous development and one encouraged by judges who have insisted not only upon their supremacy but upon their superior virtue.

The appearance of other authoritarians stronger even than the Court would be an expensive cure for the ills of radical autonomy. What joys, then, has a life in law provided? What has it taught? No doubt others would answer those questions somewhat differently. In moments of despair, I sometimes advise young people, most of whom seem headed for law school, not to go into the law. A student tells me that I advised one class to take up dermatology and another that cosmology would be preferable. But I don't really mean that (except perhaps the part about cosmology). A life in the law can provide excitement, humor, interesting problems, association with interesting people, camaraderie, the satisfaction that comes from hard work well done, and money, sometimes lots of money. The academic branch of the profession provides many of the same benefits (law school professors are surprisingly well paid) and, for the ambitious, the endless pleasures of intellectual striving to understand reality in ways the courts have not. For the others, the academic life provides what some genius called the leisure of the theory class. There is the danger in both practice and teaching of middle-age burnout, but that is not inevitable and can happen in any line of work. I am going to stop telling the young to avoid the law, which was meant only half seriously anyway.

The lessons learned are somewhat more gloomy. As subjects like antitrust improved in the courts, constitutional law deteriorated, becoming increasingly little more than a cultural and political playground for judges and professors. The difficulty is that they are playing with the most profound questions of our culture, government, and social order. And, on the whole, their frivolity, and it can only be called that, has produced regrettable results. There may be hope for the academy. The students of the late Sixties and early Seventies who went on to teach constitute a lost generation of constitutional scholarship, but recently some young professors have appeared who take the study of the Constitution quite seriously, as more than a form of advocacy for desired social results. They may just conceivably make that body of law respectable intellectually in the schools. It will take a very long time to accomplish that in the courts, if it can be done at all. Because it is taking so many topics out of the hands of the people in order to please the elites, the Supreme Court has gone from being what Alexander Bickel called "the least dangerous branch" to a place where it can lay a fair claim to being the most dangerous branch. It bears endless repeating that we are now being ruled in some of our most crucial cultural and moral issues by the majority vote of a committee of nine lawyers who have the power, but certainly not the legitimate authority, to take those decisions out of our hands. There is good reason to believe that this authoritarianism has become an inherent characteristic of most judges, foreign and domestic, ever since the time they realized the full extent of their power and their relative invulnerability.

What is true in the United States is also true in other Western nations and, ominously, in international tribunals. We should resist the drive to cede control of more and more issues to such tribunals, not only because they will prove, and have proven to be anti-American, but also because the judges of such courts, often inspired by the American model, are proving to be imperialistic, eager to take issues away from representative governments, including our own. Whether the courts are American or international, we may come at last, though perhaps too late, to see the wisdom of Judge Learned Hand's observation about "the fatuity of the system which grants such powers to men it insists shall be independent of popular control."

Institutionalizing our demise: America vs. multiculturalism

Roger Kimball

*Here individuals of all nations are melted into a new race of men,
whose labours and posterity will one day cause great changes in the world.*
—J. Hector St. John de Crèvecoeur, *Letters from an American
Farmer*, 1782

*There is no room in this country for hyphenated Americanism. When I
refer to hyphenated Americans, I do not refer to naturalized Americans.
Some of the very best Americans I have ever known were naturalized
Americans, Americans born abroad. But a hyphenated American is not
an American at all. This is just as true of the man who puts "native"
before the hyphen as of the man who puts German or Irish or English or
French before the hyphen.*
—Theodore Roosevelt, 1915

*The delicate task that faces our civilization today is not to reform the
secular, rationalist orthodoxy, which has passed beyond the point of
redemption. Rather, it is to breathe new life into the older, now largely
comatose, religious orthodoxies—while resisting the counterculture as best
we can, adapting to it and reshaping it where we cannot simply resist.*
—Irving Kristol, "Countercultures," 1994

O N A RECENT TRIP to Maryland, I stopped at Baltimore
Harbor with my wife and five-year-old son to see Fort
McHenry. This was the site, in September 1814, of the Battle of

Baltimore, a decisive episode in the War of 1812. The late April afternoon was glorious: the sky an infinite azure punctuated by a flotilla of stately white clouds.

Our first stop was a modern outbuilding adjacent to the eighteenth-century fort. We crowded into a small theater with about thirty fourth-graders and their teachers to watch a short film. We learned about the origins of the war, about how the British took and burned Washington, about how at last a thousand U.S. troops under George Armistead at Fort Mc-Henry successfully defended their bastion against the British naval onslaught, saving Baltimore and turning the tide of the war.

It was (as the Duke of Wellington said of Waterloo) a "damn near thing." The British ships, anchored out of range of Armistead's cannons, pounded the fort with mortar and Congreve rocket fire over the course of twenty-five hours. Sitting on a truce ship behind the British fleet was a young American lawyer and amateur poet named Francis Scott Key. He watched as the battle raged, dappling the night sky with noisy coruscations.

Sometime before sunrise, the bombardment suddenly stopped. Key was uncertain of the battle's outcome until dawn broke and he saw the American flag fluttering above Fort McHenry. (When he had taken command, Armistead asked for an extra large flag so that "the British would have no trouble seeing it from a distance.") There would be no surrender. The Brits abandoned their plans to invade Baltimore. The war would soon be over. As soon as he caught sight of Old Glory, Francis Scott Key began scribbling what would become "The Star-Spangled Banner" on the back of a letter. He finished it in a hotel in Baltimore a day or two later. The poem was an instant hit and was soon set to "The Anacreontic Song," an eighteenth-century English drinking tune. It became the official national anthem in 1931.

The film ended and strains of the song began floating out from the loudspeakers—softly at first, then louder and louder. Everyone in the room scrambled to his feet.

O say, does that star-spangled banner yet wave
O'er the land of the free and the home of the brave?

The schoolchildren stood reverently, each with his right hand over his heart. A floor-length curtain wheeled back, flooding the room with light. There was Fort McHenry. And there, rising above it, was the American flag, waving gently in the breeze. With the possible exception of our son, who was busy attacking The Enemy with his toy F14, there wasn't a dry eye in the house.

OF COURSE, that calculated piece of theater was in part an exercise in sentimentality, a deliberate effort to manipulate our emotions. Is that a bad thing? Wallace Stevens may have been right that, in general, "sentimentality is a failure of feeling"—a sign of counterfeit emotion rather than the real thing. Nevertheless, there is a place for a bit of affirmative sentimentality in the moral economy of our society. Among other things, it provides emotional glue for our shared identity as Americans. These days, perhaps more than ever before, that identity needs glue. The essays in this book have traversed many American institutions, from music, the visual arts, and poetry to religion, law, and the military. But as we contemplate the prospects for America and its institutions in the twenty-first century, it is not only particular cultural and social institutions that deserve scrutiny. What we might call the institution of American identity—of who we are as a people— also requires our attention.

It is often said that the terrorist attacks of September 11 precipitated a new resolve throughout the nation. There is some truth to that. Certainly, the extraordinary bravery of the firefighters and other rescue personnel in New York and Washington, D.C., provided an invigorating spectacle—as did Todd "Let's roll" Beamer and his fellow passengers on United Airlines Flight 93. Having learned from their cell phones what had happened at the World Trade Center and the Pentagon, Beamer and his fellows rushed and overpowered the terrorists who had hijacked their plane. As a result, the plane crashed on a remote Pennsylvania farm instead of on Pennsylvania Avenue. Who knows how many lives their sacrifice saved?

The widespread sense of condign outrage—of horror leavened by anger and elevated by resolve—testified to a renewed sense of national purpose and identity after 9/11. Attacked, many Americans suddenly (if temporarily) rediscovered the virtue of patriotism. At the beginning of his remarkable book *Who Are We? The Challenges to America's National Identity* (2004), the Harvard political scientist Samuel Huntington recalls a certain block on Charles Street in Boston. At one time, American flags flew in front of a U.S. Post Office and a liquor store. Then the Post Office stopped displaying the flag, so on September 11, 2001, the flag was flying only in front of the liquor store. Within two weeks, seventeen American flags decorated that block of Charles Street, in addition to a huge flag suspended over the street close by. "With their country under attack," Huntington notes, "Charles Street denizens rediscovered their nation and identified themselves with it."

Was that rediscovery anything more than a momentary passion? Huntington reports that within a few months, the flags on Charles Street began to disappear. By the time the first anniversary rolled around in September 2002, only four were left flying. True, that is four times more than were there on September 10, 2001, but it is less than a quarter of the number that populated Charles Street at the end of September 2001.

THERE ARE SIMILAR anecdotes from around the country—an access of flag-waving followed by a relapse into indifference. Does it mean that the sudden upsurge of patriotism in the weeks following 9/11 was only, as it were, skin deep? Or perhaps it merely testifies to the fact that a sense of permanent emergency is difficult to maintain, especially in the absence of fresh attacks. Is our sense of ourselves as Americans patent only when challenged? "Does it," Huntington asks, "take an Osama bin Laden . . . to make us realize that we are Americans? If we do not experience recurring destructive attacks, will we return to the fragmentation and eroded Americanism before September 11?"

One hopes that the answer is No. The behavior of those schoolchildren at Fort McHenry—behavior that was, I am happy to report, quietly encouraged by their teachers—suggests that the answer cannot simply be No. But I fear that for every schoolchild standing at attention for the National Anthem, there is a teacher or lawyer or judge or politician or ACLU employee militating against the hegemony of the dominant culture, the insupportable intrusion of white, Christian, "Eurocentric" values into the curriculum, the school pageant, the town green, etc., etc. The demonstration of national character and resolve following September 11 was extraordinary. It did not, however, purchase immunity from the virus of cultural dissolution. The usually perceptive commentator Max Boot, writing about the issue of gay marriage, remarked in passing that "no one who saw the response to 9/11 can think we are soft or decadent" or that "America is in cultural decline." Alas, the display of national heroism and resolve following 9/11 has had little if any effect on the forces behind the fragmentation and "eroded Americanism" to which Huntington refers.

Those forces are not isolated phenomena; they are not even confined to America. They are part of a global crisis in national identity, coefficients of the sudden collapse of self-confidence in the West—a collapse that shows itself in everything from swiftly falling birthrates in "old Europe" to the attack on the whole idea of the sovereign nation state. It is hard to avoid thinking that a people that has lost the will to reproduce or govern itself is a people on the road to destruction.

Only a few years ago we were invited to contemplate the pleasant spectacle of the "end of history" and the establishment of Western-style liberal democracy, attended by the handmaidens of prosperity and rising standards of health care and education, the world over. Things look rather different now as a variety of centrifugal forces threatens to undermine the sources of national identity and, with it, the sources of national strength and the security which that strength underwrites.

The threat shows itself in many ways, from culpable complacency to the corrosive imperatives of "multiculturalism" and political correctness. (I use scare quotes because what generally travels under the name of "multiculturalism" is really a form of mono-cultural animus directed against the dominant culture.) In essence, as Huntington notes, multiculturalism is "anti-European civilization. . . . It is basically an anti-Western ideology." The multiculturalists claim to be fostering a progressive cultural cosmopolitanism distinguished by superior sensitivity to the downtrodden and dispossessed. In fact, they encourage an orgy of self-flagellating liberal guilt as impotent as it is insatiable. The "sensitivity" of the multiculturalist is an index not of moral refinement but of moral vacuousness. As the French essayist Pascal Bruckner observed, "An overblown conscience is an empty conscience."

> Compassion ceases if there is nothing but compassion, and revulsion turns to insensitivity. Our "soft pity," as Stefan Zweig calls it, is stimulated, because guilt is a convenient substitute for action where action is impossible. Without the power to do anything, sensitivity becomes our main aim. The aim is not so much to do anything, as to be judged. Salvation lies in the verdict that declares us to be wrong.

Multiculturalism is a moral intoxicant; its thrill centers around the emotion of superior virtue; its hangover subsists on a diet of ignorance and blighted "good intentions."

As Mark Steyn has shown earlier in this book, wherever the imperatives of multiculturalism have touched the curriculum, they have left broad swaths of anti-Western attitudinizing competing for attention with quite astonishing historical blindness. Courses on minorities, women's issues, the Third World proliferate; the teaching of mainstream history slides into oblivion. "The mood," Arthur Schlesinger wrote in *The*

Disuniting of America (1992), his excellent book on the depredations of multiculturalism, "is one of divesting Americans of the sinful European inheritance and seeking redemptive infusions from non-Western cultures."

A profound ignorance of the milestones of American culture is one predictable result of this mood. The statistics have become proverbial. Huntington quotes one poll from the 1990s showing that while 90 percent of Ivy League students could identify Rosa Parks, only 25 percent could identify the author of the words "government of the people, by the people, for the people." (Yes, it's the Gettysburg Address.) In a 1999 survey, 40 percent of seniors at fifty-five top colleges could not say within half a century when the Civil War was fought. Another study found that more high school students knew who Harriet Tubman was than knew that Washington commanded the American army in the revolution or that Abraham Lincoln wrote the Emancipation Proclamation. Doubtless you have your own favorite horror story.

But multiculturalism is not only an academic phenomenon. The attitudes it fosters have profound social as well as intellectual consequences. One consequence has been a sharp rise in the phenomenon of immigration without—or with only partial—assimilation: a dangerous demographic trend that threatens American identity in the most basic way.

These various agents of dissolution are also elements in a wider culture war: the contest to define how we live and what counts as the good in the good life. Anti-Americanism occupies such a prominent place on the agenda of the culture wars precisely because the traditional values of American identity—articulated by the Founders and grounded in a commitment to individual liberty and public virtue—are deeply at odds with the radical, de-civilizing tenets of the "multiculturalist" enterprise.

To get a sense of what has happened to the institution of American identity, compare Robert Frost's performance at John F. Kennedy's inauguration in 1961 with Maya Angelou's performance thirty-two years later. As Huntington reminds us, Frost spoke of the "heroic deeds" of America's founding, an event, he said, that with "God's approval" ushered in "a new order of the ages." By contrast, Maya Angelou never mentioned the words "America" or "American." Instead, she identified twenty-seven ethnic or religious groups that had suffered repression because of America's "armed struggles for profit," "cynicism," and "brutishness."

Repellent though Maya Angelou's performance was, it did seem the appropriate rhetorical embroidery to welcome Bill Clinton, a president infatuated with the blandishments of multiculturalism and who sought a third "great revolution" to emancipate America from the legacy of European civilization and its Anglo-Protestant values. It has to be acknowledged that considerable progress toward that goal was made during his administration.

A favorite weapon in the armory of multiculturalism is the lowly hyphen. When we speak of an African-American or Mexican-American or Asian-American these days, the aim is not descriptive but deconstructive. There is a polemical edge to it, a provocation. The hyphen does not mean "American, but hailing at some point in the past from someplace else." It means "only provisionally American: my allegiance is divided at best." (I believe something similar can be said about the feminist fad for hyphenating the bride's maiden name with her husband's surname. It is a gesture of independence that is also a declaration of divided loyalty.) It is curious to what extent the passion for hyphenation is fostered more by the liberal elite than the populations it is supposedly meant to serve. How does it serve them? Presumably by enhancing their sense of "self-esteem." Frederick Douglass saw through this charade some one hundred and fifty years ago. "No one idea," he wrote, "has given rise to more oppression and persecution toward colored people of this country than that which makes Africa, not America, their home."

The indispensable Ward Connerly would agree. Connerly has campaigned vigorously against affirmative action in

California. This of course has made him a pariah among the politically correct elite. It has also resulted in some humorous exchanges, such as this telephone interview with a reporter from *The New York Times* in 1997.

REPORTER: What are you?
CONNERLY: I am an American.
REPORTER: No, no, no! What *are* you?
CONNERLY: Yes, yes, yes! I am an American.
REPORTER: That is not what I mean. I was told that you are African American. Are you ashamed to be African American?
CONNERLY: No, I am just proud to be an American.

Connerly went on to explain that his ancestry included Africans, French, Irish, and American Indians. It was too much for the poor reporter from our Paper of Record: "What does that make you?" he asked in uncomprehending exasperation. I suspect he was not edified by Connerly's cheerful response: "That makes me all-American."

The multicultural passion for hyphenation is not simply a fondness for syntactical novelty. It also bespeaks a commitment to the centrifugal force of anti-American tribalism. The division marked by the hyphen in African-American (say) denotes a political stand. It goes hand-in-hand with other items on the index of liberal desiderata—the redistributive impulse behind efforts at "affirmative action," for example. Affirmative action was undertaken in the name of equality. But, as always seems to happen, it soon fell prey to the Orwellian logic from which the principle that "All animals are equal" gives birth to the transformative codicil: "but some animals are more equal than others."

AFFIRMATIVE ACTION is Orwellian in a linguistic sense, too, since what announces itself as an initiative to promote equality winds up enforcing discrimination precisely on the grounds that it was meant to overcome. Thus we are treated to the delicious, if alarming, contradiction of college applications that declare their commitment to evaluate candidates "without regard to race, gender, religion, ethnicity, or national origin" on page 1 and then helpfully inform you on page 2 that it is to your advantage to mention if you belong to any of the following designated victim groups. Among other things, a commitment to multiculturalism seems to dull one's sense of contradiction.

The whole history of affirmative action is instinct with that irony. The original effort to redress legitimate grievances—grievances embodied, for instance, in the discriminatory practices of Jim Crow—have mutated into new forms of discrimination. In 1940, Franklin Roosevelt established the Fair Employment Practices Committee because blacks were openly barred from war factory jobs. But what began as a Presidential Executive Order in 1961 directing government contractors to take "affirmative action" to assure that people be hired "without regard" for sex, race, creed, color, etc., has resulted in the creation of vast bureaucracies dedicated to discovering, hiring, and advancing people chiefly on the basis of those qualities. White is black, freedom is slavery, "without regard" comes to mean "with regard for nothing else."

Had he lived to see the evolution of affirmative action, Tocqueville would have put such developments down as examples of how in democratic societies the passion for equality tends to trump the passion for liberty. The fact that the effort to enforce equality often results in egregious inequalities he would have understood to be part of the "tutelary despotism" that "extends its arms over society as a whole; it covers its surface with a network of small, complicated, painstaking, uniform rules through which the most original minds and the most vigorous souls cannot clear a way to surpass the crowd."

Multiculturalism and "affirmative action" are allies in the assault on the institution of American identity. As such, they oppose the traditional understanding of what it means to be an American—an understanding hinted at in 1782 by the French-born American farmer J. Hector St. John de Crèvecoeur in his famous image of America as a country in which "individuals of all nations are melted into a new race of men." This crucible of American identity, this "melting pot," has two aspects. The negative aspect involves disassociating oneself from the cultural imperatives of one's country of origin. One sheds a previous identity before assuming a new one. One might preserve certain local habits and tastes, but they are essentially window-dressing. In essence one has left the past behind in order to become an American citizen.

The positive aspect of advancing the melting pot involves embracing the substance of American culture. The 1795 code for citizenship lays out some of the formal requirements.

> I do solemnly swear (1) to support the Constitution of the United States; (2) to renounce and abjure absolutely and entirely all allegiance and fidelity to any foreign prince, potentate, state, or sovereignty of whom or which the applicant was before a subject or citizen; (3) to support and defend the Constitution and the laws of the United States against all enemies, foreign and domestic; (4) to bear true faith and allegiance to the same; and (5) (A) to bear arms on behalf of the United States when required by law, or (B) to perform noncombatant service in the Armed Forces of the United States when required by law . . .

For over two hundred years, this oath had been required of those wishing to become citizens. In 2003, Huntington tells us, federal bureaucrats launched a campaign to rewrite and weaken it.

I SHALL SAY more about what constitutes the substance of American identity in a moment. For now, I want to underscore the fact that this project of Americanization has been an abiding concern since the time of the Founders. "We must see our people more Americanized," John Jay declared in the 1780s. Jefferson concurred. Teddy Roosevelt repeatedly championed the idea that American culture, the "crucible in which all the new types are melted into one," was "shaped from 1776 to 1789, and our nationality was definitely fixed in all its essentials by the men of Washington's day."

It is often said that America is a nation of immigrants. In fact, as Huntington points out, America is a country that was initially a country of *settlers*. Settlers precede immigrants and make their immigration possible. The culture of those mostly English-speaking, predominantly Anglo-Protestant settlers defined American culture. Their efforts came to fruition with the generation of Franklin, Washington, Jefferson, Hamilton, and Madison. The Founders are so denominated because they founded, they inaugurated a state. Immigrants were those who came later, who came from elsewhere, and who became American by embracing the Anglophone culture of the original settlers. The English language, the rule of law, respect for individual rights, the industriousness and piety that flowed from the Protestant work ethic—these were central elements in the culture disseminated by the Founders. And these were among the qualities embraced by immigrants when they became Americans. "Throughout American history," Huntington notes, "people who were not white Anglo-Saxon Protestants have become Americans by adopting America's Anglo-Protestant culture and political values. This benefitted them and the country."

Justice Louis Brandeis outlined the pattern in 1919. Americanization, he said, means that the immigrant "adopts the clothes, the manners, and the customs generally prevailing here . . . substitutes for his mother tongue the English language" and comes "into complete harmony with our ideals and aspirations and cooperate[s] with us for their attainment." Until the 1960s, the Brandeis model mostly prevailed. Protestant, Catholic, and Jewish groups, understanding that assimilation was the best ticket to stability and social and economic success, eagerly aided in the task of integrating their charges into American society.

The story is very different today. In America, there is a dangerous new tide of immigration from Asia, a variety of

Muslim countries, and Latin America, especially from Mexico. The tide is new not only chronologically but also in substance. First, there is the sheer matter of numbers. More than 2,200,000 legal immigrants came to the U.S. from Mexico in the 1990s alone. The number of illegal Mexican immigrants is staggering. So is their birth rate. Altogether there are more than 8 million Mexicans in the U.S. Some parts of the Southwest are well on their way to becoming what Victor Davis Hanson calls "Mexifornia," "the strange society that is emerging as the result of a demographic and cultural revolution like no other in our times." A professor of Chicano Studies at the University of New Mexico gleefully predicts that by 2080 parts of the Southwest United States and Northern Mexico will join to form a new country, "La Republica del Norte."

The problem is not only one of numbers, though. Earlier immigrants made—and were helped and goaded by the ambient culture to make—concerted efforts to assimilate. Important pockets of these new immigrants are not assimilating, not learning English, not becoming or thinking of themselves primarily as Americans. The effect of these developments on American identity is disastrous and potentially irreversible.

Such developments are abetted by the left-wing political and educational elites of this country, whose dominant theme is the perfidy of traditional American values. Hence the passion for multiculturalism and the ideal of ethnic hyphenation that goes with it. This has done immense damage in schools and colleges as well as in the population at large. By removing the obligation to master English, multiculturalism condemns whole sub-populations to the status of permanent second-class citizens. By removing the obligation to adopt American values, it fosters what the German novelist Hermann Broch once called a "value vacuum," a sense of existential emptiness that breeds anomie and the pathologies of nihilism.

As if in revenge for this injustice, however, multiculturalism also weakens the social bonds of the community at large. The price of imperfect assimilation is imperfect loyalty. Take the movement for bilingualism. Whatever it intended in theory, in practice it means *not* mastering English. It has notoriously left its supposed beneficiaries essentially monolingual, often semi-lingual. The only *bi* involved is a passion for bifurcation, which is fed by the accumulated resentments instilled by the anti-American multicultural orthodoxy. Every time you call directory assistance or some large corporation and are told "Press One for English" and "Para español oprime el numero dos" it is another small setback for American identity.

Meanwhile, many prominent academics and even busi-nessmen come bearing the gospel of what John Fonte has dubbed "transnational progressivism"—an anti-patriotic stew of politically correct ideas and attitudes distinguished partly by its penchant for vague but virtuous-sounding abstractions, partly by its moral smugness. It is a familiar litany. The phi-losopher Martha Nussbaum warns that "patriotic pride" is "morally dangerous" while Princeton's Amy Gutmann reveals that she finds it "repugnant" for American students to learn that they are "above all, citizens of the United States" instead of partisans of her preferred abstraction, "democratic human-ism." New York University's Richard Sennett denounces "the evil of a shared national identity" and concludes that the ero-sion of national sovereignty is "basically a positive thing." Cecilia O'Leary of American University identifies American patriotism as a right-wing, militaristic, male, white, Anglo, and repressive force, while Peter Spiro of Hofstra University says it "is increasingly difficult to use the word 'we' in the context of international affairs."

Of course, whenever the word "patriotism" comes up in left-wing circles, there is sure to be some allusion to Samuel Johnson's observation that "patriotism is the last refuge of scoundrels." Right on cue, George Lipsitz of the University of California sniffs that "in recent years refuge in patriotism has been the first resort of scoundrels of all sorts." Naturally, Dr. Johnson's explanation to Boswell that he did not mean to dis-parage "a real and generous love of our country" but only that "pretended patriotism" that is a "cloak for self-interest" is left out of account.

The bottom line is that the traditional ideal of a distinctive American identity, forged out of many elements but unified around a core of beliefs, attitudes, and commitments is now up for grabs. One academic epitomized the established attitude among our left-liberal elites when she expressed the hope that the United States would "never again be culturally 'united,' if united means 'unified' in beliefs and practices." Nor is this merely an academic crotchet. Many politicians—and, as Robert Bork shows earlier in this volume, many courts—have colluded in spreading the multicultural gospel. The nation's motto—*E pluribus unum*—was chosen by Franklin, Jefferson, and Adams to express the ideal of faction- and heritage-transcending unity. America forged one people out of many peoples. Vice President Al Gore interpreted the tag to mean "Within one, many." This might have been inadvertence. It might have been simple ignorance. It might have been deliberate ideological provocation. Which is worst?

The combined effect of the multicultural enterprise has been to undermine the foundation of American national identity. Huntington speaks dramatically but not inaptly of "Deconstructing America." What he has in mind are not the linguistic tergiversations of a Jacques Derrida or Michel Foucault but the efforts—politically if not always intellectually allied efforts—to disestablish the dominant culture by fostering a variety of subversive attitudes, pieces of legislation, and judicial interventions. "The deconstructionists," Huntington writes,

> promoted programs to enhance that status and influence of subnational racial, ethnic, and cultural groups. They encouraged immigrants to maintain their birth-country cultures, granted them legal privileges denied to native-born Americans, and denounced the idea of Americanization as un-American. They pushed the rewriting of history syllabi and textbooks so as to refer to the "peoples" of the United States in place of the single people of the Constitution. They urged supplementing or substituting for national history the history of subnational

groups. They downgraded the centrality of English in American life and pushed bilingual education and linguistic diversity. They advocated legal recognition of group rights and racial preferences over the individual rights central to the American Creed. They justified their actions by theories of multiculturalism and the idea that diversity rather than unity or community should be America's overriding value. The combined effect of these efforts was to promote the deconstruction of the American identity that had been gradually created over three centuries.

Taken together, Huntington concludes, "these efforts by a nation's leaders to deconstruct the nation they governed were, quite possibly, without precedent in human history."

THE VARIOUS movements to deconstruct American identity and replace it with a multicultural "rainbow" or supra-national bureaucracy have made astonishing inroads in the last few decades and especially in the last several years. And, as Huntington reminds us, the attack on American identity has counterparts elsewhere in the West wherever the doctrine of multiculturalism has trumped the cause of national identity. The European Union—whose unelected leaders are as dedicated to multicultural shibboleths as they are to rule by top-down, anti-democratic bureaucracy—is a case in point. But the United States, the most powerful national state, is also the most attractive target for deconstruction.

It is a curious development that Huntington traces. In many respects, it corroborates James Burnham's observation, in *Suicide of the West* (1964), that "liberalism permits Western civilization to be reconciled to dissolution." For what we have witnessed with the triumph of multiculturalism is a kind of hypertrophy or perversion of liberalism, as its core doctrines are pursued to the point of caricature. As the Australian philosopher David Stove pointed out, we in the West "set ourselves to achieve a society which would be maximally-tolerant. But that resolve not only gives maximum scope to the activities of those who have set themselves to achieve the maximally-intolerant society. It also, and more importantly, paralyzes our powers of resistance to them." "Freedom," "diversity," "equality," "tolerance," even "democracy"—how many definitive liberal virtues have been redacted into their opposites by the imperatives of political correctness? If a commitment to "diversity" mandates bilingual education, then we must institute bilingual education, even if it results in the cultural disenfranchisement of those it was meant to benefit. The passion for equality demands "affirmative action," even though the process of affirmative action depends upon treating people unequally. The French philosopher Jean-François Revel put it well when he observed, in 1970, that "Democratic civilization is the first in history to blame itself because another power is trying to destroy it."

If there is a bright spot in the portrait that Huntington paints, it revolves around the fact that the centrifugal forces of multiculturalism are espoused chiefly by the intellectual and bureaucratic elite, not ordinary people. Of course, one might ask how the beliefs of ordinary people can prevail against the combined forces of the courts, the educational establishment, the "mainstream" media, and much popular culture? It is hard to say—at least, it is hard to say anything cheerful. But Huntington does provide several rays of hope. There are many movements to "take back America," to resuscitate the core values that, traditionally, have defined us as Americans. Indeed, Huntington's book may be regarded as a manifesto on behalf of that battle. The home-schooling movement is one example. Only a few years ago, it was a fringe phenomenon, allied almost exclusively to certain conservative evangelical sects. Today, home schoolers come from every religious and social background. In 1990–1991, 76,000 children were home-schooled. The estimate for 2004 is about 2 million. That explosion is not only evidence of disenchantment with the intellectual failure of public schools: much more it betokens disenchantment with the moral tenor of public education.

We stand at a crossroads. The future of America hangs in the balance. Huntington outlines several possible courses that the country might take, from the loss of our core culture to an attempt to revive the "discarded and discredited racial and ethnic concepts" that, in part, defined pre-mid-twentieth century America.

Huntington argues for another alternative. If we are to preserve our identity as a nation we need to preserve the core values that defined that identity. This is a point that the political philosopher Lord Patrick Devlin made in his book *The Enforcement of Morals* (1965):

> [S]ociety means a community of ideas; without shared ideas on politics, morals, and ethics no society can exist. Each one of us has ideas about what is good and what is evil; they cannot be kept private from the society in which we live. If men and women try to create a society in which there is no fundamental agreement about good and evil they will fail; if having based it upon a common set of core values, they surrender those values, it will disintegrate. For society is not something that can be kept together physically; it is held by the invisible but fragile bonds of common beliefs and values. . . . A common morality is part of the bondage of a good society, and that bondage is part of the price of society which mankind must pay.

What are those beliefs and values? They embrace several things, including religion. You wouldn't know it from watching CNN or reading *The New York Times*, but there is a huge religious revival taking place now, affecting just about every part of the globe except Western Europe, which slouches towards godlessness almost as fast as it slouches towards bankruptcy and demographic collapse. (Neither Spain nor Italy are producing enough children to replace their existing populations, while the Muslim birthrate in France continues to soar).

Things look different in America. For if America is a vigorously secular country—which it certainly is—it is also a deeply religious one. It always has been. Tocqueville was simply minuting the reality he saw around him when he noted that "On my arrival in the United States the religious aspect of the country was the first thing that struck my attention." As G. K. Chesterton put it a century after Tocqueville, America is "a nation with the soul of a church." Even today, America is a country where an astonishing 92 percent of the population says it believes in God and 80 to 85 percent of the population identifies itself as Christian. Hence Huntington's call for a return to America's core values is also a call to embrace the religious principles upon which the country was founded, "a recommitment to America as a deeply religious and primarily Christian country, encompassing several religious minorities adhering to Anglo-Protestant values, speaking English, main-taining its cultural heritage, and committed to the principles" of political liberty as articulated by the Founders.

Naturally, Huntington has been sharply criticized for prescribing a return to "Anglo-Protestant values" as an an-tidote for faltering American identity. For example, Michiko Kakutani, reviewing *Who Are We?* for *The New York Times*, dismissed it as a "portentous," "crotchety," "highly polemical book" that merely "recycl[ed] arguments from earlier thinkers" while imparting to them a "bellicose new spin." Oh dear. Kakutani was particularly exercised by Huntington's criticism of multiculturalism and his advocacy of Anglo-Protestant values. But she misses something important. For Huntington is careful to stress that what he offers is an "argu-ment for the importance of Anglo-Protestant culture, not for the importance of Anglo-Protestant people." That is, he argues not on behalf of a particular ethnic group but on behalf of a culture and set of values that "for three and a half centuries have been embraced by Americans of all races, ethnicities, and religions and that have been the source of their liberty, unity, power, prosperity, and moral leadership."

American identity was originally founded on four things: ethnicity, race, ideology, and culture. By the mid-twentieth century, ethnicity and race had sharply receded in importance.

Indeed, one of America's greatest achievements is having eliminated the racial and ethnic components that historically were central to its identity. Ideology—the package of Enlightened liberal values championed by the Founders—are crucial but too thin for the task of forging or preserving national identity by themselves. ("A nation defined only by political ideology," Huntington notes, "is a fragile nation.") Which is why Huntington, like virtually all of the Founders, explicitly grounded American identity in religion.

Opponents of religion in the public square never tire of reminding us that there is no mention of God in the Constitution. This is true. Neither is the word "virtue" mentioned. But both are presupposed. For the American Founders, as the historian Gertrude Himmelfarb points out, virtue, grounded in religion, was presumed "to be rooted in the very nature of man and as such . . . reflected in the *moeurs* of the people and in the traditions and informal institutions of society." It is also worth mentioning that if the Constitution is silent on religion, the Declaration of Independence is voluble, speaking of "nature's God," the "Creator," "the supreme judge of the world," and "divine Providence."

We are often told that the Founders were, almost to a man, Deists listing toward atheism. Michael Novak has done much to disabuse us of that idea. Himmelfarb carries his work further in her book *The Roads to Modernity: The British, French, and American Enlightenments* (2004). She shows how a distinctively American form of Enlightenment, deeply informed by the British Enlightenment and differing sharply from the anti-clerical rationalism of the French variety, nourished the Founders' understanding of politics and what constitutes the good life for man. It was a form of Enlightenment that, Himmelfarb observes, regarded religion as an indispensable ally of reason, not an enemy of reason. In America, Tocqueville observed, unlike in France, the "spirit of religion" and "the spirit of freedom" support rather than oppose each other. "Religion," he wrote, sees in civil freedom a noble exercise of the faculties of man; in the political world, a field left by the Creator to the efforts of intelligence. . . . Freedom sees in religion the companion of its struggles and its triumphs, . . . the divine source of its rights. It considers religion as the safeguard of mores; and mores as the guarantee of laws.

Today, we are encouraged to interpret "freedom of religion" to mean "freedom from religion"—unless, of course, the religion in question is suitably exotic. (One recalls Chesterton's observation that "Religious liberty might be supposed to mean that everybody is free to discuss religion. In practice it means that hardly anybody is allowed to mention it.") The ACLU is tortured by the thought of school children uttering the phrase "under God"; in June 2002, the Ninth Circuit Court of Appeals in California ruled that the phrase violated the principle of the separation of church and state. Yet Florida (among other states) allows Muslim women to pose for their driver's license photographs with their faces veiled. The Founders would have been astounded—not to say alarmed— at this selective exclusion of religion from public life. They would have been even more astounded that it has been carried forward under the aegis of the First Amendment, perhaps the most wilfully misinterpreted text in America legal history.

Notwithstanding the ACLU and their allies, Himmelfarb is surely right that "The separation of church and state, however interpreted, did not signify the separation of church and society." Benjamin Rush, one of the signers of the Declaration of Independence, summed up the common attitude of the Founders toward religion when he insisted that "The only foundation for a useful education in a republic is to be laid in religion. Without it there can be no virtue, and without virtue there can be no liberty, and liberty is the object of all republican governments." George Washington concurred: "Reason and experience both forbid us to expect that national morality can prevail in exclusion of religious principles."

Even Benjamin Franklin, one of the least religious of the

Founders, wanted some mention of God in the Constitution and, according to Himmelfarb, proposed that the proceedings of the Constitutional Convention begin with a daily prayer. Militant secularists will quote Jefferson's brusque dismissal of religion in *Notes on the State of Virginia*: "It does me no injury for my neighbor to say there are twenty gods or no god. It neither picks my pocket nor breaks my leg." But they somehow never get around to quoting the passage that occurs a few pages later: "Can the liberties of a nation be thought secure when we have removed their only firm basis, a conviction in the minds of people that these liberties are the gift of God?" As president, Himmelfarb notes, Jefferson was even more respectful of religion, and specifically Christianity, as the foundation of liberty and public virtue. On his way to church one Sunday, Jefferson was met by a friend.

> "You going to church Mr. J. You do not believe a word in it."
>
> "Sir [Jefferson replied], no nation has ever yet existed or been governed without religion. Nor can be. The Christian religion is the best religion that has been given to man and I as chief Magistrate of this nation am bound to give it the sanction of my example. Good morning Sir."

It is sometimes objected that, whatever lip-service the Founders gave to Christianity, their conception of religion was (the word "merely" implicitly supplied) pragmatic or utilitarian. Well, there was no doubt that the Founders thought religion was pragmatic, that is, socially useful, i.e., not merely a private affair with God. But why the implicit "merely"? As Himmelfarb argues, "this view of religion is not unworthy."

> To look upon religion as the ultimate source of morality, and hence of a good society and a sound policy, is not demeaning to religion. On the contrary, it pays religion—and God—the great tribute of being essential to the welfare of mankind. And it does credit to man as well, who is deemed capable of subor-

dinating his lower nature to his higher, of venerating and giving obeisance to something above himself.

No nation lasts forever. An external enemy may eventually overrun and subdue it; internal forces of dissolution and decadence may someday undermine it, leaving it prey to more vigorous competitors. Sooner or later it succumbs. The United States is the most powerful nation the world has ever seen. Its astonishing military might, economic productivity, and political vigor are unprecedented. But someday, as Huntington reminds us, it too will fade or perish as Athens, Rome, and other great civilizations have faded or perished. Is the end, or the beginning of the end, at hand? No one's crystal ball is sufficiently clairvoyant to allow us to say. For decades —no, longer—we have been getting bulletins about the decline of the West, the rise and (especially) the fall of great powers, etc., etc.

So far, the West—or at least the United States—has disappointed its self-appointed undertakers. How do we stand now, at the dawn of the twenty-first century? It is worth remembering that besieged nations do not always succumb to the forces, external or internal, that threaten them. Sometimes, they muster the resolve to fight back successfully, to renew themselves. Today, America faces a new external enemy in the form of militant Islam and global terrorism. That minatory force, though murderous, will fail in proportion to our resolve to defeat it. Do we still possess that resolve? Inseparable from resolve is self-confidence, faith in the essential nobility of one's regime and one's way of life. To what extent do we still possess, still practice that faith?

AMERICA ALSO FACES numerous internal threats, from the rise of immigration without assimilation to the dissolute forces of cultural decadence and radical multiculturalism. The forces of multiculturalism preach the dogma of bureaucratic cosmopolitanism. They encourage us to shed what is distinctively American in order to accommodate the quivering sensitivities of "humanity"—that imperious abstraction whose exigent mandates are updated regularly by such bodies as the United Nations, the World Court, and their allies in the professoriate and the liberal media. Huntington is right that "America cannot become the world and still be America." We face a choice between a multicultural future and an American future. Which will it be?

In *Washington's Crossing* (2004), his marvelous book on George Washington's leadership in the Revolutionary War, David Hackett Fischer argues that America won the war against a much larger, better trained, and better equipped army partly because of the "moral strength of a just cause" and partly because of "religion": "Americans," he notes, "were a deeply spiritual people, with an abiding faith that sustained them in adversity." Americans are still a deeply spiritual people, though many of our intellectual, cultural, and political leaders would have us forget that fact. In 1973, the commentator Irving Kristol observed that

> for well over a hundred and fifty years now, social critics have been warning us that bourgeois society was living off the accumulated moral capital of traditional religion and traditional moral philosophy, and that once this capital was depleted, bourgeois society would find its legitimacy ever more questionable. These critics were never, in their lifetime, either popular or persuasive. The educated classes of liberal-bourgeois society simply could not bring themselves to believe that religion was that important to a polity. *They* could live with religion or morality as a purely private affair, and they could not see why everyone else—after a proper secular education, of course—could not do likewise.

As the twenty-first century begins, we have a glorious opportunity—perhaps it is the last such opportunity—to start replenishing some of the moral capital we have been so profligate with in recent decades. Some sages assure us that our fate is sealed, that inevitable forces have scripted the (unhappy) denouement of American civilization. I do not believe them. Those children I saw at Fort McHenry are—potentially—insurance against that gloomy prognostication. They, and thousands like them, are potent weapons against the dissolutions that threaten us. Will we have the wit to use those weapons effectively? Samuel Huntington urges us to foster "those qualities that have defined America since its founding," above all the Anglo-Protestant values that wed liberty to order. Many in the liberal, multicultural establishment have rejected Huntington's vision of American unity as nativist or worse. I believe that his critics are wrong. Benjamin Franklin got to the nub of the matter when, more than two hundred years ago, he observed that "We must all hang together or assuredly we shall all hang separately."

Contributors

ROBERT H. BORK is currently a professor at the Ave Maria School of Law in Ann Arbor, Michigan and the Tad and Diane Taube Distinguished Visiting Fellow at the Hoover Institution. His most recent book, *Coercing Virtue: The Worldwide Rule of Judges* (2003), examines judicial activism and the practice of national and international courts.

DAVID B. HART is a writer and Eastern Orthodox theologian hidden in the wilds of rural Maryland. He is a frequent contributor to *First Things* and the author of *The Beauty of the Infinite: The Aesthetics of Christian Truth* (2003).

FREDERICK W. KAGAN is an associate professor of military history at the U.S. Military Academy at West Point. He is the author of *The Military Reforms of Nicholas I: The Origins of the Modern Russian Army* (1999) and is currently working on a multi-volume history of the the Napoleonic Wars. The views expressed in his chapter are his own and do not necessarily reflect those of any department or agency of the U.S. government.

ROGER KIMBALL is the managing editor of *The New Criterion* and the author, most recently, of *The Rape of the Masters: How Political Correctness Sabotages Art* (2004) and *Art's Prospect: The Challenge of Tradition in an Age of Celebrity* (2003).

HILTON KRAMER is the editor and publisher of *The New Criterion* and an art critic of *The New York Observer*. His books include *The Age of the Avant-Garde* (1975), *The Revenge of the Philistines* (1985), and *The Twilight of the Intellectuals* (1999). His book *Abstract Art: A Cultural History* is forthcoming from Yale University Press.

MICHAEL J. LEWIS, professor at Williams College, is a regular contributor to *Commentary* and *The New Criterion*. His books include *Frank Furness: Architecture and the Violent Mind* (2001) and the prize-winning *August Reichensperger: The Politics of the German Gothic Revival* (1993).

JAY NORDLINGER is managing editor and music critic of *National Review*. He is also music critic for *The New Criterion* and *The New York Sun*.

ERIC ORMSBY is currently the director of the Institute of Islamic Studies at McGill University, Montreal. His poetry has appeared in *The New Yorker*, *The New Republic*, *Paris Review*, *Descant*, *Parnassus*, and *The Oxford American*. His fifth collection of poems, *Daybreak at the Straits*, was published in 2004.

MARK STEYN is Senior North American Columnist for Britain's Telegraph Group and North American Editor of *The Spectator*. In the U.S., he is theater critic of *The New Criterion* and a columnist for *The Atlantic Monthly*. His most recent book is the anthology *Mark Steyn from Head to Toe*.

KEITH WINDSCHUTTLE, publisher of Macleay Press, Sydney, is a frequent contributor to *Quadrant* and *The New Criterion*. He is author of *The Killing of History: How Literary Critics and Social Theorists Are Murdering Our Past* (1996), *The Fabrication of Aboriginal History: Volume One, Van Diemen's Land 1803–1847* (2002), and five other books.

Acknowledgments

T HE EDITORS would like to take this opportunity to thank the people who helped make *Lengthened Shadows* possible. We are particularly indebted to the staff of *The New Criterion*; to Peter Collier, the publisher of Encounter Books; and to the Achelis and Bodman Foundations, which generously supported the original series of essays in *The New Criterion* and their publication in this volume.

This book is about the health of certain crucial American institutions. Institutions are animated by ideas. Ideas cannot exist in a vacuum: they require support and nurture. It gives us great pleasure to acknowledge The Lynde and Harry Bradley Foundation, The John M. Olin Foundation, and The Sarah Scaife Foundation. For more than twenty years, their stalwart support has made our battle in the world of ideas possible.

We have dedicated this book to our friend James Piereson, Executive Director of the Olin Foundation. Since its founding a quarter century ago, the Olin Foundation has been on the front lines of the culture wars, supporting with remarkable vision an extraordinary range of conservative ideas and initiatives. Next year, in accordance with the terms of its original bequest, Olin will close its doors. By the standards of liberal philanthropy, whose expenditures dwarf conservative initiatives, Olin is a small foundation. Yet it has made a tremendous difference on the American cultural landscape, making it possible for conservative ideas to find a forum in the university and in the larger cultural conversation. Like many others, we are immensely grateful to Jim Piereson. His support has been indispensable to *The New Criterion* as to so many other conservative institutions. We are delighted to have this opportunity to salute the man whose philanthropic leadership helped change the character of intellectual debate in America.

Index

ABC (television network), 16
Abrams, Creighton, 46–47
Abstract Expressionism, 36
Abyssinia, 4, 24
Adams, John, 219, 239
Afghanistan, 4, 8, 17, 43, 45–46, 48, 65
Africa, 15–17, 21, 131, 232; religion in, 159–160; scramble for, 15, 23
Agresto, John, 130
al-Asadi, Salam, 185
al Qaeda, 22, 133
Al-Usbu (weekly), 121
Alabama Symphony, 98
Alexandria Library, 121
Algonquin Indians, 124, 140
Allen, Woody, 192
Alwan, Dr. Ala, "A Curriculum of Inclusion," 132–133
American Academy of Achievement, 176
American Bar Association (ABA), 200–201
American Civil Liberties Union (ACLU), 123, 127, 162, 200, 229, 245
American Indian Center, 123, 126

American Prospect (magazine), 17
American Symphony Orchestra League, 97, 105
American University, 238
Amiel, Henri-Frédéric, 144
Amis, Kingsley, 32; *Lucky Jim*, 204
Angelou, Maya, 231–232
Arad, Michael, "Reflecting Absence," 88
Aristotle, *Poetics*, 180, 185
Armistead, George, 226
Armory Show (1913), 32, 38, 39
Australia, 135
Austria, 55–56; Austro-Hungarian empire, 7; Hapsburgs, 7, 9
Avery Fisher Hall, 109
Azusa Street Mission (Los Angeles, CA), 148

Baath party, 119–121, 129, 142, 185
Bach, Johann Sebastian, 163
Bagehot, Walter, 195
Balkans, the, 8, 140
Balzac, Honoré, 165
Balliol College, 14, 17
Barney, Matthew, 36
Barr, Alfred H., 71

Bart, Lionel, 12

Bass Hall (Fort Worth, TX), 99

Bauhaus, the, 71–73

Beamer, Todd, 227

Beethoven, Ludwig van, 106, 117; *Ninth Symphony*, 27

Beinart, Peter, 5, 15–17

Benaroya Hall (Seattle, WA), 99

Bentham, Jeremy, 208

Berlin, Irving, 127

Berman, Paul, *Terror and Liberalism*, 17

Berns, Walter, 207

Bickel, Alexander, 203, 211, 223

bin Laden, Osama, 228–229

Bishop, Elizabeth, 171

Black, Justice Hugo, 197

Blackmun, Justice Harry, 207

Blackmur, R. P., 185

Blair, Tony, 5, 17, 18

Bloom, Allan, *The Closing of the American Mind*, 126, 136

Bloom, Harold, 186; *The American Religion*, 151–152, 154

Bly, Robert, 183

Bocelli, Andrea, 114

Boer War, 19

Bohème, La (opera), 100

Boot, Max, 5, 229

Bork, Robert, 239

Bosnia, 15, 43, 47, 65

Boston City Hall, 76

Boswell, James, 238

Bowman, Ward, 203

Brandeis, Justice Louis, 199, 236

Braque, Georges, 25, 29–30

Brennan, Justice William J., Jr., 208

Breton, André, 180

Breyer, Justice Steven, 217

Bright, John, 13

Britain, *see* United Kingdom

Broch, Hermann, 237

Brodsky, Jascha, 116

Brown v. *Board of Education*, 209

Bruckner, Pascal, 230

Budapest String Quartet, 96, 108

Burke, Edmund, 203

Burnham, James, *Suicide of the West* 240

Bush, George, 107

Bush, George W., 8, 139, 142

Bush, Laura, 182

Cahn, Sammy, 127

California, Ninth Circuit Court of Appeals of, 245

Canada, 135–136, 138

Cantwell v. *Connecticut*, 206

Carnegie Hall, 95, 98, 105, 107

Carson, Anne, 181–182

Carter, Jimmy, 48

Cebrowski, Arthur, 50

Celan, Paul, 191

Cézanne, Paul, 39, 72

Chamber Music Northwest, 110

Chamber Music Society of Lincoln Center, 109

Chamber Music Society of Philadelphia, 109

Chamberlain, Joseph, 14

Chandos (recording company), 114

Chang, Han-Na, 116

Charter of Virginia, 150

Chechnya, 140

Chesterton, G. K., 243, 245

ChevronTexaco Corporation, 103

Chicago Tribune, The (newspaper), 122

Childs, David, 89

China, 6, 9, 14, 24, 51, 61, 135

Chomsky, Noam, 134

Christian Science Monitor, The (newspaper), 114

Christmas celebrations, 126–128

Chrysler Building, 68

Church, Charlotte, 114
Churchill, Winston, 3–4
Cicero, 141, 177
Civil War (American), 55, 83, 93, 209, 220–221, 231
Clark, Sedgwick, 100, 105, 117
Clifton, Lucille, 184
Clinton, Bill, 18, 135, 176, 232; administration, 15, 138
CNN (cable network), 62, 242
Cobden, Richard, 13
Coburn, Alvin Landon, 178
Cohen, William, 49
Colburn School (Los Angeles), 110
Cold War, 18, 20, 24, 57; post-Cold War, 47
Coleridge, Samuel Taylor, 185
Collins, Billy, 174
Colorado Symphony, 98
Columbine High School (Littleton, CO), 136
Communism, 41, 72, 81, 141
Congo, 16
Connerly, Ward, 232–233
Coutz, Bernard, 114
Covent Garden, 102
Covington, Dennis, *Salvation on Sand Mountain*, 148
Crane, Hart, *The Bridge*, 190
Creative Associates International, Inc., 130
Crèvecoeur, J. Hector St. John de, *Letters from an American Farmer*, 225, 234–235
Crimean War, 56
Cromwell, Oliver, 140
Cuba, 19–20
Cubism, 30
Curtis Institute of Music, 94, 110

Dadaism, 26, 40
Dante, 163, 191, 207
David, Jacques-Louis, 73

Davis, Pete, 123–126, 132
Davis, Stuart, 40
Deconstructionist architecture, 85–87
Degenerate Art (1937 exhibition), 42
Denver Symphony Orchestra, 98
Derrida, Jacques, 239
Dervishes, 3–4, 24
Descartes, René, 7
Deutsche Grammophon (recording company), 115
Devlin, Lord Patrick, 203, 215; *The Enforcement of Morals*, 242
Dial, The (magazine), 33
Disney Hall, 99–100
"Diversity Week," 128–129
Documenta (art show), 37
Domingo, Plácido, 113, 116
Douglas, Justice William, 197
Douglass, Frederick, 232
Dove, Rita, 173–177, 183, 187; *On the Bus with Rosa Parks*, 173; *Thomas and Beulah*, 174
Dove-Viebahn, Aviva, 176
Downtown Gallery, 40
Drake, Sir Francis, 132
Duchamp, Marcel, 26
Durham, Lord, 12

East India Company, 130
Egypt, 15, 23, 121–122
Eisenman, Peter, 84; Wexner Center for the Visual Arts, 85
Elderfield, John, 37
Eliot, T. S., 33, 143; "Love Song of J. Alfred Prufrock," 177; "Tradition and the Individual Talent," 31–32; *The Waste Land*, 29
Ely, John Hart, 211
Emancipation Proclamation, 231
Emerson String Quartet, 100, 115
EMI (recording company), 113
Emory University, 130

Empire State Building, 68, 70–71
Etlin, Richard, 79
Euripides, *The Bacchae*, 143
European Union, 146

Fair Employment Practices
   Committee, 234
Ferguson, Niall, 8, 133; *Empire*
   (book and TV series), 10, 12, 21
Fiddler on the Roof (musical), 203
Financial Times, The (newspaper), 5
Finkel, David, 115
Fischer, David Hackett,
   Washington's Crossing, 248
Fleming, Renée, 104, 113, 116
Florida, 245
Fontaine, Jean de la, 175
Fonte, John, 16, 238
Ford corporation, 49
Fort McHenry, 225–227, 229, 249
Foucault, Michel, 239
France, 11, 23, 51, 57, 126, 135, 242,
   244
Franco-Prussian War, 55
Franklin, Benjamin, 236, 239,
   245–246, 249
Freud, Sigmund, 28
Friedman, Milton, 15
Frost, Robert, 231
Fundamental Orders of
   Connecticut, 150
Furness, Frank, 83

Gallagher, Tess, 183–184
Gaza, 17
Gehry, Frank, 77, 85, 99
Germany, 22–23, 51, 56–58, 64, 74,
   135, 145; Imperial, 56, 58; Nazi,
   41, 55–56, 58, 71, 73;
Gershwin, George, 93
Getty Museum, 84
Gettysburg, 88
Gettysburg Address, 231

Giamatti, A. Bartlett, 207
Gide, André, 182, 195
Gier, David Delta, 111–112
Glück, Louise, 174
Gorbachev, Mikhail, 75
Gordon, General Charles George, 4
Gore, Al, 127, 239
Gottschalk, Louis Moreau, 93
Graffman, Gary, 94–96, 117
Graglia, Lino, 210
Graham, Jorie, 188–189
Grant, Charles, 142
Graves, Michael, 78, 80, 83
Great Britain, *see* United Kingdom
Great Depression, 70–71, 139, 197
Green, T. H., 14
Greenberg, Clement, 39, 74
Greene, Chief Wilfred "Eagle
   Heart," 124
Greenhouse, Linda, 218
Griswold v. *Connecticut*, 203
Gropius, Walter, 68, 71, 73
Guggenheim Foundation, 171
Guggenheim Museum, *see* Solomon
   R. Guggenheim Museum
Gulf War, 48, 61, 120, 133
Gutmann, Amy, 238

Hacker, Marilyn, 172
Hahn, Hilary, 116
Hale, Pamela, 184
Halpert, Edith, 40
Hamburger, Philip, 207
Hamill, Sam, *Poets Against the War*
   (ed.), 182–185
Hamilton, Alexander, 236
Hamilton, George Heard, *Painting
   and Sculpture in Europe 1880–1940*,
   27–28
Hampson, Thomas, 108
Han, Wu, 115
Hank, Judge Learned, 224
Hanks, Tom, 134

Hansen, Betsy, 129

Hanson, Victor Davis, 237

Harley-Davidson motorcycles, 36

Harmonia Mundi (recording company), 114

Harries, Karsten, 82

Harries, Owen, 21

Harth, Robert, 98–99, 105, 107, 114–115

Hartley, Marsden, 39

Harvard University, 186, 188; Graduate School of Design, 71–74

Hass, Robert, 172; *Field Guide*, 181

Haussmann, Baron, 70

Hayek, Friedrich von, 15

Hazlitt, William, 185

Heaney, Seamus, 189–190

Hegel, G. W. F., 14

Heifetz, Jascha, 95, 115–116

Heinz family, 98

Henry V, 132

Herbert, George, 163

Heymann, Klaus, 114

Himmelfarb, Gertrude, 216; *The Roads to Modernity: The British, French, and American Enlightenments*, 244–247

Hitchcock, Henry Russell, 71

Hitler, Adolf, 41–42, 57

Hofmann, Hans, 39

Hofstra University, 238

Holmes, Oliver Wendell, 199

Holocaust, the, 122

Hood, Raymond, 83

Hopkins, Gerard Manley, 189

Horne, Marilyn, 96, 99, 107–108, 111–114

Horowitz, Vladimir, 94–95

Horowitz, Wanda Toscanini, 94-95

Howard, Richard, 186; "The Ghettoization of Poetry," 174

Howe, George, 70

Hudson Review, The (journal), 33

Hughes, Chief Justice Charles Evans, 206

Human Rights Watch, 16

Hungary, 73

Huntington, Samuel, *Who Are We? The Challenges to America's National Identity*, 228–229, 231–232, 235–236, 239–244, 247, 249

Hussein, Saddam, 5, 18, 48, 64, 119–122, 126, 128, 185

Ignatieff, Michael, 5–6

Ikeda, Patricia, 183

Illinois Institute of Technology (IIT), 71

Impressionism, 27; in France, 70

India, 21, 23, 130–132, 141–142; Amritsar massacre, 10; Mughal empire, 11, 21, 23; mutiny, 10; Supreme Court of, 217

Indonesia, 22, 140

Ingersoll, Earl G., 175

International Criminal Court, 16, 162

International Exposition of Surrealism (1938), 38

International Monetary Fund, 11

International Style, 71, 77, 86

Iran, 44, 120

Iraq, 4–5, 8, 17, 21–22, 43–47, 52, 61, 63–64, 119–122, 126, 128–130, 132–133, 142, 184

Iroquois Indians, 126

Isacoff, Stuart, 116

Islam, 3–4, 24, 121; Shi'ites, 185; fanaticism within, 22, 134, 135, 140–141, 247

Italy, 22, 23, 121, 139, 145, 242

Ivry, Benjamin, 114

Jackson, Jesse, 132

Jacobs, Jane, *The Death and Life of Great American Cities*, 74
Jacoby Hall (Jacksonville, FL), 99
Jahn, Helmut, 80
Jamaica, 13; Privy Council of, 217
James, Henry, 177–178, 193
Japan, 6, 8, 21, 23, 64, 135–138, 141
Jarrell, Randall, 185
Jay, John, 235
Jefferson, Thomas, 132, 235–236, 239; *Notes on the State of Virginia*, 246
Jeffersonians, 220
Jenkins, Philip, *The Next Christendom*, 159
Jim Crow laws, 234
Johnson, Paul, 5–6
Johnson, Philip, 71; AT&T Building, 78
Johnson, Samuel, 185, 238
Joyce, James, *Dubliners*, 28; *Ulysses*, 28
Judd, Donald, 30
Juilliard School, 110–111
Just, Richard, 17

Kagan, Frederick W., "War and Aftermath," 53
Kahn, Louis I., 76
Kakutani, Michiko, 243
Kallmann, McKinnell, and Knowles (architecture firm), 76
Kandinsky, Vasily, 36
Kaplan, Lawrence, *The War over Iraq: Saddam's Tyranny and America's Mission*, 17–18
Keats, John, 170, 186
Kennedy, Justice Anthony, 213–214, 216
Kennedy, John F., 231
Kennedy, Paul, 5–6
Key, Francis Scott, "The Star-Spangled Banner," 226–227

Khalifa, 3–4
Kahnweiler Gallery, 39
Khartoum, 3–4
Kimmel Center, 99
Kimbell Art Museum, 76
Kirk, Russell, *Eliot and His Age*, 143
Kitchener, General Herbert Horatio, 3–4, 23–24
Kolakowski, Leszek, 195, 215
Kooning, Willem de, 25, 29–30; *Women* paintings, 29
Korea, 44
Kosovo, 15, 43, 36, 65, 138
Kramer, Hilton, "The Age of the Avant-Garde," 28, 30
Krauthammer, Charles, 212
Kristol, Irving, 248; "Countercultures," 225
Kristol, William, *The War over Iraq: Saddam's Tyranny and America's Mission*, 18
Kruvant, Charito, 130
Kurds, 121; in Iraq, 185
Kyoto protocol, 16

La Scala, 102
Lachaise, Gaston, 39
Larkin, Philip, 181
Lawrence v. Texas, 213–214
Lambeth Conference, 160
Le Corbusier, 70, 76; *Vers une architecture*, 68; Villa Savoye, 84; Villa Stein, 84
Leatherbarrow, David, 82
Lebrecht, Norman, *Who Killed Classical Music?*, 114
Lever House, 73
Levine, James, 102
Levittown, 75
Liberal Party, 13–15
Liberia, 16
Libeskind, Daniel, 87–88; Jewish Museum (Berlin), 87

Ligeti, Gyorgy, 106
Lincoln, Abraham, 220–221, 231
Lipovšek, Marjana, 108
Lipsitz, George, 238
Liscio, Keith, 123–124
Lithuania, 135
Lochner v. *New York*, 196
Locke, John, 12
Logan, William, 186, 189
Longinus, 185
Loos, Adolf, "Ornament and Crime," 27
Los Angeles Philharmonic, 99
Louis, William Roger, *Oxford History of the British Empire*, 10, 12, 21
Lower Manhattan Development Corporation, 88

Ma, Yo-Yo, 116
MacArthur Awards, 188
Macaulay, Thomas Babington, 90, 130–131, 141
Madison, James, 236
Madison School (Skokie, IL), 122–126, 129
Magdala, battle for, 4, 24
Malatare, Leonard, 123–125
Manchester School, the, 13
March of Dimes, 100
Marilyn Horne Foundation, 107
Marin, John, 39
Massachusetts, Board of Education, 137–138; state constitution, 219; Supreme Judicial Court, 220–221
Massasoit, 124
Matisse, Henri, 39
Maurer, Alfred, 39
Max M. Fisher Center (Detroit, MI), 99
Max Protech Gallery, 86
Maya, 69
Mayflower Compact, 150

McAuliffe, Jack, 97–98, 105–106
McIntosh-Round, Wilden, 183
McDonald's, 79
McNamara, Robert, 49–51
Mehta, Zarin, 95–96, 106, 111
Mehta, Zubin, 95
Meier, Richard, 84
Metropolitan Museum of Art, 117
Metropolitan Opera, 102–105
Meyerson Center (Dallas, TX), 99
Michelangelo, 75, 79
Mies van der Rohe, Ludwig, 30, 71, 73, 75–77
Mill, John Stuart, 12, 203; *On Liberty*, 215–216
Millay, Edna St. Vincent, 171
Mills, Billy, 124
Milosevic, Slobodan, 65
Milstein, Nathan, 95, 116
Minogue, Kenneth, 210, 218
Misérables, Les (musical), 99–100
Modernism, 25–42, 67–91
Mondrian, Piet, 30
Montale, Eugenio, 191
Moore, Charles, 78, 80, 83
Moore, Marianne, 25, 29–30, 193; *Marriage*, 23–30
Moore, Michael, 134
Morning Post (newspaper), 3
Morris, Herbert, 177–180; *Peru*, 177; *What Was Lost*, 177–180
Mozart, Wolfgang Amadeus, 93
Multiculturalism, 234–244
Museum of Modern Art (MOMA), 36–37, 71, 75, 117
Museum of Non-Objective Painting, 36
Music Academy of the West (Santa Barbara), 111
Musical America (magazine), 95, 100

Napier, Sir Robert, 4, 24
Napoleon Bonaparte, 56–58, 70, 73

Nash, Ogden, 172–173
National Assessment of Education Progress, 136
National Book Award, 183
National Defense University, 54
National Education Association (NEA), 133, 136, 138
National Interest, The, 5
National Review (magazine), 5
Native American Educational Services College, 123
Naxos (recording company), 114
Neoconservatism, 18–19
Network-Centric Warfare (NCW), 50–53
New Brutalists, 75
New Criterion, The (journal), 6, 33, 135
New Criticism, 33
New Jersey Performing Arts Center, 99
New Left, 197–198
New Republic, The (magazine), 5, 15
New York Philharmonic, 95, 111
New York State Regents, 132–133, 141
New York Times, The (newspaper), 5, 197, 218, 223, 242–243
New York University, 238
New Zealand, 135
Newman, Barnett, 39
Newman, Paul, 134
Newton, Sir Isaac, 132
Nietzsche, Friedrich, 146
Nightline (TV news show), 16
Nisbet, Robert, 208
Novak, Michael, 244
Nussbaum, Martha, 238

O'Connor, Justice Sandra Day, 217–218
Oglala Lakota Indians, 123–124, 133, 137

O'Leary, Cecilia, 238
Oldenburg, Claes, 86
Oliver! (musical), 127
Oliver, Mary, 190
Olympic Games, 124
Omaha Beach, 88
Omdurman, Battle of, 3–4, 23–24
Opera America, 101
Opium Wars, 14
Organisation for Economic Co-operation and Development, 135
Orwell, George, 233
O'Sullivan, John, 5, 133, 210
Ottoman empire, 7
Owens, William, 50
Oxford University, 14; Press, 10

Pakistan, 140
Palestinian Authority, 122, 126
Palestrina, Giovanni Pierluigi da, 163
Palmerston, Lord, 14
Pan Am Building, 73
Papua New Guinea, 132
Parker, Dorothy, 172
Parks, Rosa, 231
Parkway High School (LA), 128–129
Parsons, Betty, 39
Partisan Review (magazine), 33
Patriot missile system, 47–48
Pavarotti, Luciano, 116
Peabody Institute, 110
Peace Center, 99
Pearl Jam (rock group), 111
Pentagon, 49, 52, 54
Perlman, Itzhak, 116
Phantom of the Opera (musical), 99
Philippines, 20
Piatigorsky, Gregor, 95
Picasso, Pablo, 30
Pickens, Buford, 72
Pine Ridge Oglala reservation, 124

Pioneer High School (Ann Arbor, MI), 128–129
Pittsburgh Plate Glass, 73
Pittsburgh Symphony, 98
Plains Indians, 124
Planned Parenthood v. *Casey*, 216
Plato, 141
Policy Review (journal), 53
Polisi, Joseph, 110–111, 113
Pollock, Jackson, 36, 39
Porter, Cole, 93
Post-Impressionism Show (1910), 38
Postmodernism, 40–41, 78–81
Pound, Ezra, 33
Pousette-Dart, Richard, 39
Powell, Colin, 131–132
Powell, Thomas Reed, 197
Princeton University, 238
Protocols of the Elders of Zion, The, 121–122
Prussia, 55–56
Pulitzer Prize, 171, 188

Quasthoff, Thomas, 108

Radicalism, in 19th-century England, 13
Rattle, Simon, 105
RCA Victor (record company), 94–95
Reagan, Ronald, 15, 48, 80
Redgrave, Vanessa, 134
Reed, Henry Hope, 81
Reiner, Fritz, 93
Reinhardt, Ad, 30
Revel, Jean-François, 241
Revere, Paul, 140
Revolution in Military Affairs (RMA), 53–55, 57
Revolutionary War, 248
Ricks, Christopher, 185
Robbins, Tim, 134
Roberts, Justice Owen, 206

Robinson, Gene, 158
Rockwell, Norman, 36
Rodgers, Richard, 93
Roe v. *Wade*, 207, 214
Roman empire, 9, 13, 19
Ronsard, Pierre, 163
Roosevelt, Franklin Delano, 139, 197, 234
Roosevelt, Theodore, 225, 235
Root, John Wellborn, 83
Rose, Stephen Peter, 5
Rosen, Charles, 94
Rosenkavalier, Der (opera), 104
Rostropovich, Mstislav , 116
Rothko, Mark, 39
Rousseau, Jean-Jacques, 208
Rubinstein, Anton, 95, 116
Rudolph, Paul, 76
Rumsfeld, Donald, 44, 51–53, 62–63, 65, 119
Rush, Benjamin, 245
Russia, 24, 51, 56; empire, 7; Revolution, 72–73; under Stalin, 41; *see also* USSR

Saarinen, Eero, 76–77
Saatchi, Charles, 35
St. John's College (Santa Fe, NM), 130
Saladin, 121, 126, 142
Salk Institute, 76
Samoset, 124
San Francisco Conservatory, 110
São Paulo Biennial, 37
Saudi Arabia, 121, 122, 126, 140
Schade Michael, 108, 113
Schafer, Christine [sp], 108
Schlesinger, Arthur, Jr., 197; *The Disuniting of America*, 230–231
Schlieffen Plan, 5
Schneider, Alexander, 96
Schulman, Grace, *The Poems of Marianne Moore*, 30

Schuster Center (Dayton, OH), 99
Scorca, Marc, 101–102
Scott, Sir Walter, *Marmion*,
    169–170, 179, 187, 189–190, 193
Seagram Building, 73
Sennett, Richard, 238
September 11, 17, 18, 22, 44, 86, 88,
    97, 133, 139, 227–232
Serkin, Rudolf, 95
Serota, Sir Nicholas, 35
Seussical (musical), 100
Seven Years War, 23
Severance Hall (Cleveland, OH), 99
Shakespeare, William, 132, 163, 170,
    180, 186; *Julius Caesar*, 189;
    Sonnets, 187
Shaw, George Bernard, 18
Shifrin, David, 109, 112, 115
Shingle Style, 77, 79, 90
Sidney Janis Gallery, 29
Sills, Beverly, 100, 102–103
Silver, Ron, 134, 139
Silverstein, Larry, 88
Singapore, 132
Smith, Adam, 7, 13, 18–19, 21
Smith, Dinitia, 187–188
Smith, Thomas Gordon, 80–81
Socialism, 197
Solti, Georg, 93
Solomon R. Guggenheim Museum,
    35–36
Solzhenitsyn, Aleksandr, 106
Solzhenitsyn, Ignat, 106–107,
    109–110
South Dakota Symphony, 112
Southard, John, 130, 132
Spain, 20, 136, 145, 242
Spanish-American War, 84
Spencer, David, 123
Spiro, Peter, 238
Spong, John, 159–160, 164; *Why
    Christianity Must Change or Die*,
    159

Squanto, 124
Staatsoper (Vienna), 102
Stalin, Joseph, 41–42
Stern, Robert A. M., 78
Sternfeld, Harry, 72
Stevens, Justice John Paul, 217
Stevens, Wallace, 25, 29, 187, 227
Steyn, Mark, 230
Stieglitz, Alfred, 39
Stiles, Amanda, 128
Stonewall Riots, 84
Story, Joseph, *Commentaries on the
    Constitution of the United States*,
    209
Stove, David, 240
Stravinsky, Igor, 117
Streisand, Barbra, 134
Stuffed Owl, The (poetry anthology),
    185
Styne, Jule, 127
Sudan, 3–4, 135, 140
Suharto, General, 22
Sullivan, Louis, 83
Surrealism, 38, 40, 182
Switzerland, 136
Symbolism, 26
Syria, 122
Szell, George, 93

"291" (gallery), 39
Tacitus, 141
Taliban, 5
Tallmadge, T. E., *Story of Architecture
    in America*, 70
Tate Britain, 35
Tate Gallery, 35
Tate Modern, 35
Tchaikovsky, Peter, 117
Tennyson, Alfred, Lord, 170
Terfel, Bryn, 103, 116
Texaco Corporation, 103
Thanksgiving celebrations, 122–126,
    133

Thatcher, Margaret, 15, 181
Theodore, emperor of Abyssinia, 4
Thibaudet, Albert, *Histoire de la littérature française de 1789 à nos jours*, 26
Thompson, William Irwin, 183
Thucydides, 141
Time (magazine), 116
Tisquantum, 124
Tocqueville, Alexis de, 243–245
Tory Party, 13, 15
Toscanini, Arturo, 94, 105
Traviata, La (opera), 104
Trilling, Lionel, "The Function of the Little Magazine," 33
Tubman, Harriet, 231
Turner Prize, 35, 162
TWA Terminal, 73, 76

United Kingdom, 51, 57, 64, 145; constitution of, 195; education in, 126, 135–136; empire of, 3–15, 23–24; enlightenment in, 244; Liberal Imperialism in, 14–15; poet laureateship of, 173; religion in, 145; Royal Navy, 8, 142
United Nations, 8, 16, 145
United States, Congress, 5, 44, 173, 220–221; Constitution, 126, 195–224, 235, 239, 244; education in, 119–142; empire, 5–24; military, 43–66, 174; Poet Laureateship of, 172–177; solicitor general of, 205–208; Supreme Court of, 195–224
University of California, 238
University of New Mexico, 237
Univesity of Notre Dame, 81
University of Pennsylvania, 72, 82
USSR, 23, 45, 48, 57, 60, 73

Vendler, Helen, 175, 186–190; *The Breaking of Style*, 189

Vengerov, Maxim, 107, 116
Venice Biennale, 37
Venturi, Robert, 76–79; *Complexity and Contradiction in Architecture*, 75, 78–79; Mother's House, 77, 79
Verlaine, Paul, 193
Victoria, as Empress of India, 14
Viebahn, Fred, *Dove-Viebahn Newsletter*, 176–177
Vietnam War, 20, 43, 46, 48–49, 64
Voigt, Deborah, 113
Vollard Gallery, 39
Volpe, Jeseph, 102–105, 115

Wagner, Richard, *Ring* cycle, 96, 113
Wahhabism, 3–4, 140
Walker, Peter, "Reflecting Absence," 88
Wall Street Journal, The (newspaper), 5
Wampanoag Indians, 124–125
War of 1812, 84, 226
Warren, Earl, 197, 208; Warren Court, 197–198, 209
Washington, George, 132, 236, 245
Washington Post, The (newspaper), 16
Washington University, St. Louis, 72
Webster, Noah, 137
Weinberg, Adam D., 37
Weiner, Myron, 11
Wellesley, Arthur, Duke of Wellington, 132, 226
West Indies, 131–132
West Point, 54
Weyhe Gallery, 39
White, Justice Byron, 206
Whitney Museum of American Art, 36–37; Biennial, 38
Whyte, William H., 74
Wilson, Woodrow, 18

Wordsworth, William, 132, 144, 170

World Trade Center site, 86–89

World War I, 15, 19, 55–56, 64, 69

World War II, 8, 11, 20, 23, 27, 55, 64, 93

Wright, Charles, 190–192; *Black Zodiac*, 191; *Negative Blue*, 190, 192

Wright, Frank Lloyd, 90

Wunderlich, Fritz, 113

Yale University, 6, 82, 186; Art and Architecture Building, 76;

Law School, 197, 203–205; School of Architecture, 67–68

Yeltsin, Boris, 48

Yemen, 140

Young British Artists (YBAs), 35

Ysaÿe, Eugène, 116

Zankel Hall, 107

Ziedan, Dr. Yousef, 121–122

Zimbabwe, Supreme Court of, 217–218

Zimbalist, Efraim, 116

Zweig, Stefan, 230